Yrs Very Truly
John McLonnie

A WEEK WITH JESUS,

OR

LESSONS LEARNED IN HIS COMPANY.

BY

JOHN M. LOWRIE, D.D.,

AUTHOR OF "ESTHER AND HER TIMES," "ADAM AND HIS TIMES," AND "THE HEBREW LAWGIVER,"

AND PASTOR OF THE FIRST PRESBYTERIAN CHURCH, FORT WAYNE, INDIANA.

And what if my feet may not tread where He stood,
Nor my ears hear the dashing of Galilee's flood,
Nor my eyes see the Cross which he bowed him to bear,
Nor my knees press Gethsemane's garden of prayer,

Yet, loved of the Father, thy Spirit is near
To the meek, and the lowly, and penitent here;
And the voice of thy love is the same even now
As at Bethany's tomb or on Olivet's brow.

WHITTIER.

PHILADELPHIA:
PRESBYTERIAN BOARD OF PUBLICATION,
No. 1334 CHESTNUT STREET.

STEREOTYPED BY WESTCOTT & THOMSON.

PREFACE.

IN the Life of Julius Cæsar, recently given to the world by the Emperor of France, occurs the following thoughtful paragraph:—

"By what sign are we to recognize the greatness of a man? In the sway of his ideas, when his principles and his system triumph in spite of his death or his defeat. Is it not in fact the prerogative of genius to outlive destruction and to extend its empire over future generations? Cæsar disappeared, and his influence predominates still more than during his lifetime. Cicero, his adversary, is obliged to exclaim, 'All the acts of Cæsar, his writings, his words, his promises, his thoughts, are more powerful after his death than if he were still alive.'"

In this book, one who ranks among the first of living monarchs, for remarkable success achieved, for political sagacity displayed, and for actual power now in his possession, has written of another, whose genius and sagacity and ambition can scarcely find their parallels. It matters little to our present purpose whether the royal writer had some special object in view in this significant quotation, touching the political aspects of things in our own times: nor yet whether, as thus rendered, the words express the exact meaning of the great orator; or whether Tully is not rather complaining that words uttered in the name of Cæsar—purporting to be his, though falsely ascribed to him—were used, in the excitement following his violent death, to carry measures which the living Cæsar would not have dared to propose. For, apart from the attempted application of it, the thought is legitimate and forcible. It IS the high prerogative of true greatness to triumph in spite of apparent defeat and to extend its fame and authority to later generations.

But we are by no means ready to agree that this principle properly applies to men like Cæsar, or Napoleon I. During his lifetime each of these remarkable men rose to the summit of greatness among his own people. They won their power by the splendour of military genius, with the clash of arms, and in the carnage of a hundred battles; and the death of the one, and the exile of the other, served but to increase the enthusiasm that already burned for them in ten thousand hearts. The highest standard of true genius must find better examples than these. Indeed there is but ONE NAME in all the history of the world that can successfully abide the test of eminent greatness, thus shrewdly suggested by the royal writer.

The life of Jesus of Nazareth is, beyond all comparison, the most remarkable that finds record in the annals of humanity. No biography has within a hundred fold been so abundantly re-written; whether by those who humbly follow his footsteps, or by those who have no single tie of sympathy with him that could enable them to comprehend or appreciate his character. No reasonable mind can question, whether from the direct teachings of simple history, or the various concessions of his bitter foes, that we have the true record of this great life; and the facts and the influences flowing from them are equally remarkable. We have here brought before us a young man, born in lowly life, having no advantages of position, or even education, to lift him above the mass of men, and contenting himself by instructing, with the voice merely, the humbler classes in society in one of the meaner provinces of the Roman Empire. For three or four years he spent his time in these pursuits; he gathered about him a meagre band of disciples, not above his own state; he awakened only persecution and contempt among the influential men of his own nation; and before he reached the middle age of life he was condemned as a malefactor, and put to a violent and shameful death. And now let the test be applied for truth and true greatness, in the succeeding influence of his sentiments and character. He was not the idol of his nation, overborne by force as hostile to them as to himself, nor did he leave ten thousand wakeful hearts upon the watch for the earliest moment of a sweet revenge. He had not caught and promoted the spirit of his age; rather, he was in all respects out of sympathy with the general mind of the world; and, most of all, his plans were in direct opposition to the long cherished prejudices of the Jewish people. We can reckon nothing upon the influence already gained in his brief lifetime, upon the enthusiasm he had awakened in the breasts of numerous friends, or upon their indignation as able to create a re-action because he was unjustly dealt by. No case can be imagined where the power and influence of any man seemed more necessarily to die with him than when Jesus lay in Joseph's rocky tomb.

And yet, after his death the most remarkable and permanent power belonged to one whose life, up to its latest moments, had been full of humiliation. Though we have no record that he ever penned a single word with his own hand, his teachings did not perish when his voice was hushed in death. His indeed were thoughts peculiarly his own. Though the greatest of earthly teachers, he certainly was not a *learned* teacher. We have proofs in the writings of Paul that the apostle had read the writings of other men and of other lands. But we cannot gather from all the teachings of Jesus, that he ever sat at the feet of any other instructor, or that he ever read a single book in all his life; except indeed the inspired writings of the Church of God, with which he was fully familiar, to which he often appealed as sustaining his authority, and with all which his entire teachings were in complete consonance. His were the mighty words of the world. They were living and life-giving principles, which took hold upon men with regenerating power. There was nothing in his claims, his teachings, his promises, to inflame or to gratify the ordinary passions of men; no honours to be won, no ambition to be gratified, no sensual pleasures to be enjoyed. On the contrary, he ever proclaimed the cross, and called his disciples to suffer the loss of all things. Only by self-renunciation could they follow this strange leader.

Yet his words were powerful as no other teachings have been upon the earth. They went forth from the narrow boundaries of Judea, and attacked the hoary prejudices and superstitions of the Pagan world; and in a few brief centuries the gospel of the despised man of Galilee became the avowed faith of the Roman Empire. And now for many ages, during which hosts of great men have risen and been forgotten, his words, wherever received in their simplicity, have had power to cast down superstition, to change the aspects of human society, to teach men the true principles of freedom, to awaken impulses that refine and strengthen and elevate humanity, and to support true morality and true piety, that seems strangely in contrast with the feeble attainments of his life-work, and with the apparent triumph of his foes in his death upon the cross.

It is remarkably true of Jesus that all his acts, his words, his promises, his thoughts, are more powerful after his death than before. There can be no valid objection to making this the test at once of truth and of true greatness in his case, because there were no adventitious aids to give power to his empire over men; and because to admit his claims at all, seems logically to demand our acquiescence in their entire truth and in their supreme authority. A kingdom purely of moral principles, having only that power over the minds of men which springs from the proofs of its truth and its inherent excellency, and tending to results so contrary to the usual bias of man's fallen nature, could not be founded upon any misapprehension of the great things then occurring before the eyes of his disciples. Such a kingdom must be established upon principles of truth and righteousness. Happily for the world there is a consistency between his words and deeds, his claims and his avowed purposes, the purity of his personal character and the tendency of his gospel to purify its disciples, that justifies our most implicit faith, and bids us receive this Jesus as our Friend and Teacher, our Redeemer and Lord.

Yet not all who speak well of our Jesus are ready to concede the consistent pre-eminence of his claims. It is quite a remarkable feature of his fame, that men who deserve the name of infidels, because they set themselves in determined opposition to all that is distinctive in his teachings; because, touching Christ's mission to the earth, they have no faith in its necessity, in its true object, or in the exalted character that must be ascribed to him in any just understanding of the gospel; and because they are out of all sympathy with Christ's most loving followers—these men have yet been, most strikingly, the eulogists of his greatness, of his personal purity, and of the excellence of his moral teachings. They speak most inconsistently indeed; they agree not with each other, in their estimates of him, or in understanding what he says; but it would be easy to gather from skeptical writings many a decided and eloquent tribute to the excellence and dignity of Jesus Christ.

With the gospel in our hands we need not wonder at the folly and blindness of men. Man's proneness to earthly things, contrasted with the spirituality of our Lord's teachings, is a sufficient solution of these inconsistencies. Only a regenerated mind receives cordially and fully the truth as it is in Jesus. Happy are they who acknowledge the supreme claims of man's great Mediator; who, understand his mission to earth; who yield themselves to his service as cheerful and decided disciples; and who lovingly follow his footsteps. To such, flesh and blood reveals him not, but the Father. Mat. xvi. 17. It is a vital, blessed truth to us, not only that his words have more power among men than when he was on the earth; but that we may know better himself, his truth, his promises, his requirements than did the very friends who were then his associates. And love for Christ has this superiority over the respect we may entertain for the world's dead heroes, that *our Lord is living yet;* and that our study of his life on earth, is the study of principles which were designed for perpetual instruction and which are as interesting and important for us as for any that have ever pondered them.

These pages are the result of a loving effort to draw near to Jesus, by associating the teachings of the evangelists with vivid ideas of Christ as a personal and living Lord. One incident connected with their publication deserves grateful record here. The entire volume had been prepared in days of vigorous health and abundant labours; but the afflicting hand of the Master had beckoned his servant aside from active duty, just as in his providence the proof-sheets of the earlier pages were laid before his eyes. They were written several years before, without a thought of personal application at least in this form: they seemed now just as if written for this exact occasion: and hard as the trial has been to close his lips from uttering the messages he has ever loved to speak, yet at no period of life has the calm consciousness of doing just the work assigned by the Master been so complete and satisfactory, as during these trying months of inactivity. The book, before leaving the press, has begun its work upon the writer's own soul. May this be but an earnest of large blessings to be long scattered by its agency through the church of Christ. If any learn here how to walk in the Master's company, this will be a blessing.

CONTENTS.

CHAPTER I.

PAGE

Companionship with the Master........ 13

CHAPTER II.

Retiring from the World........ 22

CHAPTER III.

Reasons for Repose........ 30

CHAPTER IV.

The Miracle of the Loaves........ 44

CHAPTER V.

Divine Beneficence........ 60

CHAPTER VI.

Providential Troubles........ 76

CHAPTER VII.

The Redeemer's Prayers........ 84

CHAPTER VIII.

Delivering Grace........ 90

CHAPTER IX.

PAGE
The Cry of the Perishing 106

CHAPTER X.

Cleaving to Christ 124

CHAPTER XI.

Divine Concealments 139

CHAPTER XII.

Faith Seeking for the Healer 156

CHAPTER XIII.

Faith Severely Tested 173

CHAPTER XIV.

Faith Earnest and Persevering 188

CHAPTER XV.

Faith Triumphant and Commended 203

CHAPTER XVI.

The Great Claims of Christ 220

CHAPTER XVII.

Various Opinions respecting Christ 229

CHAPTER XVIII.

The Church Founded on the Rock 241

CHAPTER XIX.

The Scriptures Fulfilled in Christ's Death 262

CHAPTER XX.

The "Must be" of the Death of Christ 273

CHAPTER XXI.

PAGE

Taking up the Cross 286

CHAPTER XXII.

Bearing the Cross 296

CHAPTER XXIII.

The Saviour's Great Question 308

CHAPTER XXIV.

Scenes of Transfiguration 328

CHAPTER XXV.

It is Good for us to be here 345

A WEEK WITH JESUS.

CHAPTER I.

COMPANIONSHIP WITH THE MASTER.

"Did not our heart burn within us while he talked with us by the way?"

No more important writings can man ever study than the simple records given us by the four evangelists, concerning the Lord Jesus Christ. In the lowest view we can take of these writings, as giving us a portraiture of him far more accurate than that we have of any other eminent character of times so ancient, and as giving this in terms of so great simplicity and verisimilitude, they are testimonials of extraordinary interest. But these writings are still more wonderful and interesting in a higher and better view. We should consider the exalted character he sustained, the wonderful teachings he gave, the magnificent works he wrought, and the surprising influence he has exerted upon every generation since his own: we should regard the claims he made and sustains to Divine dignity, the peculiar position he holds as the only person who ever professed to be the Saviour of sinful men, and the warm affections he has gathered to him of holy men in all the ages: and weighing all these things, and the demands he makes upon us individually, our interest should be absorbing in the instructions of the GREAT BIOGRAPHY.

It is true indeed of Jesus Christ, as it is true of Socrates, one of the purest and greatest of the ancient sages, that not a word of his teachings has come down to us as penned by his own hand, or even as caught immediately from his lips. Important as it is to have a full and accurate report of his life and teachings, what we have, was written by his disciples after his death; and the whole is crowded into the narrow limits that might be occupied by a modern tract. Yet as no scholar questions that we have the true sentiments of Socrates, though the reports of his disciples, Plato and Xenophon, cannot in all things be strictly accurate; far more evidently is it true that the teachings ascribed to Christ give internal proof that they are not the composition of his humble friends, but have an origin evidently above human wisdom. "The inventor would be more astonishing than the hero," exclaims the voice of worldly wisdom. These disciples of Christ indeed say that they pretend not to record *all* he said and did. John xx. 30; xxi. 25. But they declare that they wrote not from their bare remembrance of what they saw and heard. The Holy Spirit was upon them. John xiv. 26 seq. God himself bore witness to their authority. Heb.

ii. 4. And converting power still accompanies their teachings in all the earth, even until the present day.

When such a life is written; when it is comprised in so brief a compass; when the writers are divinely inspired, both to reject what they need not write, and to select what they should record: we may properly judge that nothing insignificant is here handed down for the perusal of later generations. As in the ancient Jewish tabernacle, every pillar and every pin, every curtain and every tassel, the altar of God and the meanest vessel used in the service, must be made according to the pattern shown to Moses in the mount, though the old law had but a shadow of future good things, Heb. x. 1; so, with much more propriety, may we maintain that the permanent and substantial teachings of later times are exact in every minor detail. All things are not of equal importance, but nothing is insignificant in the life of Christ. We indeed often pass hastily over the evangelists: we overlook many of their expressions as of trivial concern. Here we are not wise. Men accustomed to work in gold, gather up every minute particle of the precious dust. Every grain of gospel truth is better than gold. And sometimes a neglected expression is worth more than itself; and may be less properly compared to an unproductive grain of gold than to a priceless seed, that, sinking into the prepared and softened heart, and quickened into life by the dews of the Spirit and the shining of the Sun of Righteousness, may spring up and multiply into a harvest of eternal joy.

Instead of a single biography of our great Teacher, the Divine Spirit, speaking through as many servants, has been pleased to furnish us with four. These bear sufficiently the characteristics of their writers, and are sufficiently independent of each other, to give them greater weight as testimonials, and to impart greater interest to the details they narrate in common. They "have been likened to four portraits or four landscapes, all presenting the same objects, but in different lights and from different points of view, and illustrative of one another."* So we regard them as equally truthful witnesses of the same great history. Speaking of the same person, having the same great end in view, they often say the same things; yet they do not copy each other; in minor respects each has in view a different adaptation of the truth; and we may expect in them such diversities as are not inconsistent with the truth of their respective narratives.

It is an advantage to us when we find the same discourse or deed of our Lord, recorded by the pen of two or more of the evangelists. If we find anything only once suggested by the Holy Spirit for insertion in these permanent records, we may well consider it worthy of our thoughts; and when the same, rather than new teachings are two or three

* Alexander on Mark, Preface.

times repeated, they are certainly not less worthy of our careful study. With two distinct views of any landscape, different but equally truthful, we should better understand the scene. We can learn some things from one writer which another has omitted; and the whole matter is fully brought before us only when we compare all that is told us. We have an illustration of this in the philosophical instrument called the stereoscope. In this instrument we get views of peculiar distinctness and satisfaction and beauty; we have two pictures of the same view, yet only nearly and not precisely identical, placed so before us that they blend into one. Whether we can explain the philosophical principle of the instrument or not, we see the beauty of the scene presented. But the Scriptures, which are full of true philosophy, have adopted an analogous method of presenting before us scenes of historical interest. Some scenes and some teachings in the life and ministry of Christ are but singly recorded; as only John tells us of his interviews with Nicodemus and with the woman of Samaria; and only Luke records the delightful parable of the Prodigal Son. But other scenes are given us by two or more of the evangelists; each historian speaks with less or more diversity from the others; the narratives are manifestly independent and are not always obviously harmonious; yet the differences are no greater than would be seen in separate views of the same landscape taken from different points of observation; and indeed, as in the stereoscope, we see the scene far better when diverse views are attentively studied till they blend and harmonize in one.

It is an excellency of every meritorious picture that its beauties grow upon us; and that it affords us the more pleasure, the more carefully we study its general effect and the separate parts. A rough, coarse painting often makes a good impression when seen from a distance; but it will not bear close examination, nor can we venture to distinguish its minor details. In a better specimen of taste and skill, we can do otherwise. We admire the whole work, as a whole; and we then use simple means to confine our gaze to a single spot, excluding all the rest; and thus we please ourselves with the minuter beauties. In nature we may carry this process to the utmost limits possible for us; and this in either direction, to gain larger or more minute views, which are equally astonishing. We may look at God's great works in their vastness; and how grand appears the empire he has made as we gaze by the aid of a telescope out into space,

> "From world to luminous world, as far
> As the universe lifts its blazing wall."

Or we may look downwards, and by the aid of the microscope we may see some minute fragment of these works of God. We may take the down on the wing of a fly, which we could not even see without the help of an instrument; and we may discern skill as marvellous, adaptation as perfect, and beauty as pleasing in the least as in the greatest of the works of such a God.

The word of God is like his works; and our study may wisely be directed to its teachings as a whole, and to the precious instructions of its minor details, which, like the things of nature, give more delight the more profoundly they are known. No book in existence is at all to be compared with the Bible. We can form no conception of the blank that would be left in human thoughts, if the teachings it has given were completely blotted from the memory of man. All our clear knowledge of God and of salvation and of eternity, we learn from the sacred pages. But this great volume is entirely consistent and harmonious with itself and with its great principles. It is not always obviously so. Nature also has its apparent jarrings; and wise men are often confounded that unquestionable truths do not seem to agree together. But such apparent discrepancies call for more patient observation and thought, that our misconceptions may be corrected and the hidden harmony perceived. It gives greater interest and larger profit to our studies of nature that the gold is not found pure upon the surface; but that we must often journey far to find its place, dig deep to get it, and even then must skilfully refine it before it can be used. It gives us a better appreciation of the gospel, that it is "hid in a field;" and that we must search for it as for hidden treasure.

Sometimes at least we ought to direct our thoughts to the careful study of brief passages and isolated expressions in these sacred writings. It is the design of these pages to consider carefully a single portion of our Lord's life. Let us imagine that we had now the opportunity afforded us of spending a week with Jesus. Suppose that we could be transported away to Judea, and far back in time, till we stood before the incarnate Son of God. Perhaps it is quite impossible for us to think of him as he appeared in the eyes of the generation then about him. Even his favoured disciples did not know him; the three who stood with him on the mount of transfiguration were still ignorant of the majesty of his person and claims, as they saw these things after his ascension, and as they now appear to us. But if we do not attempt to divest ourselves of our familiar thoughts concerning him; if we look upon that meek and humble man and know still that he is the Lord from heaven; if we keep present with us the thought that words or deeds like these would the earth never know again, we will carefully engrave upon our memory every deed we see and every word we hear. To spend an hour, a day, a week with Jesus! What disciple would not desire it! How it would delight and profit all our future life; and how would the minuter events of days like these, compared with the greatest occurrences of ordinary times, be as jewels of priceless value in settings of clay.

The week of our Lord's life to which we refer, begins with the day upon which he heard the tidings of the death of John the Baptist, and ends with the scene of his Transfiguration. We do not affirm that these events all belong with chronological accuracy to the consecutive days of a single week. It is enough to know that they are placed very nearly together by these sacred writers; and that their occurrence within that time is possible. It is very evident that the evangelists have taken no special pains to give the order of time in the things they record of Christ; and thus those who have carefully attempted to harmonize the various teachings of the four gospels have succeeded in showing how the writers agree in their teachings, but have signally failed to determine the exact order of time in which the events have occurred.* The main matter is, to relate the words and works of Christ; and it is only occasionally that we need to compare these things with the precise time of their occurrence. Some of the matters we now consider, owe their significance and interest to the time of their occurrence; but the whole took place within a brief period of time, so that we do no violence to the narratives if we regard them as occurring during one week in the life of Jesus.

* Alexander on Mark, Introduction vi.

CHAPTER II.

RETIRING FROM THE WORLD.

"When Jesus heard of it he departed thence."

It is very evident that the kindest relations existed between our Lord and John the Baptist. Though they were descended of different tribes, they were kinsmen; and their respective mothers were well acquainted with each other. Luke i. 36–40. Yet we do not know that John and our Lord ever met in the early years of their lives; we are rather led to judge that they did not. Certainly the first interview of which we know anything, is when they met on the banks of the Jordan, and when the greater claimed baptism at the hands of the less. Here John knew and yet did not know his Lord. Perhaps he had never seen him before, so widely had their lives been apart; and now he did not fully know him until, after the baptism, the appointed seal from heaven was upon him. But between John and Christ there could be no disagreement. The preacher in the wilderness came as the forerunner of the Messiah; their ministries were unlike yet not discordant; and John was willing to proclaim his own decrease and the increase of his Lord. We do not believe that they were ever much together, or that the friendship of John and Jesus was maintained by personal intercourse. But they were one in the service of truth; and John's disciples were restrained by him from feeling any jealousy of the new and greater teacher.

Some, at least, and perhaps many, of John's disciples became the disciples of Christ. Some of them did so while Christ was yet alive, John i. 35; and some after his ascension. Acts xviii. 25; xix. 1–5. The ministry of John was preparatory to that of our Lord, who therefore did not fully begin his public services till John was cast into prison. How long John was kept a prisoner we cannot decide. But at last the second Elijah met a new Jezebel,* and different from the first, escaped not her power. The account of his death need not now engage our thoughts. We are told that as soon as his disciples had buried the body of their master, they came with their griefs and told them to Jesus. This is the first incident belonging to the period of time which we propose to spend in his sacred company. Just then also came the disciples whom Jesus had sent out to preach the gospel, and gave him an account of their mission. When Jesus heard these things, under the influence of various motives, he departed to separate himself and his disciples from the multitudes about them; and perhaps even went out of the country; at least he went to the borders of

* Lange on Matthew.

Tyre and Sidon. Just then more than any time in his history he seems to have shunned public observation. This itself attracts our attention and fills us with surprise. We wonder that he should ever wish to be out of the public view; and we share somewhat the feeling expressed by his unbelieving brethren, when they said, "Depart hence and go into Judea, that thy disciples also may see the works that thou doest. For there is no man that doeth anything in secret, and he himself seeketh to be known openly. If thou do these things show thyself to the world." John vii. 3, 4. We wonder to hear him charge those whom he healed, "See thou tell no man." Matt. viii. 4. "See that no man know it." Matt. ix. 30. Now for urgent reasons he wished to be away from observation. If we accompany him, he leads us first into a desert place. When there the crowds have sought him out, we must go with him as he steals by night across the stormy waters of the sea; and when again the multitudes are around him, we retreat with him to the borders of Tyre, where he enters a house and wishes that no man may know it.

Perhaps one of the reasons for our Lord's desire at this time specially to separate himself from public observation had regard to his own safety; and this regarding his deliverance from persecuting foes and injudicious friends. The early preaching of our Lord was immensely popular. An extraordinary concourse of people attended his preaching;

and his fame grew rapidly. Yet he very soon met with most violent opposition, which was the more virulent, because he neglected the ceremonial services of the Pharisees, sought his associates among the poor, ate with publicans and sinners, claimed the power of forgiving sins, and disregarded the prevalent views respecting the sanctification of the Sabbath day. At every period, from the time his ministry was fairly understood, he was closely watched by hostile eyes; and his enemies would have been glad to find any occasion against his life. He must therefore not only guard his own conduct, but take care that those who were friendly to him should not do things in his name that were contrary to the schemes of his grace.

Herod had now slain John the Baptist. He belonged to a cruel and unscrupulous family. When a child, the infant Jesus had been carried to Egypt to escape the sword of this man's father; of the malice of this Herod even the Pharisees warned him, Luke xiii. 31; and surely no scruples of conscience would hinder John's murderer from again bathing his sword in blood. Yet while he avoided Herod, the multitude gathered about him, and their gratitude formed designs that were foreign to his mind and dangerous to his life. They would have taken him by force and made him a king, John vi. 15, and he must again retire to defeat their scheme.

Let us not judge, when our Lord thus hides himself from foes and friends, that this gives proof in jurious to his claims. We expect in him superior wisdom as the Son of God: we expect the bold and manly virtues of the Son of man. But we have, neither here nor elsewhere in his history, any tokens of distrusting God's providential care over his life. We can understand the singular evidences of divine wisdom and power in him, combined with the convincing proofs of human weakness and dependence; we can see how strangely yet how harmoniously these unite in his life, only by a just recognition of his mediatorial Person, and of the estate as Mediator, which he held on earth. It was for no insignificant reason, so long as he dwelt upon earth in humiliation and in the garments of mortality, that he gave himself a name which no person among all his friends ever used respecting him. The SON OF GOD was wont to call himself the SON OF MAN.

He was a man. Though never a mere man, he was truly a man. The Word was made flesh. John i. 14. He took part of our flesh and blood. Heb. ii. The entire scope of Scriptural language marks a vital difference between him and other men; but expressly this was *not* as to the reality of his human nature. As to the manner and as to the purpose of his human existence, he differed from ordinary men. Other men are subject to the law of God by the necessities that belong to them as creatures, he by voluntary choice; they naturally, he federally. Yet he was truly a man. As if he—the Son of Man—would exemplify in his own person, all the essential elements of a true humanity, he was not only born as other men and lived as other men; but, all the difference which sin involves excepted, he was as other men. "Made under the law," Gal. iv. 4, he was truly subject to its authority, and must comply with its obligations of duty, and its restraints of dependence. He must eat and drink and sleep; he must be liable to suffering and fatigue and death; he must watch and pray and resist temptation; he must use prudent measures to ward off evil and to secure good; he must in all these things "be made like unto his brethren." So far as concerns all matters pertaining to his personal comfort and personal duty, we see no such differences between him and other men, as would seem to belong to his eminent dignity. If we stood beside him in the wilderness in the hour of his temptation, we would find him suffering from hunger; and unable consistently, in this his estate of humiliation, to put forth miraculous power to furnish himself with bread. This subjection to law marks the truthfulness and completeness of his human character; and is needful to make him our brother and exemplar. So in his obedience to moral and ceremonial law, in his dependence upon Providence, in his earnest diligence in pursuing his ends, in his carefulness to avoid needless offence, yet in his boldness to withstand the proud and to reprove the hardened, in his kindness to the lowly and the penitent, he was as his disciples should be; and has left us an example that we should follow his steps.

If now we were standing by our Lord as he was then upon the earth, we might find it difficult, with our views of his divine dignity, to conceive of his true dependence in his estate of humiliation. Yet we may neither overlook the greatness nor the lowliness of the incomparable Teacher. Both the power to do and the capacity to obey and suffer, must belong to him; dignity and condescension were both there, the one as truly as the other; and to reconcile these truths is no more strange than it is encouraging and instructive. It must be for noble purposes that such an One partakes of our infirmities. And we need both these assurances, as we look upon our Incarnate God: *that* he is mighty to save, and *that*, touched with a feeling of our infirmities, he was in all points tempted as we are.

Our Lord retired from the public gaze for the double purpose of avoiding the persecutions of Herod and the zeal of ill judging friends. Herod desired to see him; but we cannot know what the result might have been. The appetite for blood grows upon violent men; and though Herod slew John with professions of great regret, he might deem it an easier step to take a second life. Our Lord indeed knew that his hour was not yet come. And this, to his justly reflecting mind, would be a reason for retiring from the tyrant's dominions. The desert to which he withdrew was "under the mild sway of Philip, the only one of Herod's sons who deserved the name of a good prince."* Here he would be out of Herod's reach. It is neither in the true spirit of courage nor of martyrdom, that any man exposes his life to uncalled for peril. It was remarked, in the perils of early Christianity, that the men who recanted in view of death were those who had made in advance the boldest protestations of firmness. It often demands much wisdom to judge of our duty. We may retire from dangers we should rather face; and this is cowardice. Or we may face dangers from which we should retire; and this may be rashness or foolhardiness. True courage is the wise mean between the imprudence that tempts Providence, and the cowardice that fears to go forward in the path of duty. Our Lord retired from Herod; yet when his time was come, he steadfastly set his face to go up to Jerusalem; and he stood calm and meek and fearless to be mocked by this man, and to be scourged and crucified by Pilate, on the day of Calvary.

* Lange on Matthew, xiv. 13.

CHAPTER III.

REASONS FOR REPOSE.

"Come ye yourselves apart and rest a while."

WE have said that just when our Lord heard of the death of John the Baptist, he also received the report of the twelve disciples whom he had sent out to preach the gospel. Not only influenced by the prudential motives already suggested; but affected himself with grief for the death of John—with which feeling many of his disciples, as John's former friends, would deeply sympathize—and desirous of affording relief to the disciples after a season of unwonted toil, he said to them, Come ye apart and rest a while.

It is oftentimes difficult for active and earnest men, who are really interested in the ordinary affairs of life, and who feel the pressing responsibility of the duties providentially assigned to them, to persuade themselves that they need rest; or that they so need it as to justify their absence from their place of service. It is interesting for us, upon this point, to learn a lesson from the Master himself. The disciples had been sent forth for a season of earnest preaching; and they were wearied out in these delightful but exhausting labours. So Whitefield, just before his very last sermon, being told that he was more fit to go to bed than to preach, answered, "True, sir." But turning aside he clasped his hands, and looked up, and said, "Lord Jesus, I am weary *in* thy work; but I am not weary *of* it." The disciples had gone forth through the towns and villages preaching. They had taught the people; they had wrought many miracles; they had perhaps awakened an unwonted curiosity through the land to attend upon the feast of the Passover, which was now just at hand, John vi. 4; and a very large multitude of people, who may have been upon their way to Jerusalem, pressed upon Jesus and his disciples, so that their labours in teaching were greatly increased, and "they had no leisure so much as to eat." Mark vi. 31. Then the Master says, Come ye apart and rest a while. And when he gives the intimation, when true wisdom bids us rest, we are still serving the Lord as truly as in the most wearying toils.

These are feeble frames; these minds easily lose their balance. Neither of them can bear unremitting and exhausting labours. So God has providentially given us seasons of rest that are absolutely needful to the well being of every man. The earth itself is so ordered as to point out for us our regularly-recurring seasons of sleep. We need daily repose; and our revolving planet casts the shades of night around us, to mark the time of needful rest. But at longer intervals we need a different rest from our ordinary cares; a rest involving rather a change of thought than the cessation of thought. So the Sabbath comes to bid us throw off the cares of our usual life, and employ our buoyant energies in those spiritual engagements, which, as compared with our worldly avocations, are the soul's rest. We can neglect with impunity neither of these Divinely appointed seasons of repose. Let a man attempt to do without sleep; and after a few passing days of suffering, even unto agony, his mortal frame would sink in death. And though the process is less rapidly destructive, no man can neglect the Sabbath, as a period of rest in an active existence, without putting life and reason in peril. So the records of insane asylums will show; and truthful verdicts of many an early death would corroborate the proof. So William Wilberforce remarked that while some of the men who were in public life with him broke down under excessive and unremitting toil—so that insanity and suicide resulted from the over-tension of the mind—for himself, he too would have broken down, but for his habitual observance of the day of sacred rest. "I can truly declare," said he, "that to me the Sabbath has been invaluable." Well may toiling man bless God for his holy day. He who made us has provided for us necessary seasons of repose. "For he knoweth our frame; he remembereth that we are dust." Ps. ciii. 14.

But besides these common times of rest, seasons of more than usual exertion demand corresponding relaxation. Many a merchant would sink under his toils, if his busiest seasons were an exact type of the entire year. Men who till the earth could not possibly sustain, for the whole year, the efforts they put forth for the brief season of harvest. We may be justified in the extraordinary labours of any brief time; but they cannot last. After special labours through the villages and neighbourhoods of Judea, Christ said to his disciples, "Come ye apart and rest a while."

Now the teachings of Providence to bid us secure these periods of relaxation may come in different ways. If in our zeal and interest for our usual duties we pay too little attention to ordinary monitions, they may be more plainly sent; perhaps sorrow, laid in some form or other upon us, may beckon us to go apart from the busy world. We refuse to notice the milder warnings of lassitude and flagging energy; and our overtasked frames give way to an undue pressure, and disease comes upon us. The duties we could not leave, we are obliged to leave; the care we could not throw off, we must give up; and other hands must do the work which we thought belonged to us. In the chamber of feebleness and languishing, we find a change of scenes, and learn the lessons we thought we had no time to learn. There we secure leisure to look inward, that we may see the true workings of our own hearts; that we may recognize that our earthly duties are to be done, not for themselves alone, since they and we may so easily be separated, but as means to higher ends.

And indeed we are often taught these lessons of leisure and retirement quite as profitably, when yet, in our own persons, we are free from disease and feebleness. We may be called aside from ordinary cares through afflictions laid upon the persons of others. God has bound us to each other in ties of affection and kindred, so that no man is a solitary being; and thus Providence can lay hold upon us and draw us where he will, by simply touching others. As the spark of the electric battery runs through the circle of joined hands, no matter how large; so our afflictions are social, rather than personal. Death enters the circle of our acquaintance; and when a friend is called away we cannot but feel the stroke. When the visitation is upon a near friend, true affection, and even the simple proprieties of life, call us to withdraw for a time from our busy avocations, that we may render the last tribute of respect; and for a longer season we are disinclined to the merely social privileges of society. The sudden death of a friend especially, awakens serious thoughts in us; and prompts us to seek retirement. Have we not the example of Christ in this? He who wept at the grave of Lazarus has now just heard of the death of John the Baptist; and in the warmth of pious friendship, and for the proper indulgence of grief, he and his disciples would leave the world a while.

Sometimes our seasons of withdrawal are far from being times of leisure and relaxation. They are times of burdening cares, yet different from our usual avocations; but they are times when we are called to profitable thoughts and spiritual improvement. We are wise when we judge so of them. Sickness visits our household. Should we not consider every affliction that enters the abode as designed for those members of the family who are kept in health, as well as for those who languish before our eyes? Are we not often forced to believe that they are sent purely for the benefit of those that are not sick? A very large proportion of our anxious days and watchful nights are spent by the cradles of our babes; and we are far more frequently called to lay an infant down to its final rest than an older form. If the Christian poet could write, concerning all our earthly afflictions,—

> "Smitten friends
> Are angels sent on errands full of love;
> For us they languish, and for us they die,"

how much more obviously is this true of the sufferings of infant children, which must have their chief moral end in the spiritual improvement of the older friends about them? But when any member of the family, young or old, and with whatever result, whether bereavement or restoration, is laid upon a bed of languishing, it is the voice of Providence saying to stricken hearts, Come ye apart a while. There is no chance in this occurrence, in the person it affects, in the grief it occasions, in the results it reaches; and we should not undervalue these times of sorrow. They are often long enough and changeful enough to teach us a thousand alternating lessons, from the depths of desponding fear to the heights of exulting thankfulness; and, taking our whole lifetime into view, they come often enough to make us inexcusable in that guilty folly that can be contented with the mere things of earth. No portion of our experience is better fitted "to try us and to prove us and to know what is in our hearts," than these seasons of grief. A beloved one languishes before us; we are helpless, all human aid is helpless, to afford relief; if help comes, it must be from above. Then there is a God; then we need a God; then, if never otherwise, our cries are wrung forth towards God. We indeed unwisely push these thoughts away, and refuse to learn the lessons that are taught us, even when the final shadows begin to darken the room. Yet we have great lessons to learn in the chamber of affliction. How little this world is worth; how slight a hold have we upon our most valued treasures here; how near is the grave to our happiest hours; there is but a step between us and eternity!

God calls us aside again and again; he touches the tenderest places of our hearts, yet gives us many proofs that these visitations are in his mercy and for our profit. He mercifully spares those whom we feared to lose; he often mercifully prepares those that are called away. In the hour of affliction time is given for serious thought; wants are felt, to call forth our prayers: and manifold mercies mingle in sorrow's cup. The heart that softens not, under such dealings, must be hard indeed; the man who prays not in trouble must be far from God; he who makes no serious vows in adversity should be startled at his own perverseness. Precious are the seasons when God says, Come apart a while. The griefs of earth are bitter; its bereavements are often long remembered; sad are our parting hours, and desolate our darkened homes; but precious throughout eternity will be the recollection of many a time of anguish, many a silent sick chamber, many a patient sufferer, many an hour of earthly separation. "No chastisement is for the present joyous but grievous, nevertheless afterwards it yieldeth the peaceable fruits of righteousness."

"Not first the glad, and then the sorrowful,
But first the sorrowful, and then the glad;
Tears for a day—for earth of tears is full—
Then we forget that ever we were sad."

But let us not think that our times of withdrawing from the world and of serious reflection should be only those when Providence, as it were, forces us aside. As intelligent, moral, reasonable beings, we should make provision for times of solitary meditation, when we are alone with God, when we commune with our own hearts in his presence, and when time and earth are shut out, that the light of eternity may shine upon us. Every soul of man should have its direct, filial intercourse with its Maker; we all need to utter prayers and to make confessions, which only he should hear; and he invites us to draw near his throne. We need these times of retirement as the balance-wheel of our energetic age. It has often been said, in the comparison of our generation with those that have gone before us, that our modern life is characterized by restless activity, rather than by serious and deep thoughtfulness. It is not that we are not a thinking age; but there are many temptations for Christians to overlook some important things belonging to the Christian life. It has been charged upon us *that* the deep reflection, so worthy of the great truths of the gospel, and so promotive of the sterling graces of Christian character; and *that* the wrestling prayerfulness which brings the soul so near to God, do not belong to us, as they were to be seen in the sturdy piety of a former race; *that* we can scarcely even relish the teachings which more contemplative instructors have handed down for us. Let the very charge awaken us to consider the path of duty and wisdom in so great a matter: and this without needing to declare that these comparisons are all just, and without falling into the error which the wise man of even a remote antiquity so plainly rebukes, of judging that former times were better than our own. Ecc. vii. 10.

That the type of piety, *e. g.* in the seventeenth century, was different from that in our age; that it had its desirable aspects, we may readily own; and this without deciding that that was an age of deeper or more prosperous piety. Let us learn of them: but to do this profitably we need not disparage our times, nor lessen the activities of our age, nor change the tastes of our reading people. How gladly would Baxter, and Bunyan, and Howe, and Charnock have scattered their volumes as widely as we scatter them, or have known with how much delight their choicest writings are read by us, or have seen in all the earth as many people able to read as we now see, or have entered the open doors of access by which we can approach so many perishing millions! They lived in times, even after the days of the great reformation, when men of whom the world was not worthy were compelled to "steal opportunities of usefulness, and to preach the gospel in secret," or not to preach it at all. And many of their hours of retirement, spent in penning many valuable teachings, were passed, by constraint of violent men, in the gloom of imprisonment, or in days of exile, or Providence had bidden them rest a while in the chamber of sanctified affliction.

The activities of our age and the success God has graciously given to these, would have seemed inestimably precious in the eyes of such men. And we, who live in the midst of these activities, know well that the energies of the people of God are not taxed to the utmost to maintain any of Zion's schemes of giving or doing. Let not our complaints be unreasonable. How rare is the sight of a Christian who labours too hard for Christ! Rather, have we not all room for far more effort: we scarcely reach by our missionary efforts, a tythe of those we could influence; and the ability of the church is far in advance of her efforts and her contributions.

We do not wish the knowledge or the activity of the church of God any less than they are: but it may be true that we do lack the deep and serious thought and the earnest prayerfulness, that were eminent in other days. We may learn from former brethren to study the truth of God more earnestly, and to pray more fervently. It would better fit us for larger activity and better direct our energies, if we were more contemplative and devotional. Our best ideas of piety lead us to regard it as an inner life; and nothing personal to each of us is more important than to cultivate the heart.

We have witnessed in our day a special interest excited in public prayer-meetings. And these have certainly been of great profit to the cause of religion. But no public services can wisely be allowed to take the place of important private duties. We need regular seasons of communion with Him. We shall see as we accompany Jesus and his disciples apart from the multitude, that he has given us an example of private devotion. And let us learn that THE CLOSET, which he enjoins upon us by his precepts and practice, is not simply a place and time of prayer, where we may tell our wants in the ear of our Father. It is this indeed; but it is more. We even wrong our souls when our prayers are but *impromptu*. We should know far greater wants than those that rise to the surface, and thus attract even our careless notice. The closet is the place and time of reading, meditation, recollection, anticipation and self-inspection; as well as of prayer for Divine forgiveness, renewal and assistance; and of praise for mercies already received. Before our Father's eye we must strive to free ourselves from those unhappy influences which intoxicate our pride, fill us with ambition, and stimulate us to an erratic, transient, and perhaps Pharisaic activity. Before him, we should study to know what we are, and what is the prevailing temper of our hearts. Before him, we should inquire what we are to do, and how we are to do it; that so we may secure that best element of a true success, THE DIVINE BLESSING!

There is surely no danger that our energies will be paralyzed or our activities lessened, to meet the increasing demands of aggressive duty, when we are never negligent of the claims the closet has upon us. Rather, thus we renew our strength. The fountain of flowing water that is not fed from secret springs must soon dry up, and cannot bear continual draughts upon it. Men may run zealously, and speak freely in the fervour of a new profession; but they will soon be hindered, if they neglect the secret sources of pious strength. The grain that fades in the first sunbeams of tribulation has but feeble roots in the shallow soil. The secret of steadfast energy, of prolonged and increasing usefulness in the church must be sought in the strength which the soul gains in communion with God. A vigorous mind in a sound body makes the healthy man; and the best style of a Christian is found in him who lives with God apart from the world, that he may walk with God in the world. This is the prophet's ancient solution of pious activity; "Even the youths shall faint and be weary, and the young men shall utterly fall: but *they that wait upon the Lord* shall renew their strength; they shall mount up with wings as eagles, they shall run and not be weary, they shall walk and not faint." Isa. xl. 30, 31.

If we learn of Jesus, there is little danger that our piety should tend to separate us from society; lead us to shun the company of men; or bid us consider earthly and public duties as inconsistent with serious and contemplative religion. Jesus says to us, Come ye apart *a while.* There is the widest possible difference between solitude and retirement, asceticism and self-denial, a hermit's cell and a Christian's closet. Private duties may be brief compared with our social engagements: but a half hour of morning devotions may spread its precious influence over the busiest day spent in the world;

or a day of humble devotion may break us away from dangerous associations; and a sacred Sabbath kept apart from the intrusion of worldly thoughts may sanctify the week. No man ever was more industrious than Christ Jesus. From an early age he was about his Father's business. He taught sedulously, both in season and out of season, the waiting people. He did not plead fatigue or hunger as a reason for neglecting the Samaritan woman of Jacob's well: and as we accompany him now apart from busy cares, we may find him allowing his season of rest to be broken in upon; teaching the multitude; supplying their necessities; and even taking the hours of the night for his secret devotions that had been interrupted by anxieties for others. It is not to keep us from busy labours that he calls us to rest and retirement and prayer. But let us weigh the claims of public and private duties; and admit and meet them both. Let not the anxieties and excitements and pressing urgencies of our earthly cares lead us to neglect the very duties to our own souls, which fit us for the due discharge of all other engagements.

CHAPTER IV.

THE MIRACLE OF THE LOAVES.

"And they did all eat and were filled."

THE place to which our Lord retired with his disciples was a desert spot, *i. e.* not perhaps a barren, but an uncultivated and unfrequented place. So we are told that "there was much grass in the place." Jno. vi. 10. In reaching it he passed in a vessel over the sea of Galilee, and landed on the eastern side of the lake, near the city of Bethsaida. The name is twice given. First the company went to Bethsaida, Luke ix. 10: and then, at the close of the day, he sent away his disciples, "to go to the other side before unto Bethsaida." Mark vi. 45. These statements have led Scriptural geographers to believe that there were two cities of this name; though the site of neither can now be determined. Dr. Thomson argues strenuously that one city explains all the terms of the narrative.* Yet other passages of Scripture, not now calling for our notice, favour the usual view. If his starting-point was Capernaum, then it would hardly be *crossing* the sea to go to either Bethsaida. He would rather

* The Land and the Book, ii. 29–33.

pass out into the lake, and keeping along the same shore, reach his destination. So we are told that the people saw him go, and went by land, and reached the place before he did. They may not have lost sight of the vessel all the time.

It is likely that these crowds who now followed Jesus so eagerly, were, in part, composed of persons going up to the feast of the Passover. (See Jno. vi. 4.) It may seem strange that men upon a journey should be destitute of food; but it is implied in the language of the disciples that they were provided with the means of purchasing it. It would be easier to carry money upon a pilgrimage than to carry much provisions.

And now we see the plans of Jesus for retirement and repose broken in upon. The multitudes are again around him. And so we learn from him the duty of sacrificing our personal desires to the larger profit of others. Though he came there to be free from public duties, he cannot repress the warm feelings of compassion, which go forth towards a needy people. So he ascended the side of a mountain, Jno. vi. 3, and sat down and taught them concerning the kingdom of God, and healed such of them as needed it. Luke ix. 11. Rest, and even private devotion, may be delayed when providential opportunities are afforded us of doing good. We have no record of the teachings of our Lord upon this occasion, or of the miracles of healing he wrought: but there is a record of one of his most remarkable works, so interesting and significant that all four of the evangelists have mentioned it. We are almost led to judge that so deeply engaged was he in the work of teaching the people, that his disciples became uneasy at the length of his discourse; even perhaps interrupting him with the suggestions that the time was rapidly passing, that they had no means of feeding this great multitude, and that they should be sent away to the surrounding villages to buy food for themselves.

Our Lord had his own plan in view for the whole matter; but he deals with his disciples for their profit. To try their faith he asked Philip where they could procure bread enough for all. Evidently Philip had no thought of the method now about to be adopted for their supply. Some suppose that Philip and Andrew were addressed, because they belonged to the neighbouring town of Bethsaida, and knew what opportunity there might be for buying food. It seems surprising that all the food of the company is in the hands of a little lad; and that even the disciples do not seem to have taken enough to supply their own wants. Yet it may be, that a limited supply, enough for a smaller company, had been consumed in the earlier part of the day; and now towards the close of the day, all were hungry, and some had been entirely without food since the morning. That may be said, in general, of a large company, that strictly applies not to all. In this emergency, by what simple means is the supply secured. Let us not despise feeble persons or feeble means. A little lad with his scanty store furnishes that by which the multitude is satisfied. Yet we must not forget that the Divine finger gives efficacy to these feeble things. With his blessing, the small becomes great. As a little maid secured healing for Naman the leper; as out of the lips of babes may come instructions, feeble in themselves, yet powerful through Divine mercy; so here a little boy becomes a blessing.

> "What time the Saviour spread his feast
>   For thousands on the mountain's side
> One of the last and least
>   The abundant store supplied."

As the time was towards the middle oı last of March, and the spring rains had already fallen, the fields of Palestine were in their richest dress, and the grass of the place made it pleasant to seat themselves upon the ground. But if now we stood beside that wonderful teacher, as he gave command that the people should arrange themselves by companies, could our faith comprehend the great miracle which he was then about to work? Could we believe that he would attempt to supply the necessities of more than five thousand persons with these few loaves in his hands? Or that he could accomplish so great a wonder as this? Even with the supposition that the number of women and children was comparatively small, since only males were *required* to attend the Passover, put five thousand men into the streets and dwellings around you, and then try to realize the usual amount of food they would need for a single meal, that so you may form some just estimate of this supernatural miraculous supply. For it is but doing justice to the wonder, when we realize its true greatness. We should study the whole matter here written for our instruction, as we surely would ponder everything connected with it, if we stood beside the Lord and saw all this with our own eyes.

We have said already that we do not wish to look upon Jesus as he appeared in the eyes of the men of his own day. They saw him as an humble man, and were gradually lifted up by an acquaintance with his words and works, to the belief of his superior dignity. We, on the contrary, have been trained from our very childhood, in the knowledge, both of his superiority over the sons of men, and of the greatness of his mission to our earth. In these respects, therefore, they and we may be said to stand upon different sides of the miracles of Christ. To them it might seem wonderful that he should or could do such great things. They saw him as a man; and it never entered their minds that man could do a thing like this. Even to arrange the company, as if to supply their wants, would seem a strange thing in their eyes: and the disciples, who knew much already of his power, would do this, wondering what he would next attempt. Yet the presumption ought to be the reverse to us. It would be wonderful in our eyes if the Son of God should *not* work the most convincing miracles. Stand beside that Redeemer and consider for a moment who he is and what he came to do? and then reflect and decide, whether the working of miracles on his part is not just what we should look for at his hands?

If this man is merely a teacher, who instructs our race from the depths of a personal wisdom superior to other sages, and this is all: then let his wisdom be his testimonial, and it is unreasonable that he should be expected to work miracles. But if this is the incarnate Son of God, if his errand to earth is to do for man that which man could not accomplish, and to teach that which otherwise man could not know, then it may reasonably be expected and demanded, that he should give proofs of his dignity in works which no other man can do. Indeed the greatest miracle of all has already been accomplished when the "Word has become flesh." Let the dignity and work of Christ be taken into the account, and the presumption that such a person would work miracles is reasonable. Let us go forth to stand with Jesus surrounded by that hungry multitude; and we would come back disappointed, if he must send them unsupplied and fainting to seek food in the villages around.

And surely no objection can be brought against the working of such a wonder, because of the power necessary to accomplish it. For the claim is that the worker is the Son of God: the power therefore which he could put forth is infinite. It is just for us then to say that the miracles wrought by our Lord Jesus when he was upon the earth, were not the greatest things which he could do. Such works as he wrought were displays of power surpassing all created energy, and therefore sufficient and convincing proofs of his Divine commission and authority: but the works of Christ were still inferior to the works of God's creative power. To restore the dead to life; to open blind eyes; to unstop deaf ears, are not works as great as the original gifts of life and sight and hearing. That God should give good sight and hearing and health to so many thousands in Judea, was surely a greater thing than that his incarnate Son should heal the few that lacked these advantages. And the ordinary supply of food by which the teeming earth is fed, is surely incomparably greater than what might meet the necessities of a few thousands for a single meal. The power necessary to do that which Christ here accomplished, is enough to prove his divinity: and yet, in the comparison, it is not greater but less, than the energy every day put forth before us by the finger of Omnipotence. We cannot discredit these miracles on the score of their greatness. Grant that they were wrought by him "by whom also the worlds were made;" and great as they are, they seem then but "the hidings of his power."

But if we were companions of Jesus upon that occasion, esteemed worthy of record by the pens of all the evangelists, the most profound interest taken in the work of that day would be entirely in keeping with every just impression we should receive of him. It is worthy of Jesus that he should be willing to forego his own plan of leisure and retirement, and fill his hands with new duty for the sake of these multitudes. It is worthy of the great Shepherd that he should pity the sheep scattered without care, and should lead them in the pastures of truth. It is worthy of his benevolence that he should supply their wants and not dismiss them fainting. The very manner of the miracle is worthy of him, when he reverently invoked the blessing of the Father upon the food—teaching us that ordinarily we should recognize gratefully the hand from which come all our common comforts. "He that enjoys anything without thanksgiving," says the Jewish Talmud, "is as though he robbed God."* It is appropriate also that while the liberality of supply stops at nothing short of satisfying the wants of all, this should be consistent with the careful gathering up of that which remained. For it is no design of Providence to teach men wastefulness, even when the abundance around us is largest. God's gifts are to be used and accounted for, not abused or wasted.

Perhaps we cannot fully appreciate the excellence of the miracles of Christ, their entire fitness to his character and claims, and their full consistency with the wonderful workings of God's providence, unless

* Trench on Miracles, 217.

we place them in contrast with the pretended miracles of different times. The more fully such a contrast is made, the more manifestly are the claims of the gospel vindicated. We may of course expect, since the publication of the gospels, that many imitations of his wonders would appear among the alleged miracles of later times. But it is remarkably characteristic of the spurious miracle, that it is usually a stupid wonder, imposed upon admiring credulity, unnatural in every aspect, aimless in purpose, insignificant in its lessons, and of no profitable spirit. What if the moon did divide at Mohammed's bidding, and pass down the sleeve of the prophet's robe, and ascend again to the sky? What if a Romish saint did cross over the sea upon a millstone; or buoyed up upon his own cloak? These and such like, would be marvellous occurrences; but they would be unnatural in aspect, unmeaning in influence, and with no tendency to bless or instruct beholders.

If we consider this miracle of our Lord, it is just such a work as becomes the character he bears. If this is the Author of creation and the Worker of providence now dwelling among men, and putting forth his finger to prove his presence, let his new works be like those old doings which men have known from his hand since the world began: or let every diversity bear that significance in itself which vindicates its propriety and excellence. This miracle is, like the usual workings of nature around .us, a miracle of multiplication. He does not bid hands unseen spread a table before them, and cover it with abundant food, mysteriously brought from unknown quarters; nor does he command the stones of the field to become bread. But a few loaves are multiplied. Does it seem strange that they should be? Is it not just as strange that the ordinary multiplication of our food should differ from this miracle only in this, that it is more deliberately accomplished? What is the produce of the ripening wheat-field, but the providential multiplication of one grain into fifty or a hundred? Is it not still wheat when you sow and wheat when you reap? So was it then barley-bread in the Saviour's hands and barley-bread for every man's appetite. There is a difference in time. It takes months to change the seed sown into the harvest gathered; and these barley loaves were multiplied in the few passing moments of that declining day: but the work of the Mediator Incarnate is like his works in providence: in no wise conflicting with the laws, over which he exhibits his control. If we wonder how he could feed five thousand with this small supply, yet must we admit that he feeds the whole earth, and this during century after century by causing the seed sown to multiply, each after its kind.

The spirit of this miracle is equally becoming the claims of him who wrought it. The miracles of Moses and Elijah were stupendous: but they were chiefly miracles of judgment. The works of Christ were beneficent. In this case, he had withdrawn to a solitary place for retirement and devotion: the multitude were intruders upon his privacy; yet he gives no indication of displeasure. All is compassion and kindness. Pitying their scattered condition, he patiently taught them: compassionating their bodily necessities, he supplied their wants. This benevolence becomes him. This is the same hand that scatters so many providential blessings at every man's door every day.

It is not possible for us to secure the full force of the argument for the miracles of Jesus drawn from the evidence which proves their actual occurrence as historical events, by the consideration of any one of these wonders separately. Christ's life, character, reputation and influence must be taken with his preaching and his miracles as one grand whole: the separate parts may indeed admit of separate proof and vindication: but their consistent harmony greatly strengthens the just evidences of his truthfulness. It was not possible for such a teacher to secure such an influence, based professedly upon his power to work miracles, when yet no such wonders were really performed. For what he did, he did openly: it required but the use of their senses on the part of multitudes to discern the reality of these things: and it is manifest that the glory of a hundred apparent successes would have been marred by the occurrence of a single failure. But no such failure ever happened. Every miracle has evidence appropriate and sufficient to establish it, while the testimony taken altogether is peculiar and forcible. In this miracle we have just the proof we should expect. The wonder was not expected: but the parties most interested and most capable of judging were fully persuaded that it was truly wrought. Perhaps the multitude began to feel some anxiety in the desert, as the disciples certainly did. Neither of them suggested, or even expected, relief from him by any miracle. And he asked counsel of his disciples expressly that he might show how feeble were their resources for such an emergency. And this very inquiry fully revealed the destitution of the people. Yet though so small a supply could be brought forth, the entire multitude was filled. They at least were fully convinced that his power had fed them in the wilderness. And who could be better witnesses than the disciples, who distributed the multiplied loaves to the companies; and the people whose wants were so unexpectedly satisfied?

But after all, the significance of the miracle is the most important thing to which our thoughts can be turned. It is not a great wonder, to call forth our astonishment merely: it is far more and better than this. It is a revelation of our Lord himself as the true bread by which man lives. What though the people who ate these barley loaves did not think so of him: let us learn better as we listen to the teachings which he gave to them in this very matter. The next day they followed him to the other side of the sea; and he reproved them for the low views they had taken of him and of his work. They followed him, because he had fed their bodies; they should rather have hungered for the life-giving truth. He bade them seek not the food that perisheth, but that which endureth to everlasting life, and *this* he also could give.

Scarcely any more natural or expressive figures can be used to signify spiritual necessities than those which arise from our well-known natural wants. Hence hunger and thirst express the desires of the soul, and food and water are significant of their supply. Figurative language like this, is as intelgible as any plain language can be. When Christ says, "Blessed are they that do hunger and thirst after righteousness," his meaning is as simple as any expression can make it. In all ages of the church the like substantial teachings have been given by like figures. So the manna and water in the wilderness included a reference to the spiritual dependence of Israel, and an intimation that they must receive supplies from heaven for their spiritual necessities.

That men may fail to understand the true teaching of these figurative expressions is true: not because of their obscurity, but because of the depraved blindness of sinful minds towards spiritual things. So the multitudes here fed by our Lord did not understand him, when he spake of himself as the true bread from heaven, and wondered if this man could give them his flesh to eat. So the monstrous and impossible doctrine of transubstantiation has grown out of the literal rendering of our Lord's words. And yet he himself gives us their interpretation. He declares that it is not as their fathers did eat manna in the wilderness. But as bread nourishes the natural life, so Christ himself nourishes spiritual life. As to natural life, we eat bread that we may live. As to spiritual life, we believe on Christ that we may never die. *Eating* in the one case, is the exact equivalent of *believing* in the other. Christ is the bread from heaven, because he who uses this bread, in the appropriate sense in which it can be used, that is by receiving, appropriating, relying upon Christ as the Redeemer, shall live by him. Are not these his very words to this same multitude? "He that cometh to me shall never hunger, and he that believeth on me shall never thirst."

Let us not pass the day with Jesus as he feeds the hungry multitude on the side of the lake of Galilee, without repeating in his ears, and with a better understanding of them, the words with which they addressed him, "Lord, evermore give us this bread." Christ is the true bread of life. And indeed he invites us to partake of him and of his benefits that we may live. If he looked with compassion upon that multitude, because they were scattered as sheep having no shepherd, we surely cannot make the mistake of supposing that his concern for them had respect to anything else than their spiritual interests. He did indeed heal the maladies of the body; he esteemed it appropriate for him to multiply the loaves that their bodies might be fed: and when he had done this, they would have made him their king. But when they eagerly followed him, he reproved in them their low thoughts of what he was, and of what he could do. He bade them labour not for the meat that perisheth, but to labour for the meat that endureth unto everlasting life. When they asked how they must thus labour and for such an end, let us seek to comprehend his answer, even if they did not. "This is the work of God that ye believe on him whom he hath sent." Christ comes to heal the malady of the soul, and to supply those spiritual necessities which he alone can supply. He still pities these necessities, even in those who feel them not. We can easily imagine that while the heart of Jesus felt compassion so deep for that people, it formed a part of their misery that they did not recognize the very things that most affected him. So it is still. How often must he weep over guilty men, as he wept over Jerusalem, saying, "Oh, if thou hadst known!" How must he still declare in the ears of perishing men, "Ye will not come unto me that ye might have life."

Yet truly as Christ did not feed that multitude but because of the necessity thus providentially laid upon him, he has proposed himself to us as the living bread only because of our imperative necessities. If we eat not of this bread we must die. Let us learn the depth of our necessities from the very fact that infinite wisdom has made this provision for our need. Christ wrought no miracle of all his ministry for a vain display. Least of all can we judge, that his very mission to earth was needless. The bread of life is given to us in the wilderness, because without it we faint and die. And there is enough to feed all the multitude. And why should we perish with hunger, when there is bread enough in our Father's house?

CHAPTER V.

DIVINE BENEFICENCE.

"Give ye them to eat."

"How pleasant to me thy deep blue wave,
O sea of Galilee;
For the glorious One who came to save
Hath often stood by thee." McCHEYNE.

LET us linger a little longer to learn further lessons from the compassion and bounty of Jesus towards the multitude, whom he fed by the sea of Galilee. Why should we read over these wonderful pages with less thoughtfulness, than if we saw the things that are here recorded? Are there not reasons additional, in the superior knowledge we possess of that incomparable Jesus, to make us weigh with more serious reflection every recorded word and action; and especially to consider thoughtfully those significant and symbolical teachings whose permanent value belongs as much to us as to those who saw and heard them? Let us eat of the bread thus broken to so large a multitude.

We have intimated before that the moral argument in favour of the working of miracles is stronger than any presumption drawn from the constancy of natural laws against them. If the person whose footsteps we now accompany, is the Son of God, both his person and his errand justify our expectations, that he should display his power, and explain his work by wondrous doings. Shall the regularity of the laws of nature stand in the way to prevent the God of nature from putting forth his finger to prove his presence, when he would do a work greater than any he has done in nature? We do not deny the usual constancy of natural laws. We recognize and admire their constancy. So far from invalidating the usual uniformity of natural laws when we speak of miracles, we rather affirm that a miracle would lose both its intelligence and its significancy, if there was not a uniformity in natural things that was invariable, except by miracle. Yet what are these laws of nature, but the working of Almighty God by rules which his wisdom has established? Do we then degrade nature, or dishonour the great Author of nature, when we deny that any less than himself can ever work a miracle, or when we affirm that he can do as nature never does, if sufficient reasons present themselves to his mind? Nature is a vast machine, and God is its maker. He who builds a house has more honour than the house; God is greater than the machine God has made; it neither dishonours him nor his works to confess this.

Suppose a skilful mechanic has built an admirable locomotive.* Every wheel is true; every valve

* The thought is from Wardlaw.

is close; flanges of great strength and accuracy confine it to the proper track; and it goes forward on its journey with admirable speed. The chief end for which it was made is to draw its train of cars on to their destination. But as it performs this purpose, hastening on with lightning speed, the engineer discerns a little distance before them, a child upon the track. There is no possibility that he can spring out of the way. Let the engine keep right on its course, and the fatal blow will come, life will be crushed out, and the mangled form will be left upon the fiery pathway. What is to be done? Do you tell me that the wise and humane engineer will put down his brakes, and stop or reverse his engine? But what kind of a reply would it be, if he keeps on his way regardless of consequences, and tells you that his engine was made to run; that its law is "straight forward;" and that no allowance was made, in the perfect machinery he controls, to stop for anything? Would you not feel that such a kind of "perfection" was infinitely undesirable; that a human life was worth more than the stopping of a locomotive; not to say worth more than the best piece of machinery ever set in motion.

God has made the world; has established every law that works in it; and carries forward all their operations. But let us not deify nature. If it was folly for Paganism to worship four-footed beasts and creeping things, let us not choose a more dignified god, yet of the same order. Their elemental sin was worshipping the created instead of the Creator; and even if we stoop not quite so low in details, we still adopt the same bad principle when we honour the work above the Workman. Nature is the mechanism: God has made and controls nature. But into this universe which God has made and sustains, disorder has entered. The noblest of God's creatures in this lower world, has rebelled against the Divine authority; and man needs that God should interpose in mercy for his everlasting salvation.

Beyond dispute sin is here, and man needs Divine aid. And shall we presume to question the propriety and wisdom of Divine interposition, and the proof of this, even by such workings as, beyond all created power, may seem to stay the onward march of nature's great machinery? The purpose is human salvation; let the greatness of the object vindicate the variations from nature which we see in miraculous workings. The engineer, who has received his orders to go forward, may stop his course to save a life, if an emergency demands. The object in view justifies an act, that will not injure his machinery, nor long delay his trip; and that indeed is itself worth more than them both. Thus we vindicate Divine interpositions by miracle to prove indisputably the authority of Divine revelations. These are teachers sent from heaven, who do works which man cannot do. The object of this gospel is the salvation of sinful men. This is an object before the

Eternal Mind far superior to the doings of his hand in physical nature. Since then no violence is done to nature when miracles are wrought: no permanent arrest is made in nature's ordinary workings; no confession is implied of folly in nature's salutary laws: no confidence is shaken in nature's constancy, even in minds that most fully credit the miraculous, let us not enslave God to nature by presuming to deny the wisdom and propriety of miracles. We cannot imagine a more important thing for God to do, than to satisfy man that he speaks in the gospel. The grand object of miracles is a sufficient vindication of their credibility.

These are important thoughts respecting the miracles in general, recorded in the Scriptures. But there are still other lessons, most important for us to learn, as we gaze upon Christ's feeding the multitude by the sea of Galilee. Perhaps there is no other miracle wrought by Jesus that more significantly reminds us of the great things he would teach, than this. He himself seems to hold it in high estimation by repeating it; and by causing it to be recorded by all the evangelists. Christ would teach his disciples of all time a lesson of true dependence upon God's wondrous dealings, in all the times of our weakness and poverty.

We know that this is a fundamental principle of his gospel, that we must walk by faith and not by sight. We may expect him therefore to teach us lessons in the school of faith. Taught by him, we must learn to study less the resources we have in our own hands, and to study more the power of God as our efficient aid. We are not to be presumptuous, but we are to be believing: and the history of the church will prove that God has answered faith, as clearly proving his presence as by the working of a miracle. Our Lord would not have performed this wonder, if the people had not needed it. If they had come there provided with abundant food; if they could have gone to seek it without suffering and loss, no such interposition had been made. But there was due occasion for supplying their necessities, and he did not stay because the bread in his hands seemed inadequate to the purpose. And is there no meaning in the fact that the bread more than held out, to do this appropriate work? This, we judge, is one of the most important lessons of that eventful day. Selfishness would have said that there was too little bread for the supply of his own household: but he would teach faith to act by a different rule. We desire, as natural men, to have full supplies in our own hands, not only for the present, but for the future. We wish comforts not only for the sorrows now pressing upon us, but for those that threaten, and even for those that are merely conjectured, and that may never come. He would have us trust the Divine wisdom and power and mercy for the enlarging of the resources that seem so small. Let us think of this lesson of faith as taught by the bread of that wilderness; and learn that this is one of the most important for our support and prosperity.

It seems the more proper for us to study this particular matter, because there are pre-intimations of the same, in the former teachings of the Scriptures. Christ repeats and enforces the lessons taught previously by the prophets of the Old Testament: for he is their master, and they are our brethren. God led the people of Israel for forty years, in the wilderness, while all through the journey he gave them no bread in advance, but only as they needed it. No other army ever dared go forth into such a desert without making large preparations for their support there: but God wished his people to learn that they lived not by bread only, but by his favour. Though dependent every day, they had full supplies for forty years.

Of all the miracles wrought during the Old Testament times, none is more like Christ's feeding the hungry, than that of Elijah when he blessed the scanty store of a poor widow in the coasts of Zidon. The prophet was both a beneficiary and a benefactor. He asked bread of this poor woman; and found her at the last morsel that her house contained. Yet at the word of the Lord, the end of her scanty supply did not come, until plenty reigned again in the land. Just at the bottom of her barrel of meal, yet for months she never found it empty. Her family was larger than before, yet starvation had fled from her doors. How the meal multiplied, as a physical fact we do not know. Yet the moral and spiritual aspect of the entire transaction is plain enough. She had a prophet for a guest: and the faith that would not turn away his request in the hour of her poverty, found its reward in the salvation of her own house, and has transmitted its lesson of encouragement to far later days.

But let us return to the side of the mountain, and read the lesson of the widow of Zarephath, as Christ teaches us again in the barley loaves. What are these among so many? we ask as we gaze upon them through Philip's eyes of sense. We look again, and lo! the disciples are busy with the waiting companies: again, and every hungry appetite is satisfied: again, and twelve baskets full remain at the last. Astonished and thoughtful we sit down in the evening hour, and ponder the teachings of a scene like this.

This is the same lesson of our daily life, that God teaches us so often by his providence. The widow of Zarephath is far from being the only widow who is never left to want: indeed whose supplies are larger than enough for her own little household, though the scanty store has often been nearly gone, for years and years in succession. We do not call it miracle, when we see the families of the earth fed year by year from God's exhaustless stores, though so many thousands know not one day where they must find the bread of the next. But the workings of Providence for the benefit of men are as wonderful as ever was a miracle. As we now look back to the meal of barley bread given to that multitude by the sea of Galilee, we can easily decide that we would rather sit to eat with them, than to partake of the richest feast ever spread in the palace of an emperor. And the time may come, when we shall decide that no life spent upon the earth is so enviable, as that spent most in dependence upon the providence of God. How many families have been ruined by the wealth that seemed to raise them above dependence—therefore above wholesome exertion. And how remarkable is that kind rule that seems to repeat for so many in all the earth, almost this very miracle. The stores they hold in their hands are like these loaves and fishes for the multitude. And yet they pass through life never destitute, always fed, and at the end seem to have no less than at the beginning. Christ's lesson here, is like the lesson in the sermon on the other mountain side. We need take no anxious thought for to-morrow. He who feeds the raven and clothes the lily, counts us of more value than the flying birds and the springing grass. We may look up morning after morning with the prayer upon our lips, "Our Father, ... give us this day our daily bread:" nor need we fear to trust his providential care.

The teaching of these barley loaves moreover is quite as plainly a lesson of our usual Christian experience. Not for one meal only upon a special occasion, but again and again does the Master feed his disciples from supplies of grace that seem in our eyes totally insufficient. We are called into his service to live by faith upon his word. Faith is not sight, nor possession, nor enjoyment. We know not, we have not, we feel not, as our natural impulses would prompt. Instead of the needed two hundred penny-worth of bread, a little lad of the company has a few barley loaves; and yet in his hands there is more than enough. We walk by faith. Every believer, at the outset of his Christian course, is like Abraham, who went out "not knowing whither he went." He knew indeed that God called; and that God could ever sustain him. But he knew not the trials he must meet, the patience he must exercise, the duties he must discharge; nor had he strength for these things in advance. Doubtless he feared for many things before him, for this is human; but the strength for each duty came when the duty was to be done. And so God deals with all his people. As the knowledge and the strength of a child may be as well proportioned to him as the knowledge and strength of a man are to him; so is it usually, in the dealings of the Divine hand with us. When we discern a duty, though we may feel weak, let us have faith in the orderings of God's providence, and attempt to do it. When we need strength to do his will, is the very time that we are warranted to rely upon his aid. Indeed feebleness is strength, if it calls forth faith in God. Take up that cross! Heavy as it seems, it shall not weigh you down. Address yourself to that duty, so important for yourself and your family. It may prove the most profitable you have ever done. We gain strength by expending strength; we increase in faith by exercising faith; we do more good by trying to do good. The barley bread grows on our hands, as we eat it and as we give it to others. "There is that scattereth and yet increaseth." A church that does nothing because it can do but little, is an unbelieving church; and will still become weaker by such a sin against the faith that Christ demands. The lad's loaves not used at all, will mould upon his hands; selfishly used they may feed a little company; yet by faith are they enough for five thousand. The individual who in the plain path of duty still forecasts evil, counts his forces, and sits down discouraged, forgetting the promises of God, is unfaithful to the gospel. Let us study our opportunities and our duties; let us rely upon Divine assistance; let us do what we can; and we will soon do more than we now imagine.

But the Saviour teaches us a lesson of Christian benevolence. Behold him upon the mountain side, feeding the necessities of the fainting multitude with a few barley loaves; and see here a picture of those great and good enterprises that have been undertaken for the good of man. You can scarcely turn your mind to a single benevolent institution, or benevolent enterprise that does not find its type in this miracle. Jesus is unseen; but the disciples do his bidding.

Our benevolence almost always forms low conceptions of the work that is to be done; and comes to understand it only by grappling with it. We are weak to do the work; and our resources are inadequate to the needful outlay; and we often forecast failure: but how wondrous are those workings of Providence, which give us strength and means and faith and the victory, while we do his will.

When the disciples of Christ began to feed the famishing millions of the world with the bread of everlasting life, how little did they know of the great work they then undertook; and how would they have said of their resources for feeding these great multitudes, "What are these barley loaves among so many?" Yet as they went forth, how did success follow every believing effort. Strength sprang from weakness; plenty from apparent poverty; and company after company in all the lands were fed with the living food. And thus has God ever wrought, so that in the great cause of Christian effort, believing and zealous men are warranted to go forward, relying upon the Divine blessing, though quite unable to calculate every step in advance, or to see the means of success.

Many illustrations of these teachings may easily occur to the thoughtful mind. How feeble the resources in the hands of Luther for warring against that gigantic system of ecclesiastical domination which then ruled the earth! We may either compare him to the stripling David with his sling and stone, triumphing over Goliath clothed in armour; or to the disciples with their barley loaves feeding the fainting people: in either case, the efficacy was Divine. For this is the permanent lesson that God's servants by faith subdue kingdoms, out of weakness are made strong, and prove their lineage by the triumphs of feebleness.

Look at our modern missionary enterprises. No Christian can doubt that the Master calls us to these. Look at the multitudes, scattered like sheep without a shepherd, hungry and fainting, no man to feed them, and divers of them belong afar off. The night comes—the long night that knows no morrow. About the beginning of the present century a feeble band of disciples—as few and as weak and of as little fame among men as the fishermen about Jesus by the sea of Galilee,—heard his voice say to them, "Give ye them to eat!" And they might have looked with astonishment at the feeble means they could command, and have asked, "Whence shall we buy bread for these?" When Carey and his brethren contemplated the formation of a society for foreign missions, their first collection was £13 2s. and 6d.: they had no experience in such matters; they had no precedents to guide them; and worldly wisdom, even in the professed church of Christ, sneered at them and their attempts. Truly it was a barley loaf for a thousand! But they looked at the Lord's command and for the Lord's blessing; they attempted great things in his service and expected great things from his power. And never was faith more justified by its results, or the power of Christ more manifest. The miracle by the sea of Galilee was but a miniature representation of Christ's working through his servants to feed the hungry, compared with his feeding the souls of men through these missionary labours. The work grew on their hands; but the barley bread grew also, and the distributing disciples multiplied. What missionary societies, what missionary labourers, have joined them in their work; until now all Christ's true disciples acknowledge its importance. If the Divine blessing is manifest upon anything we see, it is upon the missionary work. Many a time have the managers of our societies stood fearful as they saw the few crumbs they had, wherewith to feed so many: it is preëminently a work of faith; but growing means, growing labourers, growing success have ever proved the Divine favour toward their efforts to do his will.

It is no fancy thought; no stretch of the imagination merely, to suppose that we accompany the footsteps of Jesus, and see his wondrous workings. This great work of feeding earth's fainting millions with living bread IS GOING ON NOW. Not indeed by the sea of Galilee, but on the shore of the great ocean of eternity, the immense multitudes are seated. It is a desert place, the wilderness of this world: the day will last with us but a little longer: the multitude is seated in companies, not of hundreds and fifties, but of nations and continents: China, India, the islands, yes, Asia, Africa, South America, are waiting to receive from us the bread of life. We have not bread enough for so many: but we must not use our barley-loaves for our own households. When the Master bids, let us have faith. The bread has ever multiplied as Christians give it. God has helped a thousand times, and will still help. Do much for him, and you can do more. Give from poverty, and you shall have abundance. This is the very nature of the work. The bread grows more as we distribute it.

And one lesson more let us learn as we look upon these significant workings of Jesus. If we follow him, we must be believers, and live upon his power. How often do men shrink back from engaging in the service of Christ through the fear that they may not hereafter walk as becomes his gospel. The expression of such fears may indeed indicate a heart little disposed to follow where he leads; and glad of even a miserable excuse for standing back. Christ Jesus calls no hesitating and half-hearted followers. Let those who wish, stand aside for his service. But he gives every encouragement to those who would gladly follow at his bidding. He bids them put away their fears. It may be true that we are unworthy to follow such a Lord; that we are feeble to do the work which he sets before us; seeing how many have brought reproaches upon his name, we may shrink back with pain from the fear that we too may decline. Such thoughts may make the soul humble and prayerful; but they should not hinder our faith or our duty. In an humble and sincere effort to glorify Christ, we may look for his blessing. If we wait until we can see our path clear all through the journey of discipleship, we will never start at all. If we must have now all the grace we need, for days to come, we make presumptuous demands to which he will never respond. The rule of his working is, "As thy day is so shall thy strength be." Morning by morning the manna lay around the hosts of Israel; and the camp never had enough for to-morrow. So was it by the sea of Galilee; so he deals with us. As the bread in the hands of the disciples was never at any one time large enough to supply the multitude, and yet more than sufficed to feed them all, so the grace of Christ for his people, which is never sufficient to supply them for a day in advance, yet never fails through life, and is larger at the close than at the beginning of the Christian course.

The table of his bounty is spread still, to supply the wants of the hungry. Christ even sends forth his servants to compel men, with all urgency to draw near and eat. Better food than barley loaves; better life than this mere mortal existence; larger increase than five loaves for five thousand, he now offers us. Come, buy and eat; without money and without price. Believe on him and live for ever.

CHAPTER VI.

PROVIDENTIAL TROUBLES.

"Jesus constrained his disciples to get into a ship."

THE next scene that occurs in our brief sojournings with Jesus, reminds us of the rapid and wide changes of life. We have just seen our Lord instructing the people and feeding their necessities with abundant food. In that same night his disciples are sent out upon the stormy deep, in darkness and peril. So is it in the experience of human life. Days of prosperity and enjoyment are often immediately succeeded by storm and danger; and the table of our Lord's bounty has perhaps been spread, only to give us strength for trials that hasten on. So Israel ate the Passover, and girded up their loins to go forth that very night upon their long journey; and the disciples were fed by the sea of Galilee, that they might toil that night rowing over its stormy surface.

It is quite undesirable for us to reflect upon the scene thus brought before us, without turning our thoughts towards the spiritual significance which its teachings afford. Everything said and done by our Lord Jesus Christ—everything here recorded by the pen of inspiration, is full of precious meaning beyond the letter of the record. The bread broken at the sea-side may feed us yet; the consolation given on the sea, may yet sustain us in our times of necessity. Figurative actions are as natural to Scriptural teachings, as figurative words are to any other. And so commonly do men use this kind of language, that darkness and a storm need hardly any explanation, when we use them as significant of sorrow and danger. And a storm at sea is, beyond any other tropical expression, appropriate to set forth the helplessness of man in trouble. From the violence of the waves the sailor has no refuge. Whether he rises or sinks with their tumultuous swellings, he is equally helpless. He knows not at what moment he may strike a hidden rock; or be overwhelmed by a higher wave; or be overturned by a fiercer gust. "They mount up to the heavens; they go down again to the depths; their soul is melted because of trouble; they reel to and fro and stagger like a drunken man, and are at their wits' end." Ps. cvii. 26, 27. Thus is it in the experience of life. When troubles come, we are in darkness, we are dejected, we know not the way of relief.

It is a matter of great interest to inquire how the disciples came to be in this storm?

There are many storms and troubles which men can avoid; and which they ought to avoid. It is not true courage, much less is it prudence or piety, to choose our own way and to go through with our own plans and purposes, in defiance of all threatening appearances. He may be a headstrong and bold sailor, but surely he is neither a good nor a safe one, who needlessly leaves a quiet harbour to battle with a rising tempest; or who rushes forward with all possible speed though quicksands or hidden rocks lie across his exact track. Yet there may be times when duty plainly bids us go in the very face of danger; and when our troubles spring up in the pathway of a wise obedience. It makes a great difference when our troubles are not the results of our own rashness or wickedness.

The disciples were exposed to this storm upon the lake in obedience to their Lord's express command; and it would appear, against their own wishes. Let us notice the evangelists' words: "Jesus *constrained* his disciples to get into a ship." Matt. xiv. 22. Why he must *constrain* them, we do not fully understand. But we know that believers now are backward to take up many a service to which their Lord calls them: and often are obedient only through the constraint of his express command. Perhaps these disciples were unwilling to embark, because they were experienced boatmen, accustomed to launch their fishing vessels upon these very waters: and they may have discerned in the horizon the signs of the gathering storm. Only the authority of Jesus could have led them to venture forth at nightfall, and with the prospect of a tempest. We are timid to engage in duties when we see beforehand that they are to be toilsome and afflictive. It should have been enough that he had bidden them go; even overruled their objections; and constrained them to embark. So we are often forced to take our place by constraining providences that shut us up, as if by Divine direction, even to a path that threatens early troubles.

Or, it may be, the unwillingness of the disciples arose from their desire to keep in his company. He wished to send them away, while he remained alone upon the shore. With him, they would have gone cheerfully. They had already known his power to rebuke the raging waters; and with him on the vessel, they would not fear to face the storm. They are now to learn that Christ's bidding is equal to Christ's presence.

Or perhaps they were sent away from more threatening evils to themselves and to their Lord's cause, than the rising storm on the lake. There is a danger on the shore greater than the trouble on the deep: and in this we may find the "needs be" of their present mission. The people were desirous of taking Jesus by force to make him a king. The disciples had ideas so crude of their Lord's mission, and thoughts so ambitious of the things to be accomplished by him, that perhaps they sympathized with the wishes of the multitude; and the Saviour sends them upon the sea to keep them out of the way of temptation. Better embark on these agitated waters than on the more stormy and treacherous sea of politics. It would have been indeed disastrous, to have his immediate disciples involved in these ambitious schemes, so far inferior to his real purposes.

Our Lord may have given no reasons for his command, when he constrained them to embark. Whether reluctantly or readily, they obeyed his word: and it was clearly on their part, a providential exposure to the storm. They were there by the Master's bidding. And though we are very far from saying that we put ourselves away from the protection of Providence, even when we have slighted divine commands and gone wilfully into ways of temptation, still it makes an important difference to reflect, in a time of trouble, how it has come upon us. If we have neglected the plain dictates of prudence; if, worse than this, we have turned aside from the path of duty, and thus gone into danger, we have an occasion of self-reproach more insupportable than any trouble from without. Who does not see the difference between these disciples, tossed on the sea where the command of Jesus had sent them, and the prophet Jonah as he meets the tempest fleeing from the face of the Lord? Our deepest fears and our most anxious perplexities frequently regard the settlement of this very question. We ask in the time of our trouble, "How far are these sorrows the direct or the indirect result of our transgressions?" We know indeed in all our griefs that not a sorrow is laid upon us, not a pang rends our hearts, but in infinite righteousness. We, sinful men, therefore, in every season of affliction may humble ourselves in the presence of God. Yet we cannot always see why he is pleased to lay his hand upon us, now and there. The day of abundance and enjoyment when the Lord opens his hand liberally for our good, is succeeded by the night when he constrains us to go forth, leaving him behind, while we meet the darkness and the storm.

There is a "needs be," we are assured, for these manifold tribulations. Sometimes they need no external interpreter: but the voice of the storm, like the words of the shipmaster to the slumbering Jonah, comes to arouse that sleeping prophet of our hearts, that has been lulled to repose by our seasons of prosperity, and to say to the unfaithful conscience, "Awake, O sleeper! Arise and call upon thy God!" Sometimes, like David, we have given occasion of reproach against religion and against God; and worse than he, if not in the flagrancy of our offences, yet in the obduracy that refuses to hear the voice of the reprover, the stroke of chastisement is laid in faithfulness upon us. Surely then we should bow, if with a late, yet with a genuine repentance; should meekly bear the indignation of the Lord, because we have sinned against him; should be thankful that he reproves rather than forsakes. Or, it may be, that our griefs are kindly preventive of evil. We may be upon the borders of temptation, like these disciples in danger of being carried away with the fervor of the multitude, who would make their Lord an earthly and revolutionary king; and God breaks us loose from cherished plans which his wisdom will not permit us to carry out. And besides all these vindications of his dealings, there are often designs of mercy lying through trouble and beyond its dark clouds, which we cannot discern till the storm is past. A storm at sea is the best emblem of the afflictions of life. The Divine hand alone can protect us in either, or calm their troubled waves to peace. If now we could imagine ourselves to be in the company of these disciples; if we could share their toilings while the wind is contrary to them; if three or four miles is the measure of painful progress in more than as many hours; if we could look out on the wildly tossing billows and fear with them that the storm will not allay, we might find perhaps that our thoughts were strangely kindred to the troubled and agitated feelings of our times of affliction. Could we help but wonder why one of his wisdom should send us forth just at nightfall to meet a coming storm; or indulge the regret—perhaps the murmur—that he himself had remained behind, and that we must buffet the waves alone, without the recognized presence of Jesus in the vessel; or feel almost like turning backward, that we may more quickly escape the fury of the tempest!

And yet it is a support in any time of anxiety,

that our troubles arise in the pathway of duty. The disciples might properly reflect that their Lord had sent them forth upon the sea; that his authority and not their own inclination, had constrained them to embark; and thus they might less fear the swelling of the billows. So the hand that sends us into danger will protect us in it; he who brings the storm upon us, will carry us through, and make the trial a blessing. And if even we have not the consoling reflection that he has sent us forth; if like Jonah we meet the storm fleeing from the Lord, we need not still sink into despondency. A gracious God put away the sin of repenting David; he heard the cry of Jonah from the depths of the sea; and we also, though filled with self-reproach in our times of sorrow, may cry unto the Lord in our troubles; and he will deliver us out of our distresses.

CHAPTER VII.

THE REDEEMER'S PRAYERS.

"He went up into a mountain apart to pray."

BUT let us leave the disciples in their time of peril, and return to the shore to seek the Master. He has separated himself from the people, and gone apart into the mountain to pray. The thronging multitudes had interrupted his season of retirement; but though he calmly turns to bless their necessities, he allows the hindrance to be but temporary. He secures still his devotional privilege, though at the sacrifice of his personal comfort. And who of us could not always secure his seasons of private prayer, if we were willing to use the hours of sleep rather than forego them?

But how can we accompany the footsteps of Jesus, as he retires for solitary prayer; how can we know what we now know of him, without strange thoughts of his times of devotion. We are led to ask ourselves, "Why did Jesus pray? and what were the petitions which he would offer?" And we may understand at least this much, that the prayers of Jesus both separate him from us and bind him closely to us; both prove his dependent and his exalted natures. He had his necessities, as we have ours, and therefore his prayers are our example; but his were prayers in which we could not join; and thus while he teaches us to pray, he prays not with us. He could *never* ask, as we must *always* ask, for the forgiveness of sins. But in his estate of humiliation, he asked for many things for himself, as we learn from his recorded prayers: he held sweet communion with his Father; and he offered his intercessions in behalf of his disciples. And if we feel surprised at the thought that the spotless Jesus would spend whole nights in devotion, let us learn these two lessons from the prayers of our Lord. *First,* That our necessities in prayer are far more obvious than his, and that therefore the duty seems more imperatively incumbent upon us: and, *second,* that the true spirit of piety leads him in whom it dwells to prize the privilege of intercourse with God, so that the holiest will most love the throne of grace. Thus from two opposite motives should we learn to pray. If our sins abound, we need forgiving grace; if our hearts are filled with the love of God, they will overflow with our expressions of thanksgiving. Usually our prayers are like the mourning psalms of David, they include both supplications and thanksgiving; perhaps they begin with grief and end with gratitude.

But though no record is made of the petitions of that solitary hour on the mountain, we know enough of the Saviour's prayers to believe that they were not offered for himself alone. Some, at least, of his night-wrestlings had special reference to their interests; as the night before he chose his band of apostles was spent in prayer to his Father. Luke vi. 12. He was then as he is now, the intercessor: and his prayers doubtless had regard to their present trouble. How different the reality from their conception of it. Perhaps they thought they were forgotten of him; at least that he did not realize their peril; and when the wind arose, they earnestly wished for his presence. Once before he was with them, and was asleep in the storm; and when they awaked him, he calmed the lake to peace. But he was not in the vessel now. Why had he been so urgent for their going? Could he not foresee; and foreseeing, could he not prevent the tempest?

The path of duty may be the path of difficulty. But the rising storm is neither a proof that we were wrong in going forth, nor an indication that now we should turn aside from our course. The disciples are obedient to Jesus. They did not turn back on account of the storm; but taking down their sails, they toiled in rowing against the wind to reach the appointed haven. Perhaps indeed they would have been no safer if they had turned back; for it was storm one way as well as another, backward as well as forward. But it might have been easier to drive with the wind, rather than to toil against it: and they were right in pressing on where the Master bade. This should be our permanent lesson. It is sometimes easier when difficulties press upon us, and we must toil through them, to yield to their pressure: but it is never safer in the end. Difficulties and afflictions will come wherever we live, and try to avoid them as we may: let it be our wisdom to obey our Lord's constraining authority, though against contrary winds.

For whatever are the appearances about us: however long he leaves us apparently to meet the tempest alone, he has not forgotten us. What an example is this to encourage our faith. The storm continued all the night: and so far as they could see, their Lord took no interest in the struggles of his friends. Hour after hour passed away; they were weary with their toiling; the last watch of the night came; morning was about to dawn; and still they knew not that their Lord cared for them. Did he not care? Let us connect together the lake below and the mountain above. The same hours which they passed in sorrow, he passed in prayer: they were contending with the billows, and he was pleading with the Father. If this reminds us of Israel's first battle—of Joshua's fighting in the valley and the praying of Moses on the hill-top—of alternating strength in Israel and Amalek, behold a greater than Moses is here! Nor can we doubt that the praying on the dark mountain was stronger than the rowing on the lake. We may justly judge that our times of sorrow are times of strength, chiefly because then our fervent prayers are called forth. If it is reasonable to judge that we are never stronger than when God is our strength, then prayer is our mightiest instrumentality: for by prayer we enlist on our behalf the arm of Omnipotence. And how would these disciples, who had heard their Lord's prayers, prize them now in their perils. If they had but been assured of their Lord's sympathy; if they had known that upon the neighbouring mountain he was spending the wakeful hours in prayer for them, they would have been believing, perhaps calm, in the midst of the storm. But this is the assurance which we have in all our times of trial. We are below, cloud-covered, tempest-tossed; but on the distant hills of ever glorious light, the sleepless care of our Intercessor offers his pleadings for our necessities. He bears still the sympathies he bore while he was here; and his disciples are as much his care now as then. Not a pang is felt by a believing heart, that is not known to him; he knows all our tossings, when the waves of temptation rise high; he sees all our strugglings forward against the driving storm. And now he ever liveth to make intercession for us. We can see in the case of these disciples that their anxious fears arose from their ignorance. If they had known that he cared for them and would soon appear for their help, they would have put away their fears. He saw them toiling in rowing, when he started to relieve them, he knew just where to find them; and he chose his time of deliverance.

But why should we not believe that our anxious perplexities spring from a like ignorance: why should we not cast our care upon him who has graciously assured us that he careth for us?

CHAPTER VIII.

DELIVERING GRACE.

"It is I: be not afraid."

DOUBTLESS we should gather thoughts of great consolation for our own hours of trial, from considering the methods of his kindness towards his disciples upon these occasions. Jesus our Lord is the same now as then; the necessities that belong to us, his disciples, are similar; and the principles of his gracious dealings are now as they have been. We often mourn after our absent Lord. This is the chief source of grief in our times of severest temptation, that he is not with us. Yet we are not to judge of his concern for us and his care over us, by our lively sense of his presence. God may be where we lie down to lonely slumbers, and ministering angels may ascend and descend around us, when we know it not. Gen. xxviii. 16. Jesus may walk with us by the way, and even cause our hearts to burn within us, when we discern not that it is Jesus. Luke xxiv. 16. The Master may have sent us forth alone into the storm, or have sent the storm after us; yet his absence is no proof that he is unconcerned for us, or that he will not aid us in due time.

The absence of our Lord has its meaning: but it may not mean that we are forsaken. We may long and pray for his appearance; yet should not suppose that he will suffer his faithfulness to fail. When we walk in darkness, let us trust in the name of the Lord, and stay ourselves upon our God. Isa. l. 10.

The disciples were alone, but not uncared for. Their Lord was absent in person, but his thoughts were towards them. When he withdraws from us, he has his reasons for it, to be vindicated in due time: and as we strive to do the duties that are more difficult because he is not with us, he will surely appear for our relief. Yet let us wait for him. His appearance to the disciples was delayed; and, as to the manner of it, nothing could be more unlooked for. He left them to contend with the storm during the entire night; and not until the morning dawned did he come to them. Yet not a moment of this long delay was lost to them; for the Master's prayers for them upon the mountain were as precious as the Master's presence in the ship. They were safe, though they may not have thought so. Doubtless apprehended danger not only led to greater exertions, but called forth wishes and prayers for relief. But when he appeared they were afraid of their deliverer. There was indeed a beautiful propriety in their Lord's coming; it was just like him as we often see him. From the sea their trouble sprang; of the sea they were afraid: and deliverance comes from the raging deep. He came walking upon the stormy waves, to show them his perfect control over all the sources of their fears. This is wonderfully and delightfully according to the experience of far later times. As every seed brings forth its own kind, so trouble is our seed time; and the consolations that spring up after affliction take their form from the troubles that give them their origin. Christ still walks upon the sea, in this, that he shows his power over our griefs, and from our griefs evokes his mercies. Our anticipations of deliverance are seldom realized. If we do not dictate, we at least imagine how he will appear to deliver. Yet he always chooses his way; perhaps always disappoints our thoughts; strange ways, yet ever blessed ways, are his: and it may be he will awaken new fears by his wise means of granting aid. When he came to the disciples, trampling their fears under his feet, they were afraid at his approach.

But even these apprehensions were not without their value. We ought not to be stupid and insensible in a time of affliction. There is such a thing as fearing too much; and we may indulge unbelief, or sink into despondency. But the opposite extreme of not fearing at all is unnatural, and betrays spiritual deadness, not life. It is the design of Providence that we should feel the trials that are sent upon us; and the exercise of faith is only possible, when we are neither desponding nor insensible. Faith realizes the darkness, while it looks for light;

mourns our Lord's absence, while it looks for his coming; cannot see through the gloom, but believes in spite of it. Faith and fear may dwell in the same heart; though strong faith may put down fear. To be without fear is usually to be too indifferent. Fear leads to prayer; prayer hastens deliverance. But for the fears of the disciples, the Lord would have passed by them, and left them still to struggle with the storm. But when they cried out, he came to them.

When they cried out for fear he spoke to them from the waters, "Be of good cheer; it is I; be not afraid." Notice particularly, that these words did not stay the storm. The wind still blew, and the waves heaved tumultuously around them. But his voice inspired confidence. And though we see not Jesus with our bodily eyes, nor hear his audible voice, he still speaks to us in his word, by his providence, and through his Spirit, to give confidence in trouble and to bid us put away our fears.

If we have any proper ideas of true discipleship, we must recognize that Christ is a Lord to whose directions we must be implicitly obedient: and we may be fully confident of his authority to command, of his wisdom to control, of his power to save and of his love to bless. What though our experience is different from that of others? We may not inquire "what shall this man do?" but we must hear his voice saying to us, "Follow ye me!" We may be sent where we are unwilling to go; we may meet with difficulties hard to overcome; we may not understand why changes so sudden succeed our happy hours: but we should not doubt that the same hand that has sent us forward in this way of duty can still protect and deliver us.

When we see Jesus so delivering these disciples, should we distrust his power to help us? His walking upon the stormy waters of the sea of Galilee for the relief of the labouring disciples, is emblematic of his power to help us in every possible time of need. The sea is the fittest emblem of instability. It therefore aptly represents the changes of life. Temptations within and without; seasons of persecution and affliction; hopes and disappointments; anxieties and cares; poverty, feebleness, dejection, doubts, and despondencies come upon us, like the sea's troubled waters, till we adopt the psalmist's lamentation, "All thy waves and thy billows have gone over me." Yet what need we more than the voice of Jesus, to calm all these agitations, and give our souls true peace? But we must not expect to find relief by any underestimating of our troubles. And these two things are both hard to do: to put a just estimation upon trouble when we are out of trouble: and to receive comforts readily when we are in trouble. Yet what a feeling of helplessness belongs to our times of deepest affliction—especially of spiritual distress! We struggle against contending billows; or we sink in deep waters where there is no standing. What need we then so much as the strong hand of a deliverer, stretched out to save?

Yet it is not only confidence in the power of Christ to save that is needful for our times of trouble. *Will he* deliver us? Are not our sorrows from his hand, and laid upon us in his displeasure? When we consider, we are afraid of him; and our complaint is, "Surely against us he is turned." Surely we, who know so much of the character and dealings and word of Christ, should still lift up our hopes to the Compassionate and Sympathizing; and, even in the darkest storm implore and look for his mercy and love. Before they saw him they doubtless wished for him; but they had as yet never seen any such display of his power as to lead them thus to expect delivering mercy. But we know him better than they. We know that it is just like Jesus to grant his blessing to his suffering disciples. It is just like his dealings, to suffer his people to fall into divers temptations, and to seem to have no succour. If we take the history of his church for our guide, we may know that no strange thing has happened in our experience. It does indeed often perplex us that we are exposed to trials, so many, so hard, so long continued; and yet our own calm judgment often decides that the wisdom of Christ plans our dark way. He knows that these trials are needful for us. We find great dangers in our prosperity; we become indifferent to duty; we fix our thoughts toc much on the earth; we stand in danger of being led aside from the straight path. Or our faith, though not declining, should be tested and strengthened by exposure to trial. The infinite wisdom of Divine Providence has chosen that his people shall be tried by many griefs: and we who know that this is the usual method of Divine deal ings, should be neither surprised nor discouraged. Indeed we should vindicate these methods of Providence, for we have known how often they yield the peaceable fruits of righteousness.

It is a great support to us in times of trial that we know so well the love and sympathy of Christ. Though he is absent from us, we can approach his throne, and tell him our troubles, and ask his sustaining grace. Even though we may have brought our troubles upon ourselves by folly or by sin, yet who has ever shown towards the guilty, a love to be compared with his? Or who ever sought his mercy, in humility and penitence, and yet was rejected? And when we come to him it is to one who

"Knows what sore temptations mean,
For he has felt the same."

This is a wonderful thing to know of our Lord, that he was in all points tempted like as we are, yet without sin. What wonderful varieties of sorrow met together in him; how wide was the range of his experience; how thoroughly he knew this whole circle of temptation. So the trials of his life embrace all we feel or suffer. No storm breaks more loudly over us than broke upon him; no railings are more unjust against us than the provocations he bore; no stroke falls more heavily upon us; is there any sorrow like unto his sorrow that was done to him? And all these things the better fit him to be a suitable Redeemer.

We know what a difference there is between the mere kindness of our earthly friends and their sympathy. We want more than kind intentions and friendly offices in times of affliction. We want those around us to enter into our feelings; this is more than to relieve us, or to pity us: it is to sympathize with us. Two friends may be equally sincere and kind; while one may possess, far beyond the other, the faculty of touching our hearts. We give this name of sympathy to a certain delicate discernment of the feelings, and a quiet, tender, loving, effectual way of reaching them, which is itself the result of a similar experience. Neither wisdom, nor love, nor zeal, without experience, can reach the kindly offices of sympathy. Love may temper it; wisdom may guide it; zeal may put it in exercise: but these all are not sympathy. The power of sympathy to support and comfort is beyond the mere promptings of pity or of love.

We know Jesus as loving and powerful and sympathizing. The Scriptures set it forth as one of the reasons for his unparalleled humility that he might become like unto his brethren—a merciful and faithful High Priest, and capable of being touched with the feeling of our infirmities. What a wonderful declaration is that, touching our incarnate Lord, "In that he himself hath suffered being tempted, he is able also to succour them that are tempted." Our Lord too was once a sufferer; he complained in an hour of darkness; he poured out his supplications with strong crying and tears. And the Scriptural inference, directly drawn from these truths for our support in trials, is plain and strong: "Let us therefore come boldly unto the throne of grace that we may obtain mercy and find grace to help in time of need." Heb. iv. 16.

It is by no forced analogy, but by a transition as striking, and natural and beautiful as it is instructive, that the disciples of Christ in all ages since this record was made, have learned to guide their experience from this history. Many a time since have believers felt that their Lord's hand has constrained them to meet the storm, that his footsteps were upon the tossing billows, that his voice calmed the seas to peace, as truly for them as upon the lake of Galilee. When Summerfield once addressed the friends of the Bible-cause in New York city, he encouraged them by a beautiful allusion to this scene on Lake Gennesaret, as compared with the experience of the British and Foreign Bible Society, on whose behalf his address was made. "When we first launched our untried vessel upon the deep, the storms of opposition roared and the waves dashed angrily around us, and we had hard work to keep her head to the wind. We were faint with rowing and our strength would soon have been gone: but we cried, 'Lord save us, or we perish!' Then a light shone upon the waters, and we saw a form walking upon the troubled sea, like unto the Son of God. And he drew near to the ship, and we knew that it was Jesus! And he stepped upon the deck, and laid his hand upon the helm. And he said to the winds and the waves, 'Peace, be still!' And there was a great calm."

Indeed this storm upon the lake of Galilee is a grand allegorical picture of experimental religion: and as we fix our eyes upon its shifting scenes and watch its different persons, all we have to do is to interpret. It is the same lesson always; but of different times and characters. The dark night and the sea are the same, though the clouds may sometimes break away, the stars sometimes shine, or the waves seem less boisterous. The disciples still toil in rowing against contrary winds, though Peter or John may neither of them be there. The chief personage is ever the same; only the majestic footsteps of Jesus can walk the tossing billows and calm their rage to quiet. You remember the history of Jacob's aged days! God had blessed his basket and his household; and with his twelve sons around him, he feasted upon the bounties of his providence, as our Lord fed the people on the shore of Galilee. But the shadows of night closed around this day of peace, and his Lord constrained the venerable patriarch to embark upon a stormy, troubled sea. His favourite son disappeared from his sight; and the waves and billows began to come over him. His long mourning for the absent Joseph, the days of wasting famine, the severity of the lord of Egypt, the imprisonment of Simeon, the demand that Benjamin also must go down; what were all these things to Jacob and his household but the rising storm, the contrary winds, the dark and unknown dangers: yet just when all things seem to be against him, when Simeon and Joseph and Benjamin are taken from him; in the last watch of this long, dark night a light shined upon the troubled waters; the Angel which redeemed Jacob from all evil—Gen. xlviii. 16—walked amidst the storm; the waves were at peace; and the vessel in which the church of God was embarked passed quietly into her protecting haven. As the disciples knew not Jesus and cried out for fear, so the complaint of Jacob was the language of ignorance and mistake: these things were not all against him: but when he could say, "Joseph, my son, is yet alive," the thankful patriarch only anticipated the experience of the disciples, who saw the footsteps and heard the voice of Jesus on the sea of Galilee.

And scarcely any great thing has ever been wrought for Zion or her sons in all the ages, but that Jesus constrains his disciples to meet the darkness and the storm. So Israel's song is, "Many a time have they afflicted me from my youth up:"

and the chorus of the song is, "But they have not prevailed against me." Not to meet the storm, is not to obey the commands of Jesus: it is not to follow in the pathway which he trod for himself, and which he ever marks out for his disciples. Real, the scene was on Galilee: it is none the less significant. Let us mark these methods of Providence, that the knowledge may not only sustain us in our trials, but prove more plainly the Divine favour upon the plans which he blesses through trouble. It is almost impossible for us in these days to understand that the beginnings of modern missionary enterprises, half a century ago, met with so much and with such strenuous opposition; and from those of whom better things were expected. Who would have thought that from Christian nations, indeed from the Christian church, even from Christian ministers, would spring the chief resistance to the attempts of the early missionaries. Though eighteen hundred years had passed since the great Head of the church had commanded his disciples to preach his gospel to every creature, many who bore his name would neither do this work themselves, nor suffer others to do it. And it has renewed the marvels of the apostolic age that men, as humble as Christ's original disciples, should go forth at the bidding of Jesus, to toil laboriously through a gloomy night and through swelling billows; to believe his word with so enduring faith; and to see such light spread over the dark waters as their

Saviour walked upon them. Picture this scene on Galilee: see again the stormy waters and the tossing vessel: see again obedient disciples pressing forward where the winds are contrary: and though we do not see John and Andrew and Peter, but Carey and the Judsons and Martyn, they are called and sent by the same Lord; they met the same wild dashing storm; he prayed for them upon the mountain; he walked for them upon the billows; he calmed the storm to peace; he brought them to their desired haven. And if the night has again descended, if the Messenger of Peace still encounters storms, it is never without his bidding, and ever with good hopes of his due deliverance.

As Christ deals with his church so deals he with the individual believer. The storms on the sea of life, like the storms on the ocean, may not spread far. A vessel here may be in troubled waters; while yonder another speeds on her prosperous voyage: a ship may lie becalmed, while the sails of another just in sight are spread to a favourable breeze. Troubled hearts and happy hearts may beat side by side beneath the same roof, or in the same pew. All the significancy of the scene on the lake of Galilee may belong to our individual experience. And indeed memory can call up the vivid picture of the past to many a disciple, where the Master sent us out and went not himself along; and soon the shadows of night gathered over the waters, the waves began to swell, our fears were awakened, and it all came to pass just as it is here written. Just before the morning, One walked upon the waves whom we knew not; but he bade us be of good cheer, he came in with us, and the storm was gone. And these memories strengthen our faith for new trials; and help us to look for new deliverances. So we often sing songs of thanksgiving for his kindly dealings with our souls. The experience of our brethren, and that we ourselves have had, may alike assist our faith as we recognize the hand of Jesus in every trial.

But we ought not to forget this other lesson of these impressive scenes: that our Jesus only, is able to walk upon the seas, and that his voice alone can calm the troubled waves to peace. We do not mean by this that Christ's disciples alone are exposed to troubles; that he sends them only forth. For trials, temptations, afflictions are the earthly lot of all men: and darkness and grief fall upon the evil and the good. Nor do we mean that the storm will last always, with no breaking morning and no quiet waters, unless we receive him with us into the ship. For troubles rise and pass away and are forgotten, for many who do not hear his voice, saying, "Be of good cheer!" We may not discern between them that fear God and them that fear him not, either by the mere endurance of affliction, or by the brief time it may rest upon them.

But the voice of Jesus in the storm implies two things:

1st. That the only true consolation that can be found on earth is found in Christ our Lord. In the troubles which men must bear, many expedients are adopted and called by the name of comforts. Men strive to forget their troubles; they affect a stoical indifference; they argue an iron necessity. Consolation belongs nowhere in the darkness, till the radiant form of Jesus steps forward and his voice says, "IT IS I. I sent thee forth into the deep; I sent the storm; I delayed my appearance; I prayed for thee though I was absent from thee. Be not afraid. The storm shall rise no higher and rage no longer than I bid; the vessel is still safe in my hand; the power to deliver is in me; and the time of my appearance is nigh." All is right, if all is in the power of Jesus. Infinite wisdom and power and love are the sure guarantee that all these things shall work together for our good. Peace, be still. Let fears subside; for all are safe whom Christ protects. Let passion cease to swell, for love belongs to all our disquieting fears. What else than the voice of Jesus can bid the troubled soul glory even in tribulation that the grace of his Lord may rest upon him!

2d. There are sorrows that must abide, if we find not their sole relief in the voice of Jesus. The conscience of man may indeed find a brief peace, even when it hears not the whispers of his love: but such a peace shall surely be broken. By no possible means can the agitations of a guilty conscience be truly calmed, but at his word. And when at the last day, that great and terrible storm shall burst; when the false hopes and false refuges of men can no longer avail them; when men's hearts shall fail for fear, then shall be the great and final appearance of Jesus for the deliverance of his disciples. None that trust in him shall be put to shame in that day. He will speak peace to the soul. But that storm shall wreck, in eternal disaster all that look not for his coming.

CHAPTER IX.

THE CRY OF THE PERISHING.

"Lord, save me!"

WE have seen that when our Lord's disciples saw him, through the dim light of dawning day, walking upon the water, they did not know him. This was such a miracle as had never before been wrought: they had formed no anticipations of such a method of deliverance; doubtless they could not distinctly see him; and our apprehensions rather than our hopes, are usually awakened by mysterious things. It was quite natural that they should not know him. But it was also significant. The Divine Painter, who depicted these scenes for our profit, means something by every stroke of the pencil. And if we still attempt to follow the footsteps of Jesus as he walks upon the lake, let us, who know more of his grace and power, and who have a larger acquaintance with his methods of mercy, desire to exercise a stronger faith in the mysteries by which we are often surrounded. For as it was here, so is it often in the experience of our life. Christ comes to us as we do not expect him, alarms us by his very methods of relief, and is near us when we know him not. So we cry out for fear just at the moment when we should be filled with thanksgiving. Here are lessons to correct vain thoughts. Let us not indulge the false views of religious experience which bid us judge by our feelings of the Lord's favours. We are not only ignorant often of our greatest mercies, when they are very near; but even we are afraid of them. Mary stood by the sepulchre weeping for her missing Lord, and she asked, as she supposed, the gardener; yet a well-known voice dispelled her fears. It seemed a stranger who talked with the two disciples on their way to Emmaus; their hearts burned within them at his discourse: but in the breaking of bread they knew their Lord. It seemed only a spirit that could walk upon these wildly tossing waves; and the disciples feared; but their Lord's voice said, "It is I."

The disciples were glad to welcome their Master into the ship. When they knew who it was, they felt safe. Doubtless a new confidence in his power would be felt, as he made this exhibition of it. They could hardly but recall the scene in the former storm, when he had been asleep in the vessel, and had spoken the waters to peace. As yet he has not bidden the waves subside; when he calmed their fears, he was not even, as yet, in the ship: but to know that it was Jesus fills the disciples with joy. It is hard to say whether our hopes of safety are not sometimes as joyful and happy as deliverance itself. Liberty, to the prisoner long sunk in despair, can scarcely itself be sweeter than the tidings of deliverance before his prison doors are opened. The disciples were filled with joy at the voice of their Lord, before he entered the ship and before he stayed the storm.

But here Peter starts forward to teach us other lessons. Could we see this new scene,—the apostle walking on the water—and not judge that here was something well worthy of our thoughts? We are not so much surprised that the Son of God can control the elements; but we ask ourselves in amazement, "Can he impart this power to his disciples?"

Let Peter teach us some things that may be profitable for our own religious experience. And when we think of him we can scarcely overlook the reflection that our earthly experience is always greatly affected by our personal peculiarities. How much this is so; how many blemishes may be introduced into a Christian character; how far we may vindicate these modifications of piety; are matters by no means easy to settle. We must admit that the great, essential principles of religion, every believer should adopt. The foundation principles of the law of God and of the gospel of Christ cannot change to suit man's wishes; but man must change to embrace and love them. Yet these principles when fully adopted do not suppress what is human in the believer; they do not destroy the disposition that is natural to any individual; they renew and sanctify the mind. When the soul is renewed, there are important senses in which the man remains the same. It is the same intellect, and not another one; it is the same temperament, and not a different one; no new faculties are added; no old powers are removed; though indeed the quickening and sanctifying power of new thoughts and affections, may develope valuable capacities quite unknown before. Yet every change retains the characteristics of the individual. The power of God's Holy Spirit in its largest influences upon the believer's heart, still gives free exercise to all the natural faculties; and the greatest changes of regenerating grace are consistent with leaving the man intellectually much as he was before. The great change is a moral change: and we see as many diversities in God's workings of grace as we do in his works of nature. The normal, natural powers of a man are not exchanged, or subverted. The child does not become a man; nor the wise man a fool: and though to enter the kingdom of heaven a man must become as a little child, this is to be in temper and spirit, not in intellectual attainments. When a man is born again the change is from above; and though it is *super*natural, it is yet not *un*natural.

Men may believe and adopt substantially the same religious principles, yet retain their individual peculiarities. Some men are constitutionally timid; and though such men, through the force of religious principles, may be bold enough to face the martyr's stake, yet every step of their way would be through fightings against their natural feelings. Such men may do the bravest things, yet would they never be forward. So the indolent may learn industry, but would never become energetic; the sluggish would not become active, nor the phlegmatic sanguine. A man's religious feelings, impulses and engagements are still, through all his life, more or less influenced by what he is by nature; and this is the same as to say that a man is *renewed* by the grace of God: he is changed in himself, not *exchanged* for another: he still remains himself in an important sense, while he is truly made a new creature in Christ Jesus.

We can easily see that the apostles of Christ, though truly his disciples, differ among themselves; and are not like precious vessels cast all in the same mould. Thomas was slow to believe; John was amiable and loving; Nathanael simple and guileless. But no character of them all is more strikingly marked than that of Peter: and we think we can easily see just what kind of a man he was, before he knew Christ. Ardent, zealous and forward, he pushes himself into the front rank upon all occasions, ready to speak or do; his character has just the blemishes that usually belong to such a man; and his failures are just where he has been most confident. Peter was a true disciple. Though Paul, whose calling was after Christ's earthly ministry was ended, laboured more abundantly than any other apostle, yet none of those whom Jesus called to himself, showed more attachment than

Peter, was more zealous in his service, or was more energetic to spread the truth. The faults of this disciple were open and plain; like his character itself, easily read. He boldly engaged to go with his Lord to prison and to death; yet that very night he basely denied him. He drew his sword to defend him against superior numbers; yet was afraid at a maid-servant's voice. He first admitted the Gentiles to the Christian church; yet attempted to conciliate Jewish prejudices by withdrawing from the Gentiles. Yet the faults of such a man often spring from impulse: and we cannot question the piety that looks upon such delinquencies to confess them candidly, to mourn over them bitterly, and to draw from them new motives for a more ready and a more careful obedience. Let those who would point censoriously at Peter's sins, note carefully and copy Peter's repentance.

It may be that every disciple in the ship was glad to hear the Master's voice speaking to them from the sea; but Peter's ardent zeal hurries him to a warmer expression of his joy. He waits not till his Lord has passed to the vessel; but desires to go forth and meet him. This seems a strange and daring impulse indeed; and the request is one we would hardly expect. It may chiefly be through that impulsive rebounding of the feelings which often makes such men pass from one extreme to the other. We are unwilling to say that his words, "If it be thou," are indicative of any distrust on the part of Peter that it really was the Lord. Nor are we willing to attribute his desire to any improper motive; since nothing of this kind is here charged against him. Yet Peter is unacquainted with his own strength; and his Lord readily bade him come; for he would teach him a wholesome lesson, and through him to us all. Altogether, in this impulsive movement of this warm-hearted disciple, we see far more to admire than to censure. If he had not loved that Lord, who came thus walking upon the sea, he would not have sprung forth so eagerly to meet him. Peter's warmest affections had already been given to Jesus; and though such a man as he might be betrayed into inconsistencies that more cautious men would avoid, we have no reason to judge that Peter's heart was ever really anywhere else, till the day when he yielded up his life as his Lord predicted. And Peter's confidence was in Jesus. It is obvious to the most casual reflection that he would never have dreamed of preferring such a request as this, that he might go forth upon the water, except at the prompting of a strong faith in Christ. It was a great thing to see the Master treading the waves beneath his unyielding step. It was a greater thing to believe that he could or would enable him to do the same. If we stood now upon the deck of that vessel, and looked upon them both; if we recognized the One as the Son of God, and the other as a mere man like ourselves; we would stand in awe at the One; we would be deeply surprised at the other.

His Lord bade him come. Well knowing how and why the faith of the disciple would fail, he knew also that even this failure would be valuable to him and to others. And Peter was able to walk upon the water! Behold the power of Jesus. He could not only do this great thing, but he could enable a believer to do the like. And indeed before our own eyes do the disciples of Jesus do greater things than this, that the world may marvel. It is still to the great honour of Christ that believers in him can make sacrifices and bear trials and "do exploits," Dan. xi. 32, by his supporting grace, far beyond the ability or the endurance of merely mortal energy. Follow the extraordinary career of that Christian woman—Mrs. Ann Judson—whose piety and zeal would give lustre to any age of the church: compare her with any other female whose history the world has: and decide whether such a character could be formed upon any other than a Christian model, or such things done except through Christ's grace. Not only trials like hers but many others, incident to our more ordinary experience, are described in the Scriptures, as passing through the deep waters, and even through the kindling flames. And it oftentimes demands as firm a faith in Jesus to meet these trials of life, as for Peter to walk upon the sea. If we go forth to meet them without faith in him, or if as we meet them, we permit the distressing power of temptation to turn our thoughts away from Christ, we will as surely fail, as would any man who should attempt to walk upon the stormy deep; or as did Peter when he suffered the boisterous winds to awaken his fears.

So far as all spiritual profit is concerned, we are as unable in our own strength to meet the trials of life, as we are to walk upon the stormy lake. And just because of our weakness, we should stand here by our Lord, and know that his dealings with Peter are far more profitable for us than for him. This thing is written for our instruction. And this same apostle, who saw the wonders of Christ, yet intimates that the written page is the more sure word of prophecy. Blessed are our eyes, for they see more and better things than the ancient prophets: more even than these apostles, who looked upon the "Word of Life" and believed his gracious teachings. There are several points of our superiority as we gaze upon Jesus and his disciple walking on the sea. *First*, as we have repeatedly said, we recognize more fully than his disciples then did, the supreme dignity of our Lord; and should be better prepared to believe that no days of trial can come, when he is not both present to know our need and able to relieve us. If Peter trusted One then only but half known; One who yet wore the garments of his humiliation; One who himself, in this form of a servant, was subject to so many laws: how should we trust our well-known Lord, now exalted at the right hand of the Father, now the controller of providence, now possessing all power in heaven and in earth? *Secondly*, it is our superior ground for expecting the Saviour's aid, that the favours we ask at his hands are more consonant with the spirit of his kingdom; and such therefore as he will more readily grant. There is extraordinary encouragement in the miraculous records of the Scriptures; if we did not perversely persist in reading them backwards. We too often argue, Christ did miracles for these men of wondrous faith; and we cannot look for interventions like those he made for them? So the Scriptural writers do not reason. When they tell us that Elijah was a man of like passions with us, and yet that he opened and shut the heavens by his prayers, the argument is, "If God at man's feeble cry did extraordinary natural things in judgment, much more may we be encouraged to ask blessings of a spiritual nature, in mercy, according to the very purposes of his grace." And when we see Peter's request granted, contrary to all example, we may much more expect that Christ will grant us spiritual favours which accord with the very design of his kingdom. And, *thirdly*, our superiority to Peter, as we compare the grace we need with the request he made, pertains to the reasons which bring us forth into the waves of trouble. Peter was safe in the ship, and volunteered to meet his Lord on the sea. Even if we say that his was a stronger faith than that we exercise; if we class him among the eminent worthies who through faith "obtained promises," Heb. xi. 33; if in this we may sometimes imitate him; it remains true that ordinarily ours is a simpler faith, has more encouragements to put it in exercise, and may more reasonably be expected of us. If Peter went out uncalled, surely we should not be timid to go where Christ bids. If Peter wished to go in advance of the promise, it is an encouragement to our faith that we have the promises in advance. If Peter expected Christ to do a thing for him he had never before done for any man, may we not expect him to sustain us in trials similar to those which our brethren have often borne? If Peter volunteers and Christ says, "Come," should we not be fearless when he himself has put us in trials whither we should not have ventured but for his constraining providence? These contrasts may give Peter's faith the superiority as to strength; but they surely give ours the superiority as to encouragement; and we should cheerfully and calmly go where Christ bids, though it is on the sea, or through it.

But faith enough to undertake a duty is not always faith enough to go through with it. Faith enough to rejoice in a promise is not always faith enough to hold firmly by it, and to rest calmly upon it in the time of trial. Like Job, our words may instruct many and we may strengthen the weak hands; but when trouble touches us we faint. Job iv. 4, 5. Peter walked on the water to go to Jesus. Perhaps for a little time, the disciples in the vessel envied their brother this rare power; and it may be that Peter's heart swelled with exultation at the privilege thus given. Our perils often spring from our privileges.

> "We should suspect some danger nigh,
> When we possess delight."

Scarcely anything is harder than to receive our mercies meekly; but we lose our humility, and then lose sight of him by whom we stand.

Peter walked on the water to go to Jesus. The winds were no fiercer and the waves no higher than when he ventured out; but he saw the wind was boisterous; and he began to fear. Upon principles merely natural he might well fear the storm: but upon the principles of the faith that had sent him forth, he had no just reason to fear the boisterous wind. His Lord was as able now to save as ever: and his faith ought to have been in spite of the storm. True faith is through no undervaluing of the dangers about the believer, or of his weakness to withstand them; but it is such a confidence in Christ as overmasters the mightiest fears. If a seaman is exposed to a storm in a crazy vessel, he may well fear the violence of the waves; but he may be calm and fearless just in proportion as he has confidence in the sea-worthiness of the ship. A just confidence neither denies the strength of the storm, nor the strength of the vessel; but forms a proper estimate of both.

Peter looked in the wrong direction. He thought

more of the storm, than he did of him who ruled the storm: and no sooner did he this, than he began to sink. We may be reminded in him of that very common mistake of Christian experience touching the nature and grounds of our faith, which leads many to judge that the faith of a Christian is a personal persuasion of his own good estate before God. This serious error leads many to live upon their feelings and not by faith; upon their reading of their own experience, and not upon the promises of God: it makes their safety seemingly dependent upon their comforts. We are all prone to these changes; especially so perhaps are persons of warm impulses, like this disciple. We do not question that peace may fill the heart when a firm faith abides there; that there is no better persuasion of our reconciliation to God than that which faith gives; or that the permanent exercise of such a faith should be the object of desire and effort. But it is important for us to know that feeling and faith are by no means the same; that our fears, instead of hindering, may call forth our faith; and that not our imaginations or our apprehensions, but our principles are the guide of faith. Whatever influence our faith may exert upon the heart, the Scriptures ever teach us that the true object of faith is, not internal, but external; not anything in ourselves, but Christ to whom we look. The true object of faith is Christ. When we lose sight of him; when we watch our own hearts so closely as to lose sight of Christ—

whether we grow proud of privileges possessed, or fearful of perils seen—we begin to sink. We may look at other things; we may see the storm; we may feel our weakness; but Christ must be the chief object, and he gives us strength. Peter looked away from Christ.

But he reminds us that the very loss of our comforts may recall us to the actings of faith. Thus feeling and faith stand in contrast. Happy for us that they do: for what could we do in the dark, if there was not some light to look to; how rise above our despondency without a helping hand from without; how utter our prayers if the deep necessities of grief that can find no comfort within, must close our lips from pleading? Faith's most excellent actings are often in spite of fears and feelings. We are driven from self-confidence to feel our dependence on the Lord; and faith is looking to him for help when without him we must perish. The fears of Peter drove him from his self-complacent satisfaction, and made him renew the direct actings of faith towards Jesus. "Beginning to sink he cried, Lord, save me!"

Let Peter teach us how to believe. We are often perplexed to know just what relation our fears should bear to our faith. We cannot help but feel these troubles that beset us. It would be unnatural, unreasonable, and impossible to feel indifferent in our times of trial. Yes, and it is just as undesirable and unchristian as it is unattainable. When God lays his hand upon us in affliction, he means that we should feel it; when he takes away our comforts he gives us no lesson of apathy; when he brings us out on the stormy sea, he knows that the boisterous winds will frighten us. When by the strivings of his convincing Spirit he sets our sins in array before us, brings his terrors to bear upon our hearts, and bids us remember our solemn accountability to him, these things are designed to awaken our fears, so as only the voice of the Almighty can arouse them. Nor are they unreasonable fears. Rather they are just; and, except for the mightier power of Christ, they would be overwhelming. Let us feel these fears so far as to learn our own weakness; let us know that only the grace of Christ can deliver us; let us recognize that these very fears are wholesome just in proportion as they drive us from every feeling of indifference and complacency, and force us to apply to Christ. Faith is not the denial of our reasons to fear; it implies our fears; and it consists in our betaking ourselves to Christ as our refuge.

Let Peter teach us how to pray. Prayer is the earnest, timely utterance of the sinking heart. His need was pressing, immediate; his words were brief; but he knew that none else could help. We too should know that without him we must sink; that no other arm can save; and that he is able, and willing, and near. Perhaps as we gaze upon this scene some of us can recall the memory of his former mercy. We had passed through a stormy and toilsome night: and after many griefs, heavier sorrows settled down upon us. We seemed to sink in the deep waters; but our cry went up to him. We had no other hope; and this did not fail us. We could not pray; we could only cry, "Lord, save us, we perish;" and the words seemed more like the utterances of despair than the breathing of faith. And it *was* despair of all else than Jesus; and our faith in him was feeble. But he heard our cry and saved. He stretched forth his hand, and caught us that we did not sink; and we sang with the psalmist, "He sent from above; he took me; he drew me out of many waters." 2 Sam. xxii. 17; Ps. xviii. 16.

This short prayer, Jesus yet will hear. If the storms of trouble rise; if, worst of all, our sins remind us of our fearful exposure to the Divine displeasure, we are encouraged to cry to him. No time of trouble is so important, in no storm are we so helpless in ourselves, as when we form a just estimate of our estate as sinful men. But even from the troubles which sin gathers around the soul, Christ is able to save.

And now let us not decide that Peter's going forth upon the water to meet Jesus seems a most desperate adventure. Let us not think that the faith we need for the saving of the soul is too large a demand upon us. The just judgment we should form upon these things, may teach us that no man makes a more desperate venture in spiritual things, than he does who attempts to live and die without the supporting grace of Christ. This life is a troubled sea, to meet whose storms we must all go forth; and he is happiest who is best prepared to meet them. But especially in view of our immortal life, he only can be happy who is truly prepared to pass behind the dark clouds that separate us from the unseen world; to step down from the ship at the Lord's bidding, and to walk upon the ocean of eternity. Can we as sinners look forward to that boundless sea, and not fear that the storms of Divine wrath may heave its billows to fury? There are two ways of going forth upon these dark waters. One is going forth to meet Jesus; with an humble cry for his help; with a firm reliance upon his arm; and he will save those who put their trust in him. The man who goes forth thus, relies upon a promise that shall never fail; and though dark clouds for a little time may be around him, the voice of Jesus shall for ever calm the storm to peace.

But he takes another way of going forth, who has no hope in Jesus. If ever there can be a desperate venture the sinner makes it, when he passes into eternity without faith in Jesus. Stepping forth from a ship into the wildest tempest that ever blew, is nothing to it. Forewarned of the soul's exposure to the just displeasure of God, why will not men learn that they need this Saviour? And why should we, who know his infinite power, his boundless grace and his past willingness to bless; we who know our sinfulness, our liabilities to earthly troubles and our exposure to eternal wrath; we who know his law in its demands and threatenings, his gospel in its gracious promises, and his providence in its wondrous workings; why should not we judge that the faith he demands of us is as reasonable as it is necessary?

CHAPTER X.

CLEAVING TO CHRIST.

"Will ye also go away?"

THUS far, in our companionship with the Master, we have sought to learn the teachings of his significant actions: and the words spoken by him have been few in number. But if now we should consider the words of the next day, we might find as much as heretofore to engage our continued attention. Without designing this, we may devote a single chapter to some brief thoughts upon the instructions given by our Lord at this time of the narrative.

The disciples received their Lord into the ship; and wondered that he was able to walk upon the sea. Let it be instructive for us to read the inspired commentary upon their wonder, that "their hearts were hardened." Let us apply the words practically to our own case; and reflect that after we have known so much of our Lord's dignity, seen so much of his power, and experienced so much of his grace, nothing but the hardness of our heart can prevent our unbounded confidence in him, or allow us to be surprised at any thing he does. Let us seriously consider that even a true love to Christ, and a certain intimacy with him, and a true faith in his power such as Peter had, does not entirely prevent the hardening of the heart against higher and more truthful conceptions of him and his doings. If it seems strange, it is profitable to read that those near friends of Jesus, with hardened hearts, did not consider the miracle of the loaves, as giving just reason to anticipate that of the lake. In the usual language of the Scriptures, the heart is said to be hardened when divine truth does not make upon it its proper impressions. As melted wax receives and retains the impression of a seal, though the same substance, when hard, receives no impression: so our hearts will answer back exactly to the truth of God when they are exactly right. We have no better illustration of the readiness and fidelity with which a heart like God would receive and retain and reflect back the truth, than the sensitive plate which photography places for a few moments exposed to the sun's re flected rays; which seizes and holds for us an exact copy of any scene, to its most minute particulars. Or to change somewhat the illustration, the hearts of fallen men, like an untrue surface, never give back an impression entirely faithful and without distortion. A measure of hardness may affect the hearts of true disciples: and where indifference to the just influence of divine truth is most depraved and entire, the estate of sinful man is most lamentable.

But while generally the expression, a hardened

heart, has special reference to the grovelling and depravity of the affections, it includes also, and here perhaps specially refers to that sluggishness of perception and understanding, which prevents the just discernment of the truth. Why should we not judge that but for the darkness of our understandings, and the alienation of our tastes and affections that springs from sin, our moral perceptions would be acute and accurate to catch and comprehend, almost without any conscious reasoning, the valuable teachings of moral and spiritual truth? We know very well that the mind of man becomes wonderfully skilled in matters of knowledge, upon subjects where the interest has been aroused, where intelligence has been acquired, and where long habit has made the phenomena familiar. The perceptions of true skill are quick-witted and almost instinctive. Why do we trust the judgment of a jeweller in deciding that this is a false diamond; of a banker that this is a counterfeit note; of a general in military affairs, or of a physician in medicine? These men may have no better eyes than others who look on; they may not even be *as* intelligent in matters not relating to their own chosen sphere; and in this sphere, perhaps, they cannot always explain the exact reasons for the decisions to which they come. But we place confidence in them because the human mind, by studying and understanding special subjects, is capable of acquiring a skill and wisdom which enables men to see things not seen at all by eyes unskilled. There is as great a difference between the eyes of a skilful and an unskilful man, in looking upon anything, as there is between the eyes of two men who look upon a printed page which one cannot read and the other can. Both see the book, the lines, the letters: to the one, all is blank, stupid, and meaningless: to the other, intelligence, perhaps the most important information, flashes its life-like thoughts through the eye to the brain and the heart. The same things, externally, may differ to different observers, as life differs from death!

We may see here why it is that the preaching of the gospel affects the hearts of men so differently. From the sound of the same sermon, some go away with indifference; and some are deeply affected. Meaningless words, for all spiritual profit to some ears, are full of thought—are freighted indeed with the tidings of life everlasting—to others. The difference is in the hearts of the hearers. It cannot be in the words, for they are the same to every ear. So in the Lord's parable of the sower: the seed was fruitful or fruitless as the ground on which it fell was prepared or unprepared. And the heart of man may grow in hardness or grow in tenderness. There was a time perhaps within our remembrance when divine truth affected us more than now it does. Happy are they whose hearts are more and more interested in Scriptural teachings, and who are better able to comprehend them because they have become skilful in the Word. For there is a tact and skill in discerning moral and spiritual truths as truly as in learning any others: and a soul enlightened and interested in the truth acquires more this invaluable skill. These disciples of Christ show the hardness of their hearts—their inability to read the lessons their Lord had already taught—by the very fact that they marvel at his walking upon the sea. Men who had witnessed the power of Jesus to multiply a few loaves to supply the necessities of five thousand people, should not have wondered to see him attempt and accomplish anything. He who had power beyond nature would have power also over nature; he who could save five thousand on the shore, could relieve a handful on the deep. But they considered not the miracle of the loaves. Alas that a like hardness of heart keeps us too from reasoning as we should respecting the power and grace of Christ. Considering what he has done for us, why are we not hopeful for the aid we still need at his hands? Hardness of heart is the deep source of our wonder, our unbelief, and our discomfort.

When our Lord was received into the ship, the voyage was soon ended. They were immediately at the land. This may imply a miraculous advance, after he was with them. How little can we do without him; how much with him. In the meantime the people, whom he had left upon the shore, were perplexed to know what had become of him. They knew that the disciples had gone away alone; and there was no other vessel for his conveyance;

but they knew not where he was. Other vessels coming by the place, some of them embarked and crossed over to the land of Gennesaret. When they found him there, they were rebuked by him because their seeking for him was with inferior motives, when they should have sought that enduring bread by which the soul lives. Then occurred the conversation recorded for us in the sixth chapter of John's gospel: and of which we have already taken brief notice. Christ gives us to understand that the manna of the wilderness and the bread which he distributed were but typical of himself. For he says expressly, "I am the bread of life: he that cometh to me shall never hunger, and he that believeth upon me shall never thirst."

This is one of the most elaborate discourses recorded from the lips of our Lord. It is figurative in its language, and yet the interpretation seems the more easily made because it takes the form of a dialogue where the misconceptions of the hearers are recognized and corrected. But for the perverse misinterpretation put upon it by the church of Rome, which we know is the offspring of corruptions that entered the church at a far later date, the chapter would be easily comprehended. In itself it is no more difficult than many other passages of the sacred writings. This much ought to be plain: that our Lord here cannot design to teach that any external form can be regarded as the essence of religion. This would be at war with the entire spirit of his ministry. About this same time, as recorded in Matthew xv., he held a dispute with the Scribes and Pharisees on the subject of piety; and we take the sentiments urged by him upon that occasion as confirming his meaning in arguing of the bread of life. True religion must have its seat in the heart. External things neither sanctify nor defile the man. It was the great error of the Pharisees to lay the chief stress on external cleansings; it is the main characteristic of Christ's teachings to fix our thoughts upon the heart. Eating or drinking—no matter what is eaten—may be no proof or means of spiritual life; eating and drinking may be significant actions, but as our Lord says, for the very purpose of preventing misconception, "It is the Spirit that quickeneth; the flesh profiteth nothing. The words that I speak unto you they are spirit and they are life."

What then is the life and spirit of these teachings, clothed by our Lord in the drapery of these figurative words? He was seated as he uttered them in the synagogue at Capernaum, and to such instructions as these doubtless he referred when he spoke of that city as one exalted to heaven. Let us too form a part of his congregation, and sit at the Master's feet to hear his words. If we would esteem it a great privilege to partake of that wonderful bread, broken by his hands on the mountain side, let us regard it one, not less, but greater, that we may feed upon the living bread; indeed we must eat this bread if we would live for ever.

There are many reasons that forbid us to believe that our Lord in this discourse had any reference whatever to the ordinance of the sacred supper, which was afterwards to be established. The advocates of the doctrine of transubstantiation consider the language of the chapter as expressly teaching their absurd dogma. Yet not only was this literal interpretation entirely unknown to the apostolic church, but its own advocates cannot consistently carry it out. Exceptions must be made; and figurative interpretations must be admitted: and the most consistent is that which compares our Lord's own words with each other. He refers not to the Lord's supper, with which his hearers had no possible acquaintance; but to the bread with which he had fed this people only the day before.

But we learn from the evangelist that these teachings of our Lord were not acceptable to his hearers. Some of them declared that these were hard sayings, which they could not receive; and some of those who had actually professed discipleship, turned back from him and walked no more with him. And if we inquire why they thus forsook him, we may find the reasons are just those which still most frequently lead men to backsliding and apostasy, both secret and open. Men are willing to adopt the mysteries of religion, to accept its hard services and to pay it a costly tribute; and every system of error and falsehood in the world gives us examples of zeal and earnestness, which often put to shame the devotion of those who hold a purer faith. Self-denials of a certain class are the pride of man: he makes no objection to a religion of externals: penance suits him, penitence offends him. "It is a hard saying, who can hear it?" So the world over, just in proportion as religion is made formal and external, the larger is the proportion in any community of those professing to be religious. The grace and the spirituality of the gospel are its chief excellencies: yet indeed chiefly at these do men take offence. It is not at all unlikely that the very men who now forsook Jesus, were among the foremost of those who would have taken him by force to make him a king: and had he taken their way to establish a kingdom and given them a part to act in it, they would still have remained with him. How does self constitute the sum and substance of a human religion; how is the religion of Jesus proved to be divine by the very care he shows to empty men of self: and how many in every age walk no more with him, because they must deny *themselves* if they would cling to Christ.

We need not wonder in our times to find men departing from the Christian profession, since we find backsliders and apostates from the teachings of the most eminent prophets and apostles; and even, as here, from the teachings of Christ himself. The apparent reasons are infinitely various which seem to influence men to decline from a profession of religion: and the manner in which the decline is exhibited is different in different individuals. We sometimes see men *suddenly* drop off from the church of Christ, for some special offence they have taken: and sometimes they *gradually* give up the practices, opinions, and professions of other days. The snares and deceits of sin are manifold; and men easily learn to vindicate or excuse the altered conduct which is of so much importance as a test of their true standing before God. Doubtless there is no more dangerous form of departing from Christ than that which is prone to be the most common in lands where religion is held in respect by the community. Men still bear the name of Christ, keep up some of the forms of religion, and maintain their standing in the church, when, on the one hand, they are not truly interested in the principles or progress of the gospel; and, on the other, they share in the engagements and follies and sympathies of the ungodly world; and by their words and doings bring reproach upon religion, quite as dangerous in its influence upon the souls of men as anything they could do as the open and well-known enemies of Christ Jesus.

It is a great thing to know concerning these men, who thus went back and walked no more with Jesus, that they were not his true disciples. It is not a difficult thing for us to imagine that many of those who saw the miracles and heard the words of our Lord, could find reasons for a partial attachment to him, yet without understanding his entire claims, and without feeling for him a true-hearted devotion. Such a preacher they might wish to hear; such wondrous sights they might desire to see; and they might be willing to eat of his bread. Yet such a following of Christ would be far short of a true discipleship. And in our times, even more abundant reasons of a worldly nature may lead men to embrace and profess a religion that has taught our earliest thoughts and has forced the respect of the world for its teachings. But there are other things which a mind truly interested in Christ and his teachings could not forget; and these are far more important than any such motives. That any man could forsake a teacher who gave such irrefragable proofs of divine authority was itself proof that the discipleship of such an one was no just attachment. So we are expressly told here that their departure was no disappointment to our Lord. He charged them with a want of faith, John vi. 64; and knew before their defection that they would depart. And this should be the encouragement of the church always, that though men will forsake religion, yet we really lose none that are truly attached to the cause of Christ. They go out from us in every case, because they are not of us. 1 John ii. 19.

Yet let us not come to any such conclusion, nor take up with any such encouragement, through any indifference of the reproach thrown upon religion, or of mischief done to themselves by those who walk no more with Christ. The calm vindication of the

Divine righteousness and of the carrying out of the Divine purposes, is quite consistent with the most lively concern for religion and for the souls of men. We mourn over all defections from the true spirit of piety. We mourn over the inconsistencies of men in whom we hope yet exists the root of the matter. We lament the fall of those in whom we had placed high hopes. We enter into serious self-examinations, as we seem to hear the Saviour ask in view of these departures, "Will ye also go away?" And sometimes we fear for ourselves, because those who have fallen have seemed as intelligent, as zealous, as devotional as ever we have been; and seemed to stand as firmly as we. In all the thoughts awakened by these things we may be like the Saviour. There was a sense in which he stood unmoved by all the various murmurings of men against his teachings. He expresses no special anxiety to gain special disciples: he would not lower the tone of his teachings to secure any new follower: he would not decline from his supreme claims to suit any man's temper. He stood in that simple dignity of truth which could allow any man to separate from him as he pleased: he knew that the favour and the blessing came not upon the Master, but upon the disciple: and his words might be slighted by any, but at their peril. Yet he who called men so earnestly to come to him, who wept over Jerusalem, who died upon Calvary, was not indifferent to the conduct of those who would not come to him for life. And we also should be deeply concerned at the inconsistencies of those who bring reproach upon piety, or who depart to walk no more with Jesus, even when we are satisfied that our Lord never loses a true disciple.

The defections of others may grieve the true friends of Jesus; but their faith rests not upon man that it should be overthrown by anything that man does. Doubtless to test the spirit of his nearer followers, our Lord asked them if they also would go away. To their answer how many faithful hearts have a thousand times since responded! The reply is twofold. *First*, that without Christ the sinful soul is undone. When we know most of ourselves and most of God, we may well decide that we have nowhere else to go. If Christianity is false the world has no substitute. *Secondly*, that our Lord is a Saviour every way suitable and efficacious. This faith is expressed with the firmest confidence. "We believe and are sure that thou art Christ, the Son of the living God." The defection of others can have no influence to drive true disciples from Jesus. If his cause is reproached for others' sake, we should strive to adorn it the more. If others are drawn away to the world, we cannot afford to do without him. If they see not his excellency, yet in our eyes he is the chief among ten thousand and altogether lovely.

And should we not judge that any man who saw these wonderful works of Jesus should have received all his teachings without gainsaying or doubt. With Nicodemus, should not every one decide, that no man could do these miracles except God was with him? And shall we dispute with a divine teacher respecting either the truth or the tendency of his doctrines? Or can any man be safe in departing from one who has such claims upon our obedience? If we could now see Jesus as they saw him: if we had walked with him upon the water, as Peter did, we would be inexcusable for any unbelief or disobedience to such a teacher as this. No possible reason can be strong enough to justify these professed disciples in walking no more with Christ. Yet this is quite as true of every one that now hears the gospel.

And every man in our own times who neglects his salvation through Christ, is guilty of inexcusable folly and wickedness. If there be any man who does not recognize his guilt before God, his need of a Saviour and the excellency of Christ, as these things are described in the Scriptures: yet the topics are of such infinite importance, and the array of evidences in favour of these teachings so great, that he cannot without folly and sin neglect to make a careful and earnest investigation of the whole matter. Indifference must be a crime. And they who recognize, indolently, the value of the soul, the greatness of their sins and the necessity of salvation in Christ, should be self-convicted of the greatest folly and sin. How can the great importance of these things be recognized, and then Christ be neglected, or put to reproach, or forsaken, for any possible reason? A just view of Christ and a true attachment to him will lead us to cleave to him, in every thing and for ever.

CHAPTER XI.

DIVINE CONCEALMENTS.

"He entered into an house and would have no man know it: but he could not be hid."

WHEN we began our meditations upon this portion of our Lord's life, we found him ready to retire for a season from active duties; and we suggested various reasons, not inconsistent with each other, for his withdrawal from public engagements. These same reasons still remained in force after the scenes which have passed under our notice. The single day and night spent on the shore and on the bosom of the lake, would not change any of the circumstances to which we have alluded. If there was danger from Herod's persecutions before, there still is: if he and his friends were affected at the tidings of John's death, the wound is still fresh: if his disciples needed repose, they did not secure it upon that busy day, which was succeeded by a night so toilsome; if he sought a season of devotion, yet that single night of prayer upon the mountain would but partially gratify his desires. For these, perhaps also for additional reasons, we find him still seeking retirement. We cannot decide how long he tarried in the land of Gennesaret, where he landed after the storm upon the lake. We know that immediately upon his landing he was recognized by the people. By this time his person was familiar to many individuals, especially in these parts of Galilee. This, of course, would be quite unfavourable to his present wish to seek retirement: yet he did not withhold his aid from those who sought it. As the news spread widely of his presence, the sick were brought to him from all quarters. Wonderful power was manifested in these healings. The mere touch of the hem of his robe sufficed to give soundness to the diseased. Pursuing his original intention of seeking a retired spot, he seems to have tarried but briefly in any place: yet he took time enough to teach the people upon several occasions: and his route was thronged with the helpless forms of the suffering, carried by friendly care and laid in his pathway.

We will not delay to consider further these teachings or miracles; but will pass along with the retreating footsteps of the Master to the north-west, until perhaps he had gone entirely beyond the borders of the Holy Land. The declaration that he went into the coasts of Tyre and Sidon does not render it certain that he went out of the country. But as in his childhood his parents had carried him to Egypt to escape the persecution of one Herod, so now to avoid the hands of that Herod's son, he may have paid his next and only other visit to a foreign land. It strengthens this supposition to be told that about this same time, he kept out of the land of Judea proper, walking only in Galilee, because the Jews sought to kill him. John vii. 1. It was safe, as well as quiet, to retire to the coasts of Tyre and Sidon.

The purposes of privacy and retirement were still sought; for we are told that he entered into a house and would have no man know it. But it is time now to say that it was not only for the reasons already suggested, that our Lord did not openly proclaim himself there. Indeed it was not only now but almost always, that our Lord sought rather to be searched for, than to thrust himself forward. It seems quite proper to say that a certain concealment was a characteristic of the great Teacher. It could not be said that he shunned the public notice at proper times; but he never courted notoriety. As we have before remarked, his brethren complained of this, and thought he should more plainly show himself to the world. We know that there is a modesty that ever belongs to truth, in wide contrast with the impudence of imposture; there is a calm composure in strength, compared with the bravado of conscious weakness; there is a quietness in true virtue, unlike the boisterous publicity of rowdyism. But even these things are not enough to account for this great characteristic of Christ. He himself said, "The kingdom of God cometh not with observation." Long before his appearance a prophet said of him, "He shall not strive nor cry, neither shall any man hear his voice in the streets." This characteristic of Christ belongs to the gospels. Let every intelligent reader notice how remarkably free from all display are these evangelical narratives. There is almost an entire absence of expressed emotions or exclamatory words. Miracles are recorded without surprise, and in just words enough to bring them fairly to our notice. Malicious crimes against the meekest sufferer the world ever saw, are recorded almost without grief or even sympathy for the sufferer, or indignation against the criminals. The narratives are made up of truth told without passion or adornment; and the unbiassed reader is allowed to form his own judgment of the person and character and work of him, who is chiefly presented in these scenes.

This withdrawal of himself from the open gaze of the people may be variously noticed. There is no trace of vain-glorious display when working the most stupendous miracles. There is no room to charge an interested concealment, such as would cover up any weakness of his claims. But marvellous works of which every witness was a competent judge; wrought before friends and foes; and officially attested by his avowed enemies; works so numerous, so different, and of such influence that imposture before his contemporaries was impossible, were still never thrust forward in any boastful spirit. How jubilant would the advocates of falsehood be, if any of the various systems of professed revelation could point to the support of one single wonder, such as those that abound in the history of Christ! But though our Lord abounds in miracles he is never wasteful of them. He carefully refrained from the exercise of his supernatural powers, when human curiosity craved indulgence, or personal fame might appear the ruling motive. It can be said of him, "He went about doing good." It cannot be said that he did these things to be seen of men. His repeated charge to those whom he healed gave token of his unobtrusiveness, "See that no man know it." Matt. ix. 30. And his teachings gave evidence of this same characteristic. He chiefly taught in parables. While this form of instruction is exceedingly interesting and easily remembered, yet the meaning does not always lie upon the surface; and indeed he avows that his teachings were at times purposely mysterious. His disciples did not understand his teachings; he knew they did not; he did not expect them to; yet did he not withhold the words they comprehended so imperfectly.

There are several interesting reasons which we may assign for this reserve of our Lord, and for this peculiar mysteriousness of his communications. We may first notice that all valuable teachings must necessarily possess something of this character. In its highest form, teaching is the communication of knowledge. There is indeed great profit in being reminded in due season of truths that are not new; we acknowledge great excellence in timely and appropriate, though familiar, thoughts; and we are often delighted to see old truths set before us in new connections and aspects. But usually truths have become old and familiar before they are thoroughly learned; and that teaching which consists in the communication of new truths is rarely mastered at our first learning. We make a great mistake in supposing that teaching is unprofitable unless it is fairly understood. The more thoroughly we understand anything the better; but knowledge may be gained in imperfect measures. How did any one of us learn the language we now speak? We caught its familiar tones in our tenderest years; we had no laboured explanations of the words, but learned them from hearing them used, without ourselves knowing how we accomplished so much; and from a very imperfect state of knowledge, and with very feeble capacities, we gradually and imperceptibly advanced to maturer thoughts. And we can look back with surprise to notice how crude were our thoughts upon many subjects which yet we considered mastered. How little thoroughness there ever is in the first perusal of a school-book, the first memorizing of its rules, the first boast that we are "through!" We learned the alphabet years ago. Few men know its power yet. The mastering of knowledge is no single step: profit and perfection may stand far apart; the words we hear may instruct us, and yet mean far more than we get out of them. Many a man may not appreciate the logical argument of an eloquent discourse, and yet its main lessons may be well impressed upon him. You may perhaps have heard the reply of a poor woman, when it was thought she had not profited by a sermon she could not remember. She compared it to a web of cloth which she was bleaching upon the grass. It seemed useless to keep wetting it, since it so soon became dry; but this she noticed, the more she wet it the whiter it got. There are effects of teaching more evident than those that consist in verbal remembrance. It is a great mistake to judge that even the younger children of our households need not attend upon the public sanctuary, because they do not understand the sermon. The children of a family ought to be in the sanctuary as regularly as a father should gather them around the family altar; and they should learn these religious teachings, in the house and in the church, just as they learn the language they use; by the constant and familiar inculcation of things that are insensibly and gradually acquired. How we acquire knowledge is a strange inquiry. Teaching is the communication of truth; but the capacities and advancement of the pupils differ so much, that the same discourse is variously profitable to a thousand hearers.

We may say still further that this partial mysteriousness of teaching is one of the great stimulants to the acquisition of knowledge. We set great store upon the perspicuity and simplicity which characterizes the instructions of certain teachers. Everything is made plain to the simplest comprehension. And the power to do this, is exceedingly desirable; so inspired wisdom prefers to speak five words that are understood, rather than ten thousand in an unknown tongue. Yet this aiming at simplicity may go too far. The object of the teacher is to lead the pupil forward; and he must ever keep in advance of him. The least thing we can ask of a teacher is that, upon the present topic of instruction, he should be better informed than those he addresses. But he must not master for them the difficulties of knowledge; let him rather show them how to do it themselves. He may stand up the steep hill of science and invite them to stand where he does; but they must do the climbing. Teaching trains babes for men; education is the drawing out of the faculties; if the process does not lead the mind to think, it leaves us babes even when we are grown. And no man knows the pleasure of true knowledge, if he has not felt this stimulus of *trying to find out.* So our Lord's parables are the elements of thought; and the busy mind delights to combine them into profitable forms. So all true teaching is not matured fruit to be had for the gathering; but rather, to use his figure, it is the seed cast into the fertile heart: but it must sink there beneath the surface, and die, before it brings forth the blade and the ear and the grain. "Take heed therefore how ye hear:" for all our lessons of wisdom, though pleasant now, should be still more profitable hereafter

Now if these thoughts have their measure of truth for every teacher, they should be peculiarly true of Christ. For he is the most eminent and original of all teachers. If every teacher stands in advance of those he teaches, how far do the wisest lag behind him! Besides, he is the great Teacher for all ages; and he must be found still in advance, even when earth's most profound sages sit at his feet. How could we expect these simple fishermen, rude and uneducated and prejudiced, to fathom the depths of wisdom, at which the learned and wise of far more polished times have been amazed! What an audience did Christ address, when he sent these inimitable lessons down the stream of time, to be copied in the manuscripts of fifteen centuries, multiplied by the manifold printing of steam-presses in later times, published in so many pulpits, read in so many closets; yet among all his scholars what one has ever risen at all near the level of the teacher? Learn we never so much, we do not still master these incomparable teachings; the more we learn, the more we see there is in them still to learn. Whatever our attainments are, our teacher and the same teachings which we have studied over and over again, are always a little in advance of us: not so much before us apparently as to discourage our attempts to understand at all; but still before; and we never quite catch up. It is like ascending a mountain; a little way up we are enraptured with the extensive view; yet it is wider the higher we ascend, and if the horizon bounds us on every side, the view is still capable of indefinite expansion; and the limitation really belongs to our powers of sight. The mysteries of truth are necessary results of our ignorance and feebleness.

There are two reasons pertaining to our Lord's earthly ministry and to his special position at this time, which may further explain why his teachings were less clear to his disciples. The first is, that during his life the full scheme of his ministry could not be explained to them. Only after his suffering and resurrection did it seem proper that the mystery so long hidden should be made known. Accordingly the disciples were ignorant of many things concerning the dignity and office of their Lord, the spirituality and universality of his kingdom, and the nature of his service which are plain to all the church in our times. Thus our Lord declares the excellent dignity of John the Baptist, and yet emphatically adds, that the least in the kingdom of heaven is greater than he.

But there was another special reason just at this time why our Lord should keep himself in seclusion. "He entered into a house and would have no man know it." He had gone beyond the sphere of his appointed ministry. For the first and last time during his public life, he was outside of Judea and in a Gentile land. But he says of himself that he was not sent but to the lost sheep of the house of Israel. Whether we have or have not rightly judged of his reasons for retiring to the coasts of Tyre and Sidon, he did not go there to preach publicly. He retired quietly to a house and would have no man know it. Yet we are quite unwilling to believe that any chance dictated the place or time of his movements; or that, in the highest sense, the most interesting incident of that visit was not in his view as he came into these coasts. Indeed the instruction and encouragement we may receive from this simple narrative are peculiar. The footsteps of Jesus press a heathen soil, even before the time has come for preaching salvation to the Gentiles. Is it not a token of his eagerness to bless the heathen; and may we not expect his large favour to them in these days when he sends his gospel to them? Though he was not sent to them, yet we find him here giving a special blessing to a heathen woman. Is he not more ready to grant such blessings now that he is preached among them? Though he hides himself, he can be persuaded by the pleadings of earnest faith. Will he not ever answer faith in these times, when his own public promises are pledged for the penitent's acceptance? When we see Christ thus visiting a heathen land, and surpassing his ordinary mission to bless a Gentile woman, may we not argue for more than usual encouragement, whether we would seek for ourselves the favours he offers in the gospel, or would desire the success of his truth in those lands of Gentile darkness where he commands us to send it?

But there is one other reason for the peculiarity

of our Lord's character and teachings of which we have been speaking. He hides himself, as it were; he teaches us in parables; he does not always make his words as plain as they can be made, for in this very thing lies a test of the dispositions of those who hear the gospel. Christ's teachings are so set before men, the whole scheme of preaching the gospel is so arranged, that the men who truly desire to learn wisdom from him, can easily do so; and men who do not wish these instructions, can easily avoid them. We shall take further occasion to show how remarkably a mind truly awakened to any subject seizes by a ready tact upon all the available advantages for securing its end; for the narrative before us gives us one of the most interesting and instructive examples in all the Bible. But we see illustrations of the same thing all around us. It is not the manner of the great Teacher; it is not the method of God's providence to force the evidences and truths and motives of religion upon the minds of unwilling men. God leaves not himself without witness; but men may readily, if they so choose, turn away from the testimony. The world gives evidence that there is a God: yet the fool may say *in his heart* that there is none, and man may boast of his Atheism. The Scriptures manifest themselves to be his word, by various evidences both internal and external; yet may men turn to infidelity. The church of God may try to do her appropriate work of preaching the gospel to the perishing; her servants may go out into the highway and hedges and use urgent importunities to lead men to salvation; faithful public and private efforts may be made to win souls to God. But it must be acknowledged that the grand reason why multitudes all around our churches are not reached by the gospel, is because they themselves have no interest in these things. We may be bound to make efforts to awaken the careless: judicious efforts may ever have their measure of success; but men will still prove naturally averse to the gospel of Christ: and their carelessness and apathy will remain the grand reason why they do not receive the truth. Cavils will be made to hide this true reason from themselves and others; but if the particular ground of any man's cavilling is removed, his own indifference to the gospel will still remain as the chief reason for his unbelief. How often have we seen our churches crowded to overflowing, when some topic of special interest has been discussed. What is to hinder the same persons from a regular and constant attendance, if only they should form a just estimate of their own pressing need of the gospel? Can any topic be of more importance to a justly discerning mind than to secure his own interest in an eternal salvation? All the objections of men against the preaching of the gospel may be resolved to this foundation: "They care for none of these things." Take away single objections of men to the gospel without removing this plague in the very heart; and it is but healing an ulcer while the current of the life-blood remains still impure to break out in another and perhaps a more dangerous sore. It is not by any change of doctrines, or preachers, or names or evidences of religion that a radical cure of the evil is effected. Men make their ready objections against a particular preacher, when really they are indifferent to all preaching: they pick flaws in the lives of Christians when truly a Christian life has no charms for themselves: they object to the evidences of religion, when indeed the chief trouble is a heart averse to the claims of piety. Let such men become interested and awakened to a just sense of their own sinfulness, and these cavillings will be thrown aside. Many an infidel has thrown aside his arguments, through no logical process that has answered their apparent force; but awakened to see his need of the gospel and its adaptedness to his wants. Many an errorist has at once laid down his errors, taught by the candid and straightforward movements of a heart that feels a new interest and a true sincerity. Men find that the barriers in their way to the sanctuary have been piled up by themselves; that their chief burdens have been burdens self-imposed; that when the lips so readily said, "I can't," the inner man of the heart ever meant, "I won't."

Now when the gospel in every age has to deal with such men, it is but a righteous testing of their spirit; it is the wisdom of Christ, that his teachings are so presented as to leave them at full liberty to stand aside, at their own choice and on their own responsibility. Men may cavil at various things. The teachings may be esteemed mysterious; the duties hard; the conduct of Christians may often bring reproach upon the cause; and the evidences, claims, and doctrines of the gospel may seem to lack a sufficient clearness. But on the one hand, all these things are as they ever have been; they are allowed in infinite wisdom; and he who demands our faith in the gospel knew well that just such things as these would seem to withstand it; and on the other hand, it is plain that these things are not hindrances to others by our very side, whose external advantages for overcoming them are no greater than ours. Neither wisdom nor folly; neither riches nor poverty; neither prosperity nor adversity; neither favourable opportunities nor serious disadvantages have the controlling influence in leading men to neglect religion. The wise man can find others as wise as he, that are lovers of Jesus; the poor man can find others as poor as himself, who are not hindered by poverty; side by side with every caviller dwell his own acquaintances, who are not hindered from studying and knowing and loving the truth; who yet could find reasons for carelessness as strong as his, if they were but disposed to use them. The gospel of Christ is purposely set to test the hearts of men. This is a *stone of trial;* and whosoever shall fall upon this stone shall be broken.

While then it is the duty of the church of God and of the ministry to lay no unnecessary stumbling-blocks in the way of sinful men, we may recognize that the pure gospel proves a stone of stumbling and a rock of offence. Men stumble at all the truth is, and at all the friends of truth can be, or can do, or can leave undone. "Whereunto," said our Lord, "shall I liken this generation?" Yet let us remember the Scriptural teaching, and notice its confirmation all around us, that it is DISOBEDIENT men who stumble at the word. This it is that justifies the dealings of God's hand with the sons of men. If there are things hard to be understood, which the unlearned and the unstable wrest to their own destruction; yet "the meek will he guide in judgment, and the meek will he teach his way." Every rebellious sinner in a gospel land has around him the abundant proofs that his perdition is through his own guilt. Men of his own acquaintance, living by his very side, with no better opportunities of knowing the truth, have secured the salvation of the gospel and lived and died in the faith of Jesus, while he has filled his lips with excuses and cavillings. You are too busy; but men as busy as you are earnest Christians. You have many hindrances; but be faithful to your own soul, and you must acknowledge that some of your own acquaintances whose hindrances are as great as yours, yet press through every opposing obstacle and steadfastly and humbly follow the Lord. There is a natural tendency to magnify our own troubles; yet in the exercise of a just and candid mind every man may decide that the principal difficulty in religion lies in the indifference of his own heart.

Jesus entered a house and would have no man know it; but he could not be hid. A certain woman wanted just such a healer; and she found him out. Somehow or other, if relief is to be had, the suffering find out where to look for it. The man who laughs at physicians and medicines when he is well, calls for them as readily as any, in his time of distress. Jesus often hides himself from people now; but let any sinful soul seek for him as earnestly as this woman did; and his power and grace are as great as ever. What a solemn word is that of Paul, "If our gospel be hid, it is hid to them that are lost; in whom the god of this world hath blinded the minds of them which believe not, lest the light of the glorious gospel of Christ, who is the image of God, should shine unto them." 2 Cor. iv. 3, 4. Every hearer of the gospel is blinded by Satan, or enlightened by God's Holy Spirit. How should we fear the one; how should we desire and pray for the other. For the one is blessed and the other cursed; and their wide extremes are the loss or the salvation of the soul.

CHAPTER XII.

FAITH SEEKING FOR THE HEALER.

"For a certain woman whose young daughter had an unclean spirit, heard of him."

STRANGE and unusual conduct in one whose character we know, usually attracts our attention in proportion to its strangeness. When one speaks and does just as we expect him to do, his conduct passes without special remark; but when anything seems strikingly out of character, it cannot escape particular attention. In the scene to which our thoughts are now called, both the principal characters, our Lord and this suppliant woman, speak and act as we would not have anticipated for them. It surprises us to see here for the first time, that the merciful Jesus apparently pays no regard to one who supplicates his mercy; and we are as much surprised, not so much to see this heathen woman coming to this prophet from Judea to find healing for her child, as to see her persevering faith when she seems so decidedly, and indeed almost hopelessly, repulsed. And if our attention is fixed upon this whole matter, *we* may well wonder at the triumph of her faith in the issue, since our Lord himself decides that this is one of the most remarkable instances of faith that came under even *his* notice.

Our Lord, as we have said, was now probably in a foreign land; at least he was on the borders of Phœnicia. The woman was a Gentile, not only by nation, but also by religion. She is called a Greek; but this word in the New Testament is not used in its strict sense; but signifies a Gentile. Hence she is also called a Syrophœnician. The Phœnicians had colonies in Africa, (*e. g.* Carthage;) but she belonged to the tribes which yet remained in Syria: thus the evangelist Matthew calls her "a woman of Canaan." Perhaps she belonged to one of those tribes with whom specially the Jews were forbidden to hold intercourse; and whose great wickedness had brought upon them the curse of Jehovah. The ministry of our Lord was expressly to Israel; we cannot indeed doubt that in this case, he designs to show that his grace is for the Gentiles: yet it was not until after his resurrection that the barriers between them and the Jews were broken down: and this woman does not find ready access to him.

We are not told how this heathen mother heard of Jesus at all; or how she came to form such just conceptions of his dignity and mission, of his power and grace. She may teach us perhaps the wonderfully diffusive power of divine truth in any community and around it. As no figure is more beautiful, so none is more common or correct than that which compares truth to light. Light, we know, is wonderfully diffusive. Let a single ray into a dark room, and though it will not shine clearly, it will shine truly and really into every corner. And we know that a very little light is incomparably superior to entire darkness; that our eyes instinctively accommodate themselves to the degree of light we have, so that we can often see when the light is not clear; and that a dim light has always at least this advantage, that the closer we draw to it, the better we can see. Thus even a little light has a directing and guiding ministry. A man wandering in darkness may see, a long way off, the twinkling beam upon which he may fix his eye until he finds his path. So when Evangelist in the Pilgrim's Progress could not make the trembling sinner see the wicket gate, he could point him to "yonder shining light;" and the pilgrim could see enough to guide him to the spot. We need not wonder much that this woman seems acquainted with the claims and character of this great Prophet. It is doubtless true that no preacher from Judea had ever entered the city where she dwelt, to tell of the God of Jacob. Perhaps she never had entered the doors of a Jewish synagogue; much less had ever witnessed the solemn sacrifices of Jerusalem's great temple. Yet, living upon the borders of the land of Judea, she could not escape some acquaintance with the peculiar claims and character of the Jewish people. Compared with the Jews themselves, we might perhaps call her an ignorant woman in these things; yet she knew far more than could be known by those who lived in the distant darkness of heathenism. Especially we judge that the wonders wrought by this mighty Prophet of Galilee became known through a wide district of country; and awakened much attention to learn his character and teachings, as well as his deeds. We can only learn from this woman's own lips what were her views; and the name she gives him, as the Son of David, and the perseverance with which she urged her suit, are sufficiently remarkable. How could she address him thus, unless she knew something of the Jewish prophecies that a Messiah should come of David's line; and unless she acknowledged, what the Jewish rulers denied, that this was the long-expected Christ? Whatever were her disadvantages of land or race or education, precious light has dawned upon this darkened mind.

This woman may teach us something of the serious responsibilities resting upon the men in our own land; even those who are least directly brought under the teachings of the gospel. Our Lord upbraided the cities wherein most of his mighty works were done, because they repented not: and we decide that, by a just judgment, they are held specially accountable whose privileges have been largest and most direct. How inexcusable for any neglect of Christ are those who have been trained in Christian families, and taught all their lives in Christian sanctuaries! But let us not suppose that there are any persons dwelling in this Christian land, who are so ignorant of Christianity as to excuse them for the reproach they cast upon it, and the neglect they show towards it.

There is a sense in which we may mourn over the destitutions of our land. Dwelling beneath the very shadow of Christian temples, hearing constantly the sound of the church-going bell, mingling every day with professors of the faith of Christ, how many persons there are, who live and die in lamentable ignorance of what the true gospel is, and of what is its saving efficacy for the soul of man. There is a great diversity, we know, in this ignorance. Some of these, whose feet now never visit the sanctuary, were in earlier life accustomed to the trainings of a pious parentage; but unhappy associations, perhaps marriage with an ungodly person, perhaps the mortifying influence of sinfulness, or even of poverty, may have led to a gradual abandonment of these early habits; and for these, or for far worse reasons, many are training up their households in wide contrast with their own education. Some there are again, who have been born of infidel, or heretical, or careless, or wicked parentage: and all the various feelings of contempt and hostility to the gospel, which might be expected to flow from the miserable influences that have floated in the atmosphere of their godless homes, have become intensified by the distorted images of religion as they have seen it through the dense vapours of this wicked world.

It is right for us to say that these godless men

all around our churches will stand utterly inexcusable before the bar of a righteous Judge for their wicked rejection of the saving truths of the gospel. We have no wish to apologize for any indolence on the part of Christians, where they fail to use earnest and zealous means of acquainting men around them with the gospel; fail to urge church neglecters to visit the sanctuary; fail to put the word of God into the families of the destitute. Much less would we excuse the various inconsistencies of men who profess to be religious; and because of whose folly and wickedness, the prejudices of ungodly men are greatly increased. It is one thing to acknowledge that the errors and inconsistencies of Christians may do harm to other men, and that Christians are greatly to blame for this; it is quite another thing to justify ungodly men for the offence, which, *for any reason*, they take at the gospel. Make the errors of Christians, their apathy, their formality, their indolence, as great as the truth will warrant in the coldest and darkest days of religious decline; and it still remains true, that light enough shines in the darkest habitations of this land, to render every soul inexcusable before God for his neglect of the great salvation.

It is sometimes said of our communities, "We have heathen enough all around us." There is one sense in which these words are not true at all: and another sense in which they are more than true. It is not true that any among us are as ignorant of the true God as those that dwell in lands of heathenism. We may find mothers here who destroy their own offspring: but no man can claim that infanticide among us ever springs, as it does in heathen lands, from the biddings of religion. This is not a heathen land in any just sense. We have wicked ness: but it is not wickedness like theirs. We have light which men cannot but see. Churches rise in all this land, and the most ignorant man knows the purposes for which they are built. Sabbaths dawn on all this land; and the very men who desecrate them most, would be confined to their ordinary labours and would not find the time to profane them, if these days were not different from ordinary days: and all Sabbath breakers, as well as Sabbath keepers, know that it is as a religious day that this differs from other days. Bibles are scattered over all this land; and the men who read them least, know well the reputation of the Scriptures, know that the very reading of them has a tendency to make men religious, and have opportunities enough, at the promptings of curiosity or devotion, to learn what these teachings are, that prefer claims so high upon man's attention. Professors of religion abound in all this land; and though very many do little to commend or adorn the gospel, there is a sense in which every one of them teaches religion to every beholder. Thousands of men read the lives of their neighbours who never read the Bible; and three things are well worthy of our careful notice upon this subject:

First, The commendations which are sometimes uttered by the men of the world upon those who profess to be Christians are usually a suspicious kind of praise. The world praises Christians in proportion as they abandon the distinctive and more spiritual things of piety, and become conformed to worldly maxims and practices: they speak of such as liberal-minded, and not under the influence of bigotry: and they complain that other Christians are more strict than these. Yet it is well to recollect that at the very time that the laxness of such Christians is praised, their inconsistency is a matter of ridicule, their religious influence is mischievous, and the very persons who tempt them to such folly despise them in their hearts. It is shallow praise which ungodliness bestows upon inconsistent piety. But, *secondly*, we may notice that the general current of worldly remark respecting Christians is reproachful. Sometimes a Christian is so consistent and useful that all around are forced to confess that here is a truly good man. But this man and all other Christians are subject to reproach more readily and abundantly than reproach is ever cast upon others. Men who are not Christians are frequently commended; men who do not profess religion are often praised for being as good as Christians, or better; men of many faults are praised for single good qualities; the world thus loves its own. But if there be any failing in a Christian, the keen-eyed world is sure to discern it; even his virtues are spoken of with a sneer; the tendency of remark is to reproach the Christian. But, *thirdly*, this very tendency to reproach Christians is not only a compliment paid to the excellency of Christianity, but a proof that the world knows what this Christian ought to be. If Christianity is not better than this Christian, he cannot be reproached with hypocrisy, insincerity, or inconsistency, since he is as good as his principles; and the man, who does not know enough to make the comparison, is too ignorant to see the inconsistency. The very reproaches cast by ungodly men upon Christian men, are themselves proof that they are not ignorant of that religion, which binds them as truly as it does the men they reproach. Light enough to know what another man's virtues ought to be, is light enough to reveal what they themselves should believe and do. And thus the very prejudices, which ungodly men have formed against religion, will prove that they sinned against light, and will justify their condemnation before a righteous God. If a man should dare to plead at the judgment, that the evil example of Christians filled him with prejudices against religion, the Judge would quickly answer, "Thou hypocrite, out of thine own mouth will I condemn thee! You found fault with another man for declining from my service. Why did you not yourself, what you so clearly saw he ought to do?"

Around our Christian sanctuaries there is much ignorance of God, and much prejudice against religion, and much responsibility upon those who do aught to increase these evils in any way. But even when we say that all this is worse than heathenism, we say nothing to excuse the wickedness of those who despise the gospel. It is likely that there are souls around us, harder to reach than the heathen would be. Many a minister's commission is like that given to the prophet Ezekiel, "Surely if I had sent thee to" a people of a strange language, "they would have hearkened unto thee." Ezek. iii. 6. Many a minister's experience is like that of Christ, who reproached those that heard him most, and declared that Sodom would have repented where Capernaum was hardened. Opposition to God and truth; indifference to religion; scoffing at sacred things, may be found in Christian lands, worse than among the heathen. In heathen lands every man is religious; every man offers his prayers; every man serves the gods. How great is the wickedness, which under better teachings allows men to be irreligious, and prayerless, and godless. There is a sense in which our society exhibits forms of iniquity that cannot be found in heathen lands: but there is light enough thrown by the sun of Christianity into the darkest corners where its beams never directly shine, to leave inexcusable the guilt of those who perish here without the gospel. If this Gentile, living outside of the land of Judea, knew enough of Jesus to address him as the Son of David, that name and its power are not unknown to all the dwellers in Christian lands.

But we need something else beside the mere shining of this true light to lead men to rejoice in it. Men must feel their need of healing before their attention is given to the shining reputation of any healer. Perhaps this woman had dwelt carelessly in the twilight of truth that spread over this border land; it may be that even the visit of Jesus had done little to excite her interest, if it had not been opportunely made in the time of her deep distress. It is a frequent thing for the kind providence of God to awaken the souls of men to a sense of their need of him, by sending afflictions upon them. So it was with this woman. Yet this trouble was not upon her own person; it was upon her young daughter. As if we were here to learn lessons of deep interest and profit both for ourselves and for our households. It is not needful for us to draw the distinct line between the blessings we seek for ourselves, and the blessings we seek for our families. Suffice it to say that no parent can secure a blessing for himself, who is not desirous that it should come upon his children; and no parent can plead before God for a blessing upon his family without himself receiving one. Tender and sacred are the ties by which God has bound together the households of the earth. Through their children, how many blessings have come upon parents: and the various necessities of children have often sent parents to plead before the Son of David.

We know but little of this woman's household,

except just this: she had one afflicted daughter. Perhaps she was a widow, and had no one to come and present her case but herself. Perhaps she had a husband, who had been trained to heathenism like herself, but had not risen above this; and, it may be, he scoffed at the idea of applying to the Galilean prophet. Whatever may be true of these things, no woman could be more thrown upon her own resources, to make her way without human help, than this woman; and she comes off none the worse from her important pleading because this was so. The great object of her mission is briefly set before us. Enter into her house and you may learn her secret. No matter what kind of a house it was. Like the Shunammite, the friend of Elisha, she may have been a great woman, able to build a prophet's chamber, and to give a prophet lodgings; or she may, like Elijah's friend, have been reduced to the poverty of a handful of meal and a little oil. Little matter whether she dwelt in a palace or a cottage; was clothed in rich or in poor apparel; her's was a human habitation; and human ills and human fears and human cares came in to take up their abode with her. You may enter a thousand abodes in as many different parts of the wide earth, and find these griefs and ills, not the exact counterpart of hers; and yet such as burdened hearts like hers may carry to that same gracious Son of David, and find the relief she gained. Perhaps her case is less accurately told, as to its minuter features, just because those it should encourage, resemble it only in the great facts of necessity and of opportunity to ask relief of Jesus. Many a mother, grievously distressed for a young child, pleading for the life of her darling, has drawn near to Him who alone can help, and urged her case. What a picture of distress to bring before us; can our scenes of household wo go beyond it? a little daughter grievously vexed with a devil! She did not bring her daughter with her: she was young. Or if not too young to bring, perhaps the case was one where the violence of the possessing spirit placed the subject beyond the control of her friends.

How peculiarly distressing to consider a child under Satanic power! Such a case is only comparable to those moral instances, yet more distressing, where parents see their children going perversely in the ways of evil; bond-slaves of that same Satan; in a worse bondage; and his willing captives. We have all seen the children of mothers professing piety, refusing parental control, walking in ways of dissipation, profanity, impurity, grievously possessed of the devil; and in a far worse case than any bodily ailment could ever be. And indeed every unconverted child is a subject of parental prayer, and should be borne before God with all the earnestness and anxiety of a persevering importunity. We weep in anguish over the sick beds of our suffering children; yet faith bids us know that there is no malady of the body so dangerous and fatal as that disease of sin, which lurks through all the veins, and which knows no favourable crisis until the soul is born again to God. How easily should we know our chief cause for anxiety!

This woman was deeply in earnest, and this we see in every part of the narrative. Perhaps we may trace it on her approach to him in the house where he did not design to receive company. Yet we must not think that there was any rudeness in her coming, like an intrusion on his privacy. It was somewhat so; yet it must not be severely judged according to the standard of our western manners: for oriental customs allow a freedom of access to the house quite different from our habits. But the inspired writer intimates that it was because of her earnestness that he could not be hid. The truth is when the soul is filled with a deep anxiety to secure any object, all the faculties of the mind are quickened respecting it. Men succeed, if success is possible, in those things on which the mind is bent. The slightest hint is more profitable to an attentive and eager mind, than the plainest thoughts are to a careless one: and we easily comprehend and secure for ourselves every help put within our reach, to promote a favourite scheme; and as easily set aside every hindrance by which we refuse to be stopped. When a man is sick of any particular disease, he hears much of others who have the same affection; and much of those physicians who are specially skilful in such cases. Give a man a personal concern in anything;

let his heart be set upon it; and he learns fast, and learns under many serious disadvantages. If this Gentile woman, living on the borders of Palestine, had not just then specially needed the help of Jesus, doubtless she would have been heedless of his presence in the land; and he could have been hid in that house.

And this after all is the great secret for securing spiritual blessings, for securing the Divine forgiveness for our sinful souls: to set our hearts upon it. Men gain worldly honours and worldly wealth by earnest and undivided care. It is said that one of the Rothschilds was once asked respecting the clerks in their great banking-houses, whether he did not sometimes turn their thoughts to that eternity upon which they soon must enter. "We never allow them to think of such things," said he. "It would entirely incapacitate them for business." How true is it that this world often crowds the next out of the heart! How plain is it that a truly interested heart is the great necessity: and if men all around us had this, our sanctuaries would soon be crowded with earnest pilgrims pressing onwards with their faces toward Zion. The men all around us who now seem so ignorant of Jesus, would find out where he is: he could not be hid from them; they would press into the house and fall down at his feet. The men who are now careless of the preaching of the gospel would hear the words of life in the feeblest discourses of a faithful pastor; and learn more in an hour than they can with a careless ear in a lifetime. The men who spend so much breath in cavils against others, would look at home, and be only too glad that they may find pardon in Christ for the chief of sinners. What men need to lead them to salvation is not new or more lively teachings, nor new faculties, nor new powers of discerning truth, nor new opportunities of doing their duty, nor new companions around them. Let the heart be set on these great things. So far as the operations of our minds are concerned, scarcely anything is of more importance than a fixed purpose, which not only cannot be shaken by difficulties, but which turns obstacles into stepping-stones of advance. If such a man has not full light upon his path, he yet has enough to show him where he may find more. This woman heard of Jesus; and as to the place of his present retirement, from her he could not be hid. And does not the ancient promise run so: "And ye shall seek me and find me, when ye shall search for me with all your heart?" Jer. xxix. 13. How many fair promises have men made to themselves and to God for a future repentance that have not found their fulfilment, and are not likely to find it; because the heart is less interested than ever in the things of salvation. Not for want of privileges, opportunities, light, do men perish in our land and times. Men love darkness rather than light: the god of this world has blinded their eyes: the gospel is hid to them that are lost. Yet the word of life is not afar off. It is not in the depths: they need not descend. It is not in heaven: they need not go up. Jesus cannot be hid, if an earnest soul will find him. His own words are, "Ask and ye shall receive; seek and ye shall find; knock and it shall be opened." The blessing may not at once be given; it was not to this woman; but the reasons for his delay are wise; and they are not found in Christ's unwillingness to bless. He may test our faith and patience and perseverance; but he that endureth to the end shall find the reward the larger.

CHAPTER XIII.

FAITH SEVERELY TESTED.

"But he answered her not a word."

BUT for the trouble that befel her daughter, we might never have heard of this Gentile woman. Why should we be so much afraid of sorrow?. Wisdom tells us that the best lessons of life are learned when the head is bowed down. There are lessons of penitence and prayer and submission and faith—indeed there are lessons of thankfulness and hope, that can be learned only when the spirit is softened, and we wait meekly on God. And next to the actual experience of suffering ourselves, sympathy with those who are in any distress has a tendency to subdue our hearts, and to impress upon us salutary lessons. Let this humble woman teach us how to pray, as well as whom to approach: and let us adopt her short and direct petition in our times of need, "Lord, help me!" In our griefs we know how to seek human help: let us, above all, seek Divine mercy; which is more needed, may more certainly be found, and is more effectual. It is proper enough to seek human counsel and aid; it is eminently proper to pray. Indeed we should not wait till trouble comes upon us before we begin our trust in God: for it is only in our folly and perverseness that sorrows are God's rods to drive us to his throne. If we will but yield to his drawings, it is equally true that the goodness of God leads us to repentance. This is its design; and, upon wise hearts, its tendency. "Trust in him at all times, ye people pour out your hearts before him." But specially let us consider our spiritual necessities to drive us near to God. With these, men around us may have but little sympathy; for these, they may have no relief: therefore for them must we approach the Son of David. And not because they have no occasion, do so many refuse to seek him. As it is in some bodily diseases, so is it in the disease of the soul. Men refuse to believe their danger. Their worst symptoms are looked upon with a flattering eye. The fatal hectic flush upon the cheek, the eye brightening with the lustre of its last fires, the freedom from racking pains, are looked upon as indications of recruiting strength, when life is like a dying candle that starts up to unwonted brightness once or twice more before it is gone. Deceitful as these things are, they equal not the deceit of sin. "The heart is deceitful *above all things*." Many a soul needs redeeming help all the more, because of the self-flattery which prevents him from recognizing his true condition. Let us consider, in the light of God's holy word, our spiritual necessities; let us own that to be a sinner unreconciled to God is a more dangerous and fatal thing than any malady of the body: let us for our own souls, and for the heavy afflictions of those that are near and dear to us, seek the presence of Jesus, and pray with the woman of Canaan, "Lord, help!"

And as we consider her pleading, and now especially, the disadvantages under which she successfully approached our Lord, let us learn to come boldly, and believingly to the throne of grace. Let the lesson be even the more impressive from the humble place she held. If the land of Israel had seen the high priest at Jerusalem, who was learned in Jewish law, come and bow down before Jesus, and own him as the Messiah, how would multitudes have gazed in wonder. Yet Christ teaches all generations since, the great principles of his gospel, and lays them open to the acceptance of the humblest and the most dejected, by presenting the case of this Gentile woman. No sinner ever had more to discourage his application for mercy than this woman had; no sinner ought ever to give up his pleadings in despair, after seeing her success and the commendation of Christ; no sinner in a land where the gospel is preached, can find any valid excuse for his ignorance and impenitence, when we learn that Christ could not be hid from her. In every view of the case our encouragements are in contrast with her disadvantages.

It is difficult for us to realize the disadvantages under which this woman laboured as she came before

Jesus: these are either presented in the narrative, or may be gathered from the circumstances of the case. Many of them are still felt as deep discouragements on the part of penitents who seek for mercy; yet the fact that so many serious obstacles united to deter her, and that she secured the blessing in spite of them all, should forbid any soul that has an errand to Jesus to go empty from his presence. Let us come with confidence in him alone; and then the want of other encouragements will not affect the successful issue.

This woman had no invitation to come to Jesus. She belonged to a Gentile race, and, as he told her afterwards, he was not sent to such. Before this, indeed, our Lord had blessed one believing Gentile: but Jewish friends had plead on behalf of the Roman centurion; and it is not likely that she had ever heard of his case to encourage her application. Not a single precedent led her to judge that she would find acceptance; not a single promise encouraged her to draw near: her visit was a new interruption of the privacy which he came so far to seek. How many troubled souls are now dejected by thoughts which would have been true in her case; which can be no more true in any other; and which, in their fullest force, should not hinder us, since they did not interfere with her success. She came without an invitation; and we often fear that the invitations of the word are not addressed to us. They seem to be. Every variety of language is used to reach us, if trouble was not sometimes perverse in refusing to receive comfort. The Saviour says now and in our ears, "Come unto me all ye that labour and are heavy-laden: Ho, every one that thirsteth; he that believeth shall be saved." And lest we should not come, because we judge that we are not burdened or thirsty or believing, he uses terms we cannot escape; addresses his gospel to every creature; declares that he will cast out none that come, for any reason; and urges *whosoever will* to come. And even if we fear to appropriate any possible call he makes upon us, our case can be no worse than hers. A stranger, to all appearance unwelcome, certainly uninvited, she pressed to the Saviour's feet, the first, so far as she knew, to venture thus. But the precedents have multiplied since her day. She found all she sought; and thousands since her time, alone, unfriended, with all their fears have gone to Jesus empty, and returned full. We cannot make our case worse than hers. In reality it is incomparably more favourable. The gospel is full of promises, and history is full of examples to encourage our approach.

This uninvited woman was a stranger. Troubled souls often say within themselves, "If I was only a child of God, with what boldness would I approach the throne of grace; how patiently would I await an answer; how would I be assured of success." Men make themselves greatly unhappy by searching through their hearts to see whether they have faith to pray; instead of thinking nothing about that, but, which is infinitely more natural, just as this woman did, coming directly to God with their humble cry. It is only a day or two since I received a letter from an unhappy sinner, complaining that he was unfit to pray; and that God would not hear such an one pray. Just as if prayer ever was the appeal of merit; as if even a child of God would dare to plead for his own sake, and not rather through the Divine mercy; as if our unworthiness did not make up the chief element of that necessity that drives us to Jesus. Let us not talk about our rights, nor think about our rights, when we would come to ask for mercies. Let us not be afraid to hope or pray, because we have no sense of acceptance: but let our errand fill our hearts; and let us press, as she did, into his presence. She did not feel that she was a child of God; and our fears that we are not, should not forbid us to pray.

The only encouragements this woman had, were drawn from the reputation of the wonderful prophet whom she now approached. She knew that the power to heal her unhappy daughter lay nowhere else; she believed that he had the power to heal; she believed that his benevolence would relieve. These were the prevailing thoughts in all this persevering prayer. Yet compared with the privileges of others, perhaps she had but little evidence to support her faith. It is likely she had never seen him perform a single miracle; but she had heard of what he had done. She may never have heard a discourse from his lips; but she had heard of his claims as the Son of David. She had not learned to pray by listening to others; but she came to pray for herself. How little light, how little learning may guide a soul to salvation; yet how many are in darkness while the light shines all around! How many wander away and perish, who despise the guidings of wisdom! Sometimes we hear of souls converted by scattered tracts and Bibles in destitute places, where there is neither preacher nor sanctuary; sometimes we hear of a heathen cherishing with joy the salvation of Christ as told in the first sermon he ever heard; sometimes a degraded sinner, trained to wretchedness and sin, comes forth from his filthiness—like the man from whom the devils were cast out—to sit at the feet of Jesus, clothed and in his right mind. How this precious gospel achieves its triumphs under the most disadvantageous circumstances! An aged and ignorant negro in the West Indies came regularly some distance to a missionary to learn to read. But he made very slow progress; his teacher was disheartened, thought it was lost labour, and intimated to the old man that he had better give it up. "No, massa," was the reply, "me never give it over till me die." And pointing to John iii. 16, "God so loved the world," &c., he added emphatically, "It is worth all de labour to be able to read dat one single verse."* What a con-

* Foreign Missionary, xvii. 167.

trast there is between cases like these, and the privileges enjoyed by those who sit regularly in the sanctuary, and who all their lives have heard of Jesus. If the soul may be saved where the light is very dim, the evidences of religion feeble, and the privileges few; yet souls may be lost in the full blaze of the gospel. We ought to ponder the words of Christ to the men around him, "Many shall come from the heathen world on every side, and sit down in the kingdom of glory, while the children of the kingdom shall be thrust out." All the teachings of the Sacred Scriptures bid us beware of boasting, pride, or presumption; while they encourage us to the most earnest and persevering efforts of prayer and faith. Blessed are our privileges, if we rightly use them! The more we know of Christ the better, if we trust and love him more because we know him. And even if our early disadvantages were great, and our present discouragements great; if we never heard until now of this Saviour of sinners, let us imitate this woman, and use her pleadings for our necessities, "Have mercy on me, O Lord, thou Son of David."

But from considering the disadvantages which may have embarrassed her before she came at all, let us consider the difficulties she actually encountered when she had made her way into his presence. Her whole soul wrapped up in the great importance of her errand, she has thought little of the obstacles thus far: and now she stands in the presence of that great Prophet, whose fame had outgone Judea and come to foreign ears. She casts herself at his feet and pours out her complaint with a mother's feeling heart. And yet how different is her reception from her ardent anticipations! We are as much surprised as she at our Lord's conduct: indeed, we could not possibly explain it, if we had not the issue before us. This she did not have, and we never have it, when we come before his throne with our own pleadings. Hers is a remarkable case. It is the first example in the history of our Lord, where he even seemed to hesitate to relieve the necessities of any that came to him. Usually he readily heard and answered those who came; sometimes he wrought unasked the favours that were needed; sometimes he delayed long enough to inquire whether the applicants believed he could do the thing; and then gave according to their faith. Here is more than ordinary hesitation, here is the only refusal on record; and by the time we are done with it, we will find that this is no refusal, but a temporary and benevolent testing of this woman's faith. But how is she to know this? Why is she not to believe that the reports she had heard of him are untrue, and that she has mistaken, if not the power, yet the grace of Jesus? She stands before him. She has heard what he can do; what he has done; she tells her case; and receives her first repulse. His lips are sealed to her request; he answered her never a word.

When we make any request of a friend, perhaps silence is more embarrassing than an actual refusal. And silence is peculiarly distressing and painful when our hearts are full of grief and trouble. It is in the very nature of grief to seek for sympathy; yet it is too sensitive to demand it. Those attentions which must be sought after and asked for, in a time of affliction, we hardly wish to receive; while our hearts go out in all their warm affection to the spontaneous offer of help in a time of sorrow. The test to which our Lord put this poor woman seems wonderfully strange in him; and must be recorded thus for some purpose of more than ordinary instruction. There she stood in all her grief: how much she felt his silence: how fast her thoughts flew out to remember that she was there an uninvited and intruding stranger: but flew off also to that afflicted chamber where the suffering image of her daughter bade the mother plead still with the POWER to save! And through these anxious moments not a word escaped him. We have had an experience of something like this, too. Many a prayer poured out before God has seemed as utterly lost as the first requests of this Gentile woman. He answers us never a word. The case seems, not only discouraging, but hopeless. We write bitter things against ourselves. We are tempted to complain of the Divine dealings. We have heard of others to whom his mercy came as soon as asked; we have heard of those whom he has arrested in ways of folly and blessed with richest grace when they asked not after him; and now that he should refuse, or even delay, to hear our earnest cry, is enough almost to close our lips of entreaty and to drive us away from the place of the suppliant. Yet his dealing with us, as he dealt with her should not drive us from the mercy-seat. She did not leave him. And if we feel our need, helplessness, and unworthiness as she did; if we have her persuasion of his power and grace, we will not so easily give the matter up. After all, silence is not refusal. It may embarrass us, and make us fear; but it is not the decision of the case against us.

His silence does not seem to have stopped her praying at all. She still kept on her pleading; and this leads on to a second repulse of increasing discouragement. This change takes place, that our Lord's disciples speak up. We hardly know how to interpret, either their spirit or their request. Their interference seems rather the result of impatience and petulance than through any sympathy with her distress, or any benevolent desire for her relief. If they help her any, it is little to their credit; they simply express their own wish not to be longer troubled. Many a deed goes under the name of charity that deserves no such title. If we give to a beggar simply that we may get rid of his troublesomeness, our charity stands on a level with the justice of the judge who said, "Because this widow troubleth me I will avenge her." The disciples wished not this woman to cry after them.

There are two ways in which we can understand the words they addressed to Christ. But in either sense the result would be her deeper discouragement; and any ordinary pleader after this would give the matter up. Suppose they meant, "Send her away with her prayer unanswered." This would be to enlist the disciples against her. She would feel that this made her case more doubtful. We must remember that these disciples, though far inferior to their Master, yet shared somewhat of his reputation; they were held in high esteem; indeed, they had already been sent forth where he was not, to preach the gospel and to work miracles in his name; and it was natural to judge that they would have much influence with him. If then these good men had sympathized with her; had joined in urging her request, she would have felt greatly strengthened. But how disheartening to see that they took no interest in her case; that they petulantly complained of her troubling them; and that they even used their influence to have her sent away.

But there is a more favourable view of the disciples' words. Yet this, on the whole, rather increases than diminishes the woman's discouragement. Suppose we understand them to say, "Grant her request, and send her away." The other would not be unlikely. For these disciples had never learned, as yet, to show much sympathy for the Gentiles. Yet we may give the more favourable judgment, and believe that they plead *for* her. For they had never known him refuse before, not even to a Gentile: and the answer which our Lord gives seems more intelligible, if they plead on her behalf. "I cannot grant her request: for I am not sent but to the lost sheep of the house of Israel." Why should she cry any longer? He will not hear his own disciples in a case like this!

But she felt an urgency in the case that will admit of no rebuffs. There remained still the great necessity that had brought her before Jesus: the image of her beloved and suffering child still rose before the mother's eye; and for her relief, the mother's heart told her, no power could avail but the power of this great Deliverer. To whom could she go? This is her only hope. Desperate cases demand desperate exertions; and those who supplicate for undeserved mercy, which they cannot afford to do without, are justified in the utmost boldness of approach to him who alone can help. She felt sure there was nothing to be gained by yielding to despondency. If she gave the matter up, her daughter would not be healed.

Now we ought to feel that there is a wide difference in our favour, as we compare the pleadings of this humble female for this blessing, and the prayers we are allowed to offer in the name of Jesus. We have a far better knowledge of Christ, his power, his grace and his methods of relief, than she could have. And now he is sent to the Gentiles, and we may reasonably expect the progress of his gospel on every hand. And there is encouragement for us in the very nature of the blessings we seek; for the soul, rather than the body. There is not a single instance recorded in the gospels, where application was made to him for healing power, and the person departed without the blessing; and yet we do not know that he sent out public invitations authorizing the sick to come; or that he ever promised to heal those that did come. Every miracle of healing was spontaneous; they brought their sick to him, because he could heal them, and not because he had promised to do so: and how readily they brought them, and how sometimes the streets were thronged with the suffering, let the gospel narratives testify. But how blind and stupid are men in spiritual things. Christ is as able and more ready to heal souls than bodies. Touching these, he has sent forth his invitations, he has recorded his promises, and faith should believe that he will receive *all* who come to him. We are called, as she was not; we have promises, as she had not; we even may understand the very trying of our faith, as she could not.

We may know something of our own temper by the effect produced upon us when God seems not to answer prayer. Mere natural feeling soon gives over; faith becomes more earnest and importunate. The blessing seems more important, when it is not easily had; and the soul presses nearer to God. Indeed God designs to draw the soul nearer by these dealings. Let us keep saying to ourselves, *Delay is not denial.* It may mean a larger blessing. So the very church says of her Beloved, "I sought him but I could not find him; I called him, but he gave me no answer." And the patriarch complains, "Oh that I knew where I might find him! that I might come even to his seat!" Let us be only the more earnest, the longer he delays. He means righteousness and love in all his dealings with penitent souls. And if we set a proper estimate upon the salvation of the soul, and come before God to plead for it, what have we to gain by discouragement or despair? Among the worst things we can do, is to say, "Why should I wait for the Lord any longer?"

CHAPTER XIV.

FAITH EARNEST AND PERSEVERING.

"Truth, Lord! yet the dogs eat of the crumbs."

WE left the Syrophœnician woman in the midst of her pleadings, and thus far she seems to have gained but little from her approach to the Son of David. But let us stand near her and the Master to treasure up every expression, that we may use her importunity and perseverance in some hour of our own tearful coming before Jesus. The gathering difficulties about her, seem only the more thoroughly to awaken all her earnest energies, that she may secure the great boon she asks. Though repulsed, first by the silence of Jesus, and next by the disheartening answer he gave when the disciples interposed, she thinks not of turning away from her only hope. And yet the thing for which she plead was but a blessing for the present life. The deliverance of her daughter could but be her restoration to health; and this might be quite separate from any saving and spiritual benefit to the soul. She teaches us that true grace may be exercised in respect to temporal mercies; indeed that all our household affairs may minister to our piety, give tone to our devotions, and be the means of calling forth our faith: and that He who bids us pray for our daily bread, allows us to include in this prayer every mercy of health and soundness and protection that our children need. She teaches us moreover that still more importunate pleadings should characterize us in asking spiritual blessings. She becomes more anxious and more earnest as new difficulties rise, though her immediate object is the temporal relief of her child. Surely we should be solicitous and importunate when we ask the soul's salvation.

She increases her importunity as she goes on. She does not seem like one who says in her heart, "I will make one more effort, and if that does not succeed I will try no more." There is not a symptom of impatience; no betrayal of a single thought that she was harshly treated; no half-retiring, as if she had said all she knew how to say. Sinful men now often say, "I have prayed; it is vain to try again." They go further off, and plead more coldly, and are less in earnest every time they have no answer. This is not her example. She gets closer to that silent Lord; gives him more devout homage than before; and when she gets him to say anything, admits the truth of his every word; but turns everything into a plea to further her suit. He has just rejected her as one that belonged not to the house of Israel; and now she comes as near that character as a Gentile yet could dare. She comes before him with an act of solemn worship. She fell at his feet; she worshipped him. He had spoken of himself as one that was sent, she gave a far higher place to the Son of David: she called him Lord; she invoked his help as one able to render it. On other occasions, our Lord rejected the proffered homage of men, when the inward feeling did not correspond with the outward act, Matt. xix. 17; but he received homage from those who recognized his divinity. So we may rightly judge that her faith reached forth to the superior character of Christ.

But the severest repulse of all answers her increasing earnestness. She has at last forced him to break the silence; but his words are worse than silence. The Master speaks in terms of harshness such as we would not expect upon the lips of that meek and lowly man. He even seems to adopt the deepest prejudices of the Jewish people against the Gentiles; and to give utterance to the most opprobrious reproaches. Even among us, to call any one a dog is insulting and reproachful; but it is still worse in oriental than in western climes. It has been remarked as a singular fact that though the Bible often speaks of the dog, it makes no reference whatever to the useful and valuable qualities of that animal. We domesticate the dog, feed him, caress him, keep him about us, as they do not; and our ideas of the dog, and the attachments we form for him are quite different from oriental thoughts. We read indeed of the use of the dog by their shepherds; but even then it is a wild cur, and not to be compared with what we would call a shepherd's dog. So a modern traveller in Palestine writes thus: "Who ever saw a dog, in the east, within a house or tent? If not always without the walls of the city, they are always outside of the dwellings—a wandering race of prowlers whom no man owns, whom no man feeds, and for whom no man cares."* So we read of them in the Bible, as they may be seen now in eastern cities, finding their own food, tearing the carcass of Jezebel in the open street, licking the sores of the beggar at the rich man's gate, unclean animals, everywhere held in contempt. By this term of reproach, as the strongest they could find, the Jews expressed their contempt for the Gentiles; and, copying their prejudices, the Mohammedans still use it towards all unbelievers in their prophet.

If we can imagine ourselves standing by and witnessing this scene; if we retain our ideas of the boundless compassion of Jesus; if we even fear—after what he has just said of his personal mission to Israel—that he will not grant relief to this Gentile; yet these words seem needlessly harsh upon the Saviour's lips: "It is not meet to take the children's bread and to cast it to the dogs." If in our sympathy for her, we could wish the opportunity to join in helping her to plead, we would think it useless after this. The case is decided. Here is not only a rejection from mercy for her daughter

* Bonar's Desert of Sinai, 26.

and from all hope of it: but it is a rejection couched in reproachful and unkindly terms. Now she may give it up. Certainly many in her circumstances would have turned away, not only hopeless of any benefit, but indignant at the manner of his refusal.

But not a thought of this kind seems to belong to her. The very knowledge that she had no claim but misery, seals her lips from any complainings; and her misery sees no help in the despair of turning away. She cannot gainsay his words. "Truth, Lord." "I am not a child: I do not present myself as such." She does not expect relief by denying her true position; by opposing the truth of his declarations. But see the ready tact of an earnest and believing heart to turn every difficulty into an animating motive, every obstacle into a stepping-stone to help her forward. "Truth, Lord; I am a dog: but even the dogs get the crumbs!" What a humility and a faith are here. She makes no complaint of those mysterious divine dispensations that make so many inequalities all around us; that place one man in favourable and another in less favourable circumstances; that allow one to be a child of the covenant, trained to Israel's teachings, and another a Gentile dog, in Pagan ignorance. Recognizing the supremacy of God and the propriety of all his orderings; yet she pleads that she too is a creature of his hand and the recipient of his bounty; she tacitly says that the Lord is good to all, and his tender mercies are over all his works; and she humbly pleads that though she is a dog beneath the table which the Most High spreads for his children, yet even the dogs are fed. This is the keen vision and the holy logic of an earnest faith.

We have been attending the footsteps of Jesus. We have witnessed his deeds; have heard his gracious words, and are ready to say, "Never man spake like this man." But here is a sight worth visiting Palestine to see. The Scribes and Pharisees could not answer his pleadings; but here a Gentile woman fills her mouth with arguments, enters into the controversy with him, turns his own weapons against him, and gains the victory over him in the use of his own words. "With what joy did the blessed Teacher see himself foiled in that high argument! how gladly did he yield the victory to that invincible faith!"* And we, as we look on, may be reminded of the memorable wrestling of Jacob, when, though helpless and disabled, he would not let the angel go without a blessing. But this woman's plea is more wonderful than that; for we may expect faith in a grandson of Abraham such as we look not for in a Gentile. After this, let us never wonder again at any triumphs of faith. And the humblest need not fear to approach the throne of grace, where this success was gained.

But we must not allow our thoughts to dwell upon this scene, without turning them also to those great spiritual lessons that are taught us here; and

* Archer Butler's Sermons, i. 194.

for the sake of which chiefly these records are made. The Lord, to whom this woman came, had power on earth over the maladies of humanity; but he is chiefly known to us in a higher character; the Lord of souls and the Saviour of sinners. This woman is a representative character: and here, as in other parts of the Scriptures, a case is selected that seems to combine in a single view, such teachings as are best adapted to all those who would know the grace of Christ, the methods by which we must seek it, and the encouragements that bid us draw near. If we take the entire case in view, and make a comparison between this woman and the suppliant sinner, who asks before God for sin's forgiveness and the soul's salvation, we may learn the great principles of acceptable approach. Let sinners learn of her. Can any sinful man, in the most disheartening view of his case, have just reason to despair of the Divine mercy after reading of her success? Do we fear oftentimes that none of the rich promises of the gospel refer to us; that the believing children of God may lay hold upon these with confidence, but that we have no claim and may indulge no hope; that Christ was sent for others and not for us, and that therefore all our pleadings must be vain? Even supposing that all these things seem true, let her teach us lessons of faith that will not deny these unfavourable appearances, but will find the blessing still. In the worst view, we are no worse off than she was; and our darkness is not worse than hers. She could not know the result: only she had earnest faith to press on. She came into his presence uninvited and with every indication of being unwelcome; she plead without a promise and without a precedent; she bore his silence; she even heard him assign a reason why he could not help her: she felt all the chilling influence to which a warm and suffering heart is so sensitive, in the want of sympathy around her; she bore his harsh term of reproach that seemed to add a sting to her rejection; and then gained her triumph by trampling all these hindrances and discouragements under her feet, while she asked for a crumb. We, who know Jesus and his methods of grace so much better than she, should learn here, never to become disheartened. Are our prayers not answered; does God keep silence; does he seem to refuse; and do we incline to cease our anxious supplications? How much better to learn of her and to grow more earnest as the case seems more desperate! Indeed as our case is more important than hers, our reasons for copying her faith are correspondingly greater! Did she so plead for a daughter's bodily health, and shall we be less concerned when the souls of our children, or our own souls are the objects that send us to the mercy-seat? And if we justly think that our great sinfulness is our chief discouragement; if we fear that Divine mercy will not listen to pleadings such as ours; yet is it true that the necessities of our sinfulness may give an urgency to our pleadings infinitely beyond any prayer for earthly blessings; that eternal and infinite importance justifies the utmost boldness, solicitude, and importunity; and that we cannot afford to admit the thought of refusal or failure. In Christ alone can the sinful have any hope; in him, since her time, thousands as wretched and hopeless have found mercy; by this Jesus wonders of grace have been shown; in his dealings, delay, and even apparent rejection do not mean refusal; and the last breath of life would be wisely spent—should he delay that long his gracious approval—in calling for his mercy.

Should even the repulse of this woman reach our ears; should we be spurned from the footstool of mercy as a dog unworthy of the children's bread; even a dog's place is not hopeless, after her. Let us close our lips from all murmuring and complaint; acknowledge our unfitness for a child's place; but plead still that any portion from the table of God's grace is better provision than a sinful and perishing world can give. We assume what is not ours, when we speak of rights, and lay a claim upon mercy. We may ask large blessings; the word and the character of God encourage us to this; but all upon the footing of grace. Sinners, asking salvation, have no claims; should be impatient under no delays; and should indulge in no murmurings in any refusal to hear them. And if his word declares our sins; if our conscience reproaches us with our unworthiness; if every plea seems cut off; yet these thoughts are true, that the more completely miserable, wretched and sinful we are, the less are we able to bear our load of guilt and to look forward to eternity; the less can we afford to take offence at the teachings or dealings of Him, in whom alone we have hope; and the greater wisdom there is in pleading more humbly and more importunately for the blessing.

And not from her case only, but from others in the Bible, and from the experience of pardoned souls, let supplicants for God's mercy learn not to take counsel of their fears, nor to judge of him by apparent refusals. God said to Jacob, "Let me go," and yet gave him the blessing. He said to Moses, "Let me alone that I may consume this people," and yet heard his prayer to spare them. Prayer may be offered against the most threatening appearances; indeed we may be nearest the rich display of mercy when we seem furthest from it: and the dark hour may just precede the dawn. God leads us to mercy through the gloom; and we relish the blessing better and magnify the mercy more for these impressive lessons. Let us walk by faith and not by sight; let us judge, when it grows so dark, the dawn must be near; let us against hope believe in hope. So Abraham's watchword may be ours: Jehovah jireh—the Lord will provide.

"Just in the last distressing hour
The Lord displays delivering power;
The mount of danger is the place
Where we shall see surprising grace."

She teaches us how entirely consistent to dwell together in the same heart, are the deepest humility and the strongest faith. Had she not been humble she would have taken offence at his reproaches; had she not been of firm confidence in the Saviour's power and grace, she would have thought all further application vain; had not her whole soul been filled with a sense of her helplessness and need, and bent upon securing her end, she would not so readily have turned the very refusal itself into a plea of still stronger prevalence to gain her prayer. He calls her a dog; and submission meekly says, "Yes, it is so." He refuses her the bread that belongs to the children and she acquiesces; but modestly reminds him that he is her Master; that the table of his bounty is well supplied; and that the scraps and crumbs of the same food are given even to the dogs. Here is an importunity; here a tact in turning every discouragement into a motive for earnest pursuit; here a confidence in Him upon which it is the glory of the Redeemer to grant his blessing. Her daughter was made whole from that very hour. She turned from him and went home to embrace her beloved one. Faith and humility like hers never came before Jesus and went empty away.

Let it be carefully noted that she reached her success, because she was willing to stand just where the word of Jesus placed her. She was not a child, she acknowledged; and she made no complaint of this; but eagerly asked the crumbs. So the prodigal son, when he thought of coming back to his father's house, intended to ask a place among the hired servants. It is certainly not by the indulgence of pride or impatience or murmuring, that a sinful soul shows a prayerful spirit, or gets any nearer that great blessing which Christ alone can bestow. Indeed if we do not justify God's word in all it says of us; if we do not confess our sins with the humility it enjoins; if we do not forsake them with the sincerity which God requires, and magnify the letter and spirit of his holy law, it is useless and unreasonable to approach the throne of grace. For God to bless a murmuring, proud, impatient soul, in the very indulgence of such a temper against his law or his providence, would be to dishonour himself. But when we justify him in everything; when we confess with David, "Against thee, thee only have I sinned;" *i. e.* all the sin is on my side; when we acknowledge that the sin, wrong, unworthiness all belong to us, we glorify his name, his law and his gospel, and stand on ground where we may hope for a blessing. The man that pleads with God must be no murmurer at anything; must stand where the law places him; and wait as long as Providence delays; and plead on the terms of the gospel for mercy undeserved. And if a man has just impressions of his guilt and helplessness and of God's justice and grace, he will pray in this position, an humble supplicant for mercy.

It has been remarked that only upon two occasions did our Lord commend the faith of his hearers: and both the persons were Gentiles. The strength of their faith seemed more remarkable, because found in persons where it was not looked for. To find a true and strong faith in an Israelite who had known the prophets from his childhood, ought not to have appeared strange. But there is much more in what is said of this woman than a commendation of unlooked-for faith. The wonderful strength of her faith was shown by its triumphs over formidable difficulties. We do her injustice, and we fail to reap the benefits we should from her, if we suppose that she felt no discouragements and knew no misgivings, as she pressed earnestly on after the blessing. Religion—we have said before—is of *supernatural* origin, but not of *unnatural* operation. No doubt she felt, and keenly felt, all the disadvantages of her position as a Gentile, of her uninvited presence, of her unencouraged prayer. She felt, *and he meant she should feel*, the disheartening influence of his silence, his refusal, his reproach; and the more deeply she felt and the humbler her prayer, the stronger is the proof of faith in one who would not be turned away, even by these things. The strength of faith is not shown by the absence of fears and anxieties, but by our pressing on in spite of their worst power. The truly brave man is not reckless. He does not go forward by a mere impulse that refuses to see danger; but he uses a wise caution that sees danger, realizes its greatness, even fears it; but still in the pathway of duty calmly moves forward to meet it. True faith is not presumptuous. but the believer sees his unworthiness, mourns over his condition, fears that the Master will not receive him, and yet in spite of fears and darkness and a thousand misgivings looks up humbly to him who alone has the power and the grace to save. When we see in her that discouragements and delays were but to try her faith; that perseverance itself is victory, there seems no room left for unbelief. Darkness, sin, and trouble, fears, delays, and discouragements in their worst forms, do but prove the urgency of our case; and afford the opportunity for faith's success, in our patient waiting through them all.

And let us not fail to notice that the blessing is richer after so hard a trial of her faith. Many a one gets a blessing far more easily than she did. Some ask and receive at once. He does not keep them waiting. He does not thwart them at every step. But we—who can stand and look on; who can see through the whole case; and think that his special errand to these coasts was to meet her; and believe that his heart yearned to do her good all the time; and consider that here is an example to encourage sinners in all ages—we may esteem her case as enviable. "Would you not rather be this poor Canaanite woman, hoping against hope, struggling up into the presence of Christ, lying at his feet, and having faith enough to turn his repulse into an argument, and aim it back at his own heart—would you not rather be this poor creature, and have her experience, than to be the Roman centurion, answered almost before he began to ask?"* Christ was only trying this woman. There was something in his heart towards her, which she could not read in his silence or in his words; but he sympathized with that mother when he seemed to act so strangely. And *we* may misunderstand our Lord, but after such a lesson as this, we should never distrust him. Happy woman of Canaan to hear those words of love and admiration. Great is thy faith; be it unto thee even as thou wilt. Happy mother! Go home to thy daughter, so renewedly now thy debtor. Happy any mother that pleads so for her loved ones. Happy any sinner who so pleads for his own soul! The voice of pious experience has often said that, "One Christian well tried is worth ten thousand." And inspired wisdom declares that the trial of faith is much more precious than of gold that perisheth.

* Spencer's Sermons, i. 245.

CHAPTER XV.

FAITH TRIUMPHANT AND COMMENDED.

"O woman! great is thy faith!"

LONG as we have already delayed to reflect upon the interview of our Lord with the believing woman on the coasts of Canaan, we should scarcely be willing to leave the subject without some reflections upon the commendation he pronounced upon her. We have before remarked that only upon two occasions did our Lord commend the faith of his hearers. Though doubtless he brought no false charges against his hearers, yet this greatest of all teachers often complained of the unbelief of those about him; and even upbraided the impenitence of those who had enjoyed the most favourable opportunities of seeing his works and of hearing his words. The two persons whose faith he commended were both Gentiles: and though they both exhibited a strength of faith that would have seemed remarkable in anybody, doubtless it appeared more surprising, because it could scarcely be looked for in them. So in the case of the believing centurion the Lord said, "I have not found so great faith, no, not in Israel:" as much as to say, I might reasonably have expected it in Israel, where I find it not; I need not wonder to find an unbelieving Gentile, yet here I find the strongest faith. And then he laments that such contrasts as these will frequently occur. Men of very imperfect privileges will find salvation; and men of many privileges be lost: they will come from every quarter of the Gentile world to sit down with Abraham and Isaac and Jacob in the kingdom of heaven—how blessed this will be, but how solemn the conclusion—the children of the kingdom shall be cast out. When he speaks of the faith of this woman, he seems to refer, not so much to the fact that she was a Gentile, and therefore had enjoyed less opportunities to know him and his works; but specially to that humble perseverance that pressed forward to secure her object in spite of so many formidable obstacles. She did not allow herself to be discouraged, when the compassionate Master seemed to set himself in array against her; when he seemed to disregard; and even when he declared that it was not meet to grant her request.

An important matter to which we may now turn our thoughts is to the larger responsibility that rests upon us to lead us to the exercise of a true faith in God, when we see faith in so great exercise in such an one as this; and when we weigh our Lord's reflection upon the similar case. We have perhaps often noticed in the affairs of the world around us, that success and eminence do not always attend superior advantages; that indeed the world is filled with examples of those who have risen above their disadvantages, so that we are almost tempted to think that men rise by their disadvantages. This much certainly we ought to learn, that an earnest and faithful use of all the advantages we have, is the most important element of success in anything; and that where an earnest heart is wanting, any other advantages are of but little account. It is surely not right to make the bare conclusion, that they are ever better off who enter on life's duties with nothing but their bare faculties upon which to depend; and yet we should recognize the fact that advantages ready to our hands often forestall and prevent exertion. We may indeed say that there seems a kind of providential compensation for the inequalities of life in the very stimulus which makes the poor man's son more than a match for one who has all the advantages which wealth can buy. If inactivity forms part of an inheritance otherwise wealthy, far better earnestness and energy with poverty.

Of course it must be acknowledged that it is from no legitimate influences of the advantages any man possesses that they prove valueless to him; else it would be a perversion of terms to call them advantages. If in the famous fable, the tortoise overtakes the hare, it is through the folly, not the slowness of its competitor; and for a race, the swift is better than the slow. We lay therefore the just censure upon that folly which should have succeeded so easily, and yet lost. And if, in a career of learning, a man who has had all the privileges of good schools and suitable books and qualified teachers should be outstripped by one whose early course had been hindered at every step; because without competent instructors he must master difficulties alone, and without proper books he must gather up the fragments of knowledge as he best could, and must secure his time to learn from the broken moments snatched by a rigid economy from the pressing claims of a toilsome avocation; we may acknowledge that such a comparison is often seen among men, yet at the same time we decide that the same energy in both would have given the preëminence to him whose advantages were the best. The tendency of a man's necessities to call forth his efforts may be recognized; yet it is not of such a nature as to prevent our warm approval of his energies; nor do we withhold our censure from the failures of the man who had everything necessary to secure success except earnest energy.

Perhaps it is even an impossible thing for any of us to exercise a faith as strong as that which our Lord commended in the woman of Syrophœnicia: but the more truth there is in this, the greater must our guilt be if we do not exercise faith at all. The chief influence of her example is not so much to lead us to the same strength of faith, as to leave us inexcusable, if notwithstanding all our advantages, we remain unbelievers. If such faith was found in a Gentile, should we be destitute? The *strength* of her faith surpasses ours just in proportion as the *reasonableness* of our faith surpasses the natural expectation of finding faith in her. The errand—to secure a daughter's earthly health—what was this in comparison with the errand that should send a sinner to the feet of Jesus to plead for the life of his undying soul? Her acquaintance with the Son of David, what was it, in one who dwelt in a border land, belonged to a different race, was trained to a different religion, and had the prejudices and the ignorance of a Gentile? Surely she had not the opportunities we have of knowing the truth concerning him; born, as we have been in a Christian land, taught in a Christian sanctuary and accustomed to repeat his name with reverence from the lispings of infancy. The experience the world then had of him, was not, even for his most favoured disciples, as we now know him: his exalted character was veiled in the garments of his humanity; his glorious work was still but typified in the Jewish sacrifices; his kingdom was not yet set up, or understood, as we are able to form correct estimates of these things; and access to his throne of saving mercy, as the penitent souls of men have enjoyed it for so many centuries, gave not then the encouragement which we may draw from his well-known grace. If this humble woman who presses her way into the Saviour's presence, without an invitation, and undeterred by words that seem so stern and strange in him, is justified and even commended for her faith, surely no condemnation can be too severe upon us, if with our knowledge of Jesus, and our need of Jesus, and our invitations to come to Jesus, we are not believers at all. It had seemed no strange thing, if upon so severe a trial her faith had failed; but we have so many inducements to believe and so many supports to our faith, that the strangeness is that we can be unbelieving.

The Scriptures set before us examples of strong faith, not to say that we must imitate them; but to urge that faith is much more reasonable in us, and our lack of it much more inexcusable. If this woman not only found Jesus, and obtained her request and was even commended for her faith, no man in all this land should fail to secure the life of his soul. Who knows not as much as she? Who may not come in these days of free invitations, if she came unbidden? Who should ever be discouraged by silence or reproof or apparent reproach, if her pressing through all these, only gave him the greater honour and her the sweeter reward? Such a case as hers is both our encouragement under dejection and our warning against perverting better privileges. Sometimes we see men securing an honourable and indeed a remarkable worldly success, under circumstances so greatly unfavourable as to make us ashamed that any one born to the use of all his limbs and all his mental faculties should ever prove a drone in human society. One of the eminent historical painters of France during the present century, was physically a dwarf and a monster; and though he lived fifty years was frequently carried during all his life in his father's arms. For himself, he was born without arms; his legs were imperfect, almost without thighs, and closely united to the trunk; and he had but four toes on each foot. Surely such a child as this was born for helplessness. Not at all! He used his legs and toes as other boys do their arms and fingers. While yet a mere child, thrown on these limited resources, he could play ball and use the scissors with his toes; and one day laying hold of a pen, he pleased an old writing-master so much by the use of it, that he gave him lessons in writing. From writing he passed to drawing, and by the time he was sixteen years of age won the first prize in the Academy of Design. From drawing he went on to painting, and won the second and third medals of the Royal Academy at Paris. His manner of painting was, of course, very remarkable, but he used his brushes with singular dexterity, changing from one foot to the other, and with great ease and accuracy making the most delicate touches. His merits as a painter were considerable, but were the more popular for these extraordinary circumstances. His last historical painting was for the present emperor of France. The name of this man was Louis Cæsar Joseph Ducornet, and he died in 1856. Not every man can make a painter; but how many men, born in this helpless estate, would never have made anything; and how unreasonable is the indolence and inactivity of so many who have the limbs he would have prized so highly.

And it is not only in respect to success in worldly things that we may often stand astonished at what can be accomplished in spite of disadvantages the most discouraging; we may see examples of wonderful interest to show that the race for everlasting life may be run by the slow; the good fight of faith won by the weak. In considering such cases, we should better weigh the responsibilities of those who possess the best advantages for knowing and serving God. Perhaps one of the most remarkable examples of acquiring human and divine knowledge under circumstances the most surprising and difficult, is furnished by the case of a well-known American lady, who is yet living and has not yet reached the middle age of life. A little over thirty years ago a child was born in one of the New England states, who possessed the usual faculties until she was two years old; and then by sickness lost her sight, her hearing, and her sense of smelling, and impaired her taste; thus leaving her no other communication with the world than that which she could acquire by touch and feeling. How helpless would be such a child; blind, deaf, consequently dumb, the difficulty of communicating any knowledge beyond that which pertained to her natural wants, would seem insuperable. When she was eight years old she was introduced into the Perkins' Institution for the blind at Boston, and placed under the humane and skilful instruction of its teachers; and the laborious process of her education began. The first thing was to lead her to associate different objects with their names, and to teach her those names by means of raised letters. She was presented with a familiar object, then with the letters spelling its name, until she caught the idea that these were related to each other, and learned to distinguish letters and to spell words. After she began to understand this, she was furnished with a board full of holes and moveable types, so that she could arrange the type in the board and spell different words. After two years spent in learning names, she began to learn the qualities of things; and with almost incredible patience and perseverance pressed on from one degree of knowledge to another; learned the manual alphabet, was taught to write, became a performer of some skill upon the piano, though herself unable to hear a note, and acquired some practical knowledge of needle-work. Her ideas were not simply acquired by rote; but her curiosity to comprehend everything is intense; and her instructors were often compelled to depart from the direct line of the lesson, to answer her questions.

One day she asked her teacher this question: "Man has made houses and vessels, but who made the land and sea?" Here was an awakened mind, that had been shrouded in darkness and had now caught a few glimpses of light, eagerly looking for more. No mother's voice had taught her of the Father above; her silent lips had never breathed a prayer; and the precious soul knew not yet the power of its Creator, or the grace and salvation of its Redeemer. Her only way of communicating with the world around her, was by her sensitive fingers; and to her, if to any one, might be applied the remarkable words of the apostle Paul, that she might "feel after God" to find him. The answer of her teacher that God made all these things, and the explanation of his character and of her relations to him, opened up a new world of thought, and deeply affected her. Though her eyes were in darkness, divine light penetrated her mind. "Whatsoever doth make manifest is light." Eph. v. 13. At first doubtless she saw dimly, but her desires were strong to know more of this great Being, and she could only be satisfied when her teachers had made known to her the great truths of revelation. Before this, she had been distressed by fears of death; but she learned to know God, she became acquainted with the salvation of Christ and the hope of the resurrection; she reposed her confidence in the teachings of the gospel; and in a land where so many thousands, with opportunities so far superior, are neglectful of their souls, she found her way to the foot of the cross. She is deprived of the use of her natural faculties, but she looks forward hopefully to the period when, freed from all her physical infirmities she shall see and praise God with all her powers. She cannot share in the delights which many have around her; but she is not unhappy; she calls the room in which she lives the "sunny home;" and there is good reason to believe that God who commandeth the light to shine out of darkness has shined into her heart to bring the light of his glorious knowledge in the face of Jesus Christ.

It is doubtless not an easy thing to compare the difficulties and hindrances which oppose various minds, yet surely we may say that if such an one as this could learn the saving truths of the gospel, no one among us, who possesses the use of all his natural faculties, should be ignorant of them. Why should we not have the same anxiety to read God's holy word that they have, who can but spell out its precious lessons with their fingers, or even in other ways more laborious still. A poor blind French girl who had ears to hear of Jesus, and longed for sight to read his word, was taken under the care of a teacher who used the raised letters, that she might learn to read. She entered upon her lessons with joy, but, alas, she could not learn. The letters were raised but a little above the surface; it requires a very delicate touch to distinguish them; this poor girl was accustomed to daily labour, and her hands were not sufficiently soft and sensitive for work like this. Every effort was of no avail; she could not distinguish the letters. She then took a razor and pared down the ends of her fingers to make them tender; but still it would not do. She was filled with grief that she must give up her Bible; she knelt to pray in thankfulness that she had heard of Jesus, if she could not read of him; and in her love to the open pages she must now give up, she pressed her lips upon them. A new thought entered her heart. If her fingers were too dull, her lips were tender. She could read with them. She tried it; she succeeded; the Bible was hers. "Is it not blessed," said she, a year afterwards, "to kiss the sweet words as I read?" If there was but such a love as this to God's holy word in thousands who have so much better opportunities of making themselves acquainted with its great teachings, if those who have eyes but will not look, and ears but will not hear, would but begin to cry after knowledge, to seek it as silver, to search for it as for hid treasures, what changes would we witness in our families and communities! Surely this is a serious reflection, that men fail to secure the salvation of their souls, though possessed all their lives of the most favourable opportunities.

We do not forget, while we speak thus of the comparative privileges of men, that the influences of Divine grace are necessary for the saving power of the truth upon any heart; and that faith unto eternal life is not of ourselves but is the gift of God. A truth so vital in itself and in its influences may not properly be overlooked by the disciples of

Him who taught so plainly our need of the Spirit's regenerating power. John iii. 5. But while every sinful soul should feel his need of the grace of the Spirit, and from the depths of his need should humbly implore his blessing, it is but proper to remember that the doctrine of grace is entirely consistent with the plainest declaration of our responsibility; and that therefore all these thoughts of man's duty to improve his privileges are forcible and appropriate. All the truth respecting the Spirit's grace is no discouragement of human duty.

Two important thoughts should lead us to give our serious attention to the dangers attending neglected privileges. The first is that men are apt to misconceive the proper influence of superior privileges upon the minds of those who have them. We often see men rise above inferior opportunities and sink below superior advantages; we see the children of the rich enfeebled by a luxurious education, and outstripped in the race of life by the energetic children of poverty; we see that a little religion suffices the prosperous, while the afflicted become really eminent in piety and influence. And we are prone to draw the conclusion that to possess superior privileges is really a misfortune; and even good men have sometimes lauded the advantage of having no advantages! In so great a matter let us not be deceived by partial analogies. There may be an enervating influence in the training usually given to the children of luxury and wealth; but neither the

Scriptures, nor just reason put the possession of wealth among things intrinsically good, and we should not compare this with the privilege of religious instruction. And if there is in the sinful heart of man a tendency to undervalue familiar privileges, however excellent; yet this does not destroy their real excellence, nor diminish our guilt in perverting them; and our forewarning of such a tendency should go far to counteract it. The great thing is to have a just sense of our responsibility and a heart to use whatever advantages we possess; and then the greater they are, the larger our profit. In the praise of self-educated men, we forget to notice how much more useful they might have been, if with the same intellect and energy, they had possessed better opportunities. For when we make all the allowance we should, for the energies which our necessities call forth, no wise man ever despises advantages which he can easily secure, for the sake of reaching the same end by more difficult means. On the one hand, it is our duty to use every possible advantage to secure every good end; and on the other, it is our guilt to neglect the opportunities which God affords us for securing good and for doing good; and guilt greatly aggravated, when our very advantages are made to minister to our neglect and indifference.

The other thought is that our Lord Jesus Christ during the course of his ministry often urged upon his hearers the serious responsibility which grew out of superior advantages neglected. How can we accompany the Master and hear his words without understanding that man's depraved tendency to despise familiar privileges is no valid excuse for his sin, but rather its aggravation! When we hear him commend the centurion by declaring that he had not found so great faith, "no, not in Israel," what is the plain implication, but that in Israel such a faith might reasonably be expected? When anything occurs beyond our reasonable expectations, we express surprise and commendation; when men fall below what we may reasonably look for, we express our disapproval and their guilt. And so in yet plainer terms our Lord upbraided the cities in which most of his mighty works were done, because they repented not; he declares that they were exalted to heaven; and should fall but the lower because of privileges despised; and contrasting his own city with another city, whose reputation is the worst in the world's bad history, he declares that Sodom will find it more tolerable in the day of judgment than Capernaum. Surely in the light of these teachings, we may conclude that much will be required of those who have received much; that any tendency to think lightly of our advantages, however natural it may seem, cannot relieve us of the guilt and folly of neglecting our privileges; and that man's guilt before God will be justly reckoned according to the reasonable expectations that grow out of the teachings and opportunities he has enjoyed.

And when upon another occasion we hear the voice of this same great Teacher, reminding us that even one talent may not wisely be hidden in the earth; that thus those whose opportunities are poorest, must still give an account of themselves to God, how can we resist the conclusion that much more will be required of him to whom ten talents have been entrusted? And how should we, who are the children of the kingdom, born in the church, trained in her teachings, and invited by her mercies, fear lest even these advantages should not issue in our salvation! The lesson of all ages is, be not high-minded, but fear! And when the apostle would teach the same thing from the example of Israel, who saw the wonders of Moses and yet perished in the wilderness; at one time he tells us, "Let him that thinketh he standeth take heed lest he fall:" at another he concludes that they "entered not in because of unbelief;" and then his practical exhortation is, "Let us therefore fear lest a promise being left us of entering into his rest any of you should seem to come short of it." Let us not attempt to excel the Syrophœnician woman in the strength of her faith; but let us see to it that we are truly believers. We know the grace of our Lord Jesus Christ as she could not; we have every favourable opportunity for larger acquaintance with him; we have great blessings to ask at his hands; and he invites us to draw near to him. Let us think seriously of our responsibilities; let us acknowledge that faith may most reasonably be demanded of us; let us lay aside every excuse of indolence and folly, and humbly ask his mercy. This woman's faith will put to shame every one among us who shall at the last be found unbelievers. Doubtless many in heathen lands would repent, if they knew a tithe of what we know of Christ's grace to save. How great must be our disappointment and remorse, if at the last we shall see many saved who had not half our advantages, while we, the children of the kingdom, perish for ever.

If Jesus were even now looking around upon us; if we were in his presence feeling just as we do now, as we reflect on these things; if he should address us as he did her, his words would be, "O man! O woman, great is thy unbelief! Be it unto thee even as thou wilt!" This poor Gentile had her desire; and thou shalt have thine.

CHAPTER XVI.

THE GREAT CLAIMS OF CHRIST.

"Whom do men say that I am?"

WE have an account, not with the same distinctness, from three of the evangelists, respecting the conversation of our Lord and his disciples, when he asked what were the opinions of men concerning him; but we are not told when it occurred. We may suppose it was upon their return from the visit paid to the coasts of Tyre and Sidon. But we are told where the conversation occurred. He came near a city of upper Galilee called Cesarea Philippi — to distinguish it from another Cesarea on the coast of the Mediterranean, frequently named in the Acts of the apostles. This place is situated at the foot of Mount Hermon; it is on one of the sources of the Jordan — as Dan, the ancient Leshem, Josh. xix. 47, and Laish, Jud. xviii. 29, is a few miles off on the other — and is known now as Banias, though called by Josephus Paneas or Panium. A magnificent fountain of water issues there from the mouth of a cave to form one of the heads of the Jordan; ruins of ancient temples are there and through the vicinity; and this section of Judea had long been famous for its proneness to idolatry. Here it was that the company of Danites settled, who took the ephod, the image, and the priest from the house of Micah, Judges xviii.: in Dan also was set up one of the golden calves by which Jeroboam led the kingdom of Israel into idolatry. This region of the country, though a part of Judea, lay near the confines of paganism, and had been long influenced by pagan principles; and it may be with some significancy, that as he journeyed from a Gentile land towards the heart of Palestine, our Lord made the inquiries and called out the confessions of that memorable time. The population around him was a mingling of Syrians and Jews; these territories had long been desecrated by offerings made to idols. "Upon this border-land, Christ wished the confession of Peter put forth in the name of all the apostles, to sound out; thus intimating that the true church is built in the midst of Jews and Gentiles."*

We need not wonder that Luke tells us of his praying in this connection. In that gospel we have far more frequent mention made of our Lord's prayers than in any other. Doubtless many omissions are made in recording his devotions; but enough is written to teach us that all our affairs, those especially that pertain to spiritual things and to the advancement of religion, should be undertaken with prayerfulness.

They were by themselves and on their journey;

* Chemnitz Harm. 1598.

perhaps were resting by the wayside, and he had retired from them for purposes of devotion, when, as he joined them again, he began to make inquiries concerning the reception of himself and his claims among the people. They had opportunities of knowing this; they had mingled with the people; they had recently gone forth from him for the purpose of urging his claims. Doubtless—as a faithful ministry comes in contact with the popular mind—they knew what views the people held of him, and of this he would inquire. Yet why do we find the great Teacher interested in an inquiry like this? Not from any inferior motives, surely; not, we apprehend, from any personal motives. It would be entirely apart from the consistent dignity and humility of all else in the life of Christ to suppose that these inquiries sprang from curiosity or vanity, concerning the impressions made by his ministry upon the people around. This would have argued a weakness he never displayed. Rather, his inquiries sprang from no ignorance in him of the true state of feeling, both on the part of the masses of the people and on the part of his immediate followers. Nor should it be thought at all unreasonable that having already the information he should still press his question. We have but to recall the relation which these parties sustain to each other, and we see the full propriety of one of the most important questions which even he had ever proposed. This was a teacher, and these were his scholars. The greatest of all lessons, the most important of all sciences, is the knowledge of himself, as the long predicted Messiah; and inquiries of their views of this could not be out of place. There is no more proper or profitable method of communicating instruction, than by questioning the pupil; and when the questions are pertinent to the main object the teacher has in view, no one is surprised that he should thus call out the knowledge of his scholars. The inquiry of our Lord is tentative; so are the dealings of God's providence and God's word often, in our experience; God would ask us what we know, to draw forth and strengthen every wise conviction and judgment.

But brief reflection may assure us that the people of that land must have given many thoughts to the great wonders that belonged to the life of Jesus. It is not possible that a new prophet should rise in that land which claimed that only among the seed of Abraham were divine communications made to the sons of men; and yet that his claims should be treated with entire indifference. They were bound, and in a degree they were disposed, to consider the claims of any new prophet. The length of time that had elapsed since the close of the Old Testament canon; the evident nearness of the period when the long-expected Christ should himself appear; perhaps the intimation of Daniel that when he came he would close up the vision and prophecy; the very remarkable things that belonged to the commission of *this* prophet, would all tend to excite an uncommon interest in the minds of men. And yet it would be a very great mistake to suppose that the interest thus awakened concerning that prophet of Galilee, pertained only to the wondrous works he wrought before the eyes of that generation; could be only local or transient in its nature; or bore any character then essentially different from its workings in all ages where the name and claims, the workings and doctrines of Christ are known. No doubt that he should heal the sick, and cleanse the leper; should give sight to the blind and hearing to the deaf; should cast out devils and raise the dead to life, would fill the land with his fame, would bring around him the sons and daughters of sorrow, and would make men wonder who was this great prophet. But indeed the teachings and the claims of Christ are quite as remarkable as any of his miracles were; and the effects produced upon men where these are made known, are like the effects produced in his own time upon the men who saw and heard the living Jesus.

His teachings and his claims are as remarkable as the miracles. Of course this does not mean that you or I would think it no more strange to see a miracle than to hear the plainest exhibition of the teachings of this great Master. Teachings are permanent; once given they abide; Jesus still lives with us in his own words. Miracles are transient. We may have the record; we may credit the evidence; we may understand the design; we may recognize the authority. But the act is over. Now ACTS are never so important as PRINCIPLES. They owe their importance, when done by a reasonable being, chiefly to the principles they involve. The miracles of Christ were not half so important for what they actually accomplished for the subjects of them, as for the other designs he had in working them. It was not to save the life of Lazarus that he raised him from the dead; *that* end might have been secured possibly by a skilful physician, whose care might have saved him from premature dying; but to show the glory of God and to awaken faith in Jesus, his dead friend came forth from the grave. The moral influences of such a wonder could not belong only to that moment, nor be fastened to the scene where it took place, nor pass away when the death of Lazarus again occurred; the power could be understood, the proof acknowledged, the authority recognized, the principles maintained by those whose eyes did not see the opening sepulchre.

There is a permanence belonging to principles that cannot belong to acts. Therefore it would be strange to see a miracle when it would not be to hear a familiar doctrine. No matter how important any doctrine may be, if it is familiar it ceases to surprise. Nobody among us questions the remarkable excellence of the printing-press, and the railroad, and the telegraph, over the former modes of making books and journeys and distant communications. Yet these things have now become so familiar, that in one sense we no longer wonder at them. But we may justly distinguish between the mere emotion that attends something new, and the reasonable interest that must ever attend principles of striking and essential value. Such remarkable excellence for their purposes belongs to the inventions just named, that men will never lay them aside till they find their superiors. Now in this sense we aver that the claims and the teachings of Jesus are remarkable—not only beyond his miracles—but beyond anything the world can bring forth. As compared with his miracles, they are *familiar*, as his acts of power cannot be; we have often *heard*, we have never once *seen;* but his claims are more *peculiar* than his miracles; and both his claims and his teachings bear proofs as remarkable as any wonders, to convince men of his authority.

Notice what these claims were of this greatest of all prophets, "Whom do men say that I, the Son of man, am?" The peculiar designation he here uses, bears this sacred character, that during our Lord's life, none but himself ever made use of it; he called himself the Son of man, employing a term by which one of the most eminent of the former prophets described the coming Christ, Dan. vii. 13; affirming by it, his true assumption of our human nature; but implying also his legitimate claims to another nature of infinite dignity. By laying claim to the Messiahship promised in the Old Testament, with its inseparable attendants of divine dignity and human condescension; with the chief duty of the anointed of the Lord to make atonement for the people, this great Prophet separated himself from every other messenger to the sons of men. Other prophets have spoken in the name of God; this one speaks on his own authority; other priests have offered sacrifices upon the altar; this one alone offers up himself. Others have made high claims upon the faith of men in their own and in succeeding times; it belongs to Jesus Christ alone to claim that four thousand years before he was born, men began to look for his coming; that a long line of holy prophets spoke no higher themes than to declare what his character and work and rule should be; and that the most eminent men of a church that was as old as the race, had in vain longed to see his day. There are peculiarities in everything that pertains to this great Teacher that make his claims too remarkable to escape notice among men. Even when he wrought precisely the same miracles as others, he differs from them; in that theirs is ministerial and his original power. Even when he taught the same truths with others, with what remarkable force does he speak long-familiar thoughts. In all things, over all the sons of men, "he has the preëminence." His miracles surpass in numbers and excellence as well as in origin, all that other prophets wrought; his personal character exhibits in harmonious consistency all the graces of piety; and of his teachings may all the ages say, "Never man spake like this man." The sufficient evidence of his superior wisdom is inherent in his words; their like cannot be produced in all that man has elsewhere known; and they cannot be taught, and never have been taught among any people without attracting attention and changing the aspects of society. The teachings of Christ are as remarkable as were his miracles; they are as peculiarly his, as any wonders he ever wrought; and thus it is, that Christ belongs to all ages, and that we have the principles he taught quite as plainly set before us, as if we had seen his face and heard his voice. Indeed we know more of him, of his character and of his kingdom than did his disciples while he was yet upon the earth.

CHAPTER XVII.

VARIOUS OPINIONS RESPECTING CHRIST.

"But whom say ye that I am?"

THE inquiry of Christ may lead us to reflect upon the various opinions held by men concerning his character and claims. It is no abatement of the excellence of his claims that they were not, and are not, immediately conceded by all before whom he sets such clear and wondrous proofs. Thus it is that men ever do. We may say, for example, that it is impossible to make the inferior nations of the world acquainted with our arts and civilization without awakening their surprise, proving our superiority, and leading them to new graspings after our manifest advantages. And this is true; yet how slowly and variously the influence works. Warlike and barbarous tribes see the superiority of our arms, and eagerly lay aside the rude bow for the musket or the rifle. The natives of India, brought into close contact with their English rulers, establish printing-presses and issue Hindu newspapers. The Turks and Chinese find it needful to maintain their conflicts with European powers by adopting their improvements; and almost every maritime nation adopts the manifest advantages of steam navigation. Yet men are prejudiced, indifferent to new things, and the progress of thought is slow. So is it in regard to the things of religion. It is impossible for Christianity to come in conflict with paganism without producing great changes, as civilization must influence barbarism according to the closeness of contact. The teachings of Christ are wonderfully distinct from all else the world knows; men must be influenced where these are taught; and as it would be monstrous to find a man trained under civilizing influences preferring the degradation of barbarism, so it is impossible to find real paganism in a people where Christ's claims and teaching have long been made known. These teachings cannot be given to any land without producing important results.

But it is in every land and age as it was when Christ appeared; the reception he meets among men is wonderfully various. Then and now, some things were beyond dispute to everybody. That he wrought wondrous works all admitted. That the teachings of the gospel are excellent no man has ever had the temerity to dispute. That he healed the sick innumerable witnesses testified through all Judea. That his teachings now heal the sin-sick soul, that they effect changes of the most beneficial and permanent character, that to know and adopt his holy principles is a blessing to man, more numerous witnesses testify in many ages and in many lands. The teachings of Christ are more remarkable than his miracles. They effect benefits more important; as truly beyond human power; and more needful for the good of man.

This is a matter very easily tested. Suppose that in any family two forms of evil should come; the one natural, the other moral. One beloved child lies on a bed of sickness: painful watchings, harassing anxieties, sorrowful forebodings are appointed to the household; and they hold the fearful

> "Post of observation
> Darker every hour."

Another child is in the full vigour of health, but has become the shame and grief of the family. Wandering in sin, every reclaiming effort is ineffectual; tears are disregarded; prayers are mocked; and for the sin of this erring one the parental hearts are filled with sorrows, so weighty that the anguish of the sick chamber grows pale in comparison. Now suppose the cry was raised, which blind Bartimeus heard by the gate of Jericho, "Jesus of Nazareth passeth by;" and the parents of these children were permitted their choice, which of these two sufferers his wondrous hand should heal; that his gracious form should enter their abode and for *one* of them, should do as their faith should suggest; he would raise the dying, or he would bring back the lost; he would heal the malady of the body or the malady of the soul; he would remove their sickness or remove their shame; does anybody doubt which choice the parents should that day make? Death is not the chief calamity for a household; restoration from the grave is not the highest object of desire. It would be a better thing; it would be a greater thing, to bring back the wanderer than to raise the dying; as moral evils are incomparably worse than physical, and crime and sin worse than calamity and misfortune; as life is inferior to character; and as spiritual and eternal are better than temporal blessings. Now this better thing is what the Lord Jesus Christ still does among the sons of men. We never saw a sick man whom his miraculous power had healed; but we have seen the better sight, of souls whom his truth has converted. He still enters our abodes with his healing power; the wonders of his grace and truth are better and more remarkable than his miracles; and we would see still greater things, if our faith more earnestly sought his saving power, and cried anxiously with the believing nobleman, "Sir, come down, ere my child die."

No man could be so blind in Judea, as not to know the miracles of this wonder-working Prophet; no man can be so blind in this land as not to know the excellence of the teachings of Christ. And yet then, when our Lord asked, "Whom do men say that I am?" he elicited the truth that the people held various opinions. And the same inquiry now would find the same result. The opinions of that generation are divided by the reply of the disciples into two classes, to which we can easily add a third class; for to this Christ himself calls our attention at another time. And into these three classes may all they be divided, who now hear the teachings of the great Redeemer, as that generation saw his miracles. Just such men now live in Christian lands, as then gathered around him while he walked on earth.

The unmentioned class comprised the Pharisees, and all those who stood in hostility to Jesus. To them upon a subsequent occasion our Lord himself addressed substantially the same inquiry, "What think ye of Christ?' Matt. xxii. 42. We may wonder that he should have any enemies; we may wonder that his religion has any now. And we believe that our careful inquiries would establish that the hatred and unbelief of our later ages, spring from no insufficiency of reasonable evidences touching his claims, from no just charges of error or folly touching his doctrines, from no lack of excellent influence in his gospel; but from the same pride and depravity and inconsistency that refused, in the rulers of the Jews, to recognize the bearing of facts they could not dispute. Of opposers in our age, as truly as when he was upon earth, may Jesus say, "If I had not come and spoken unto them, they had not had sin; but now they have no cloak for their sin." Jno. xv. 22.

But to his disciples now, the Master says nothing of opposers. He asks concerning the people generally, "Whom say the people that I am?" That generation was like this. Between the decided opinions of his enemies on the one hand, and his disciples on the other, stood the multitude—just as the multitude stand now—neither disposed to reject him as an impostor, nor to receive him as a Saviour. Some thought he might be John the Baptist, risen from the dead, and therefore able to do these wonders; and these did not carry their inquiries far enough to learn that his ministry had begun while John was yet alive, and that therefore their conjecture must be incorrect. Others thought that this might be the reappearing of Elijah; for his mysterious translation gave room for many conjectures touching him; and his coming as the Messiah's herald had been foretold by the prophets. Others pretended not to decide which of the prophets this might be; but were ready to agree that he was one of them. Thus in that day, as in our day, men could admit that Christ has claims, who take no pains to ascertain, and who are not ready to admit THE CLAIMS of the Messiah of God. We may think that the men who saw the wonders of Christ, should have given their closest attention and their readiest confidence and affection to all his claims. And yet indeed there are many reasons that make it a more wonderful thing that so many in Christian lands and in Christian congregations and families, should hear so much of what he teaches; should have their need of him as a Saviour so clearly pressed upon them; and should be ready to recognize so much of truth and interest and duty; while yet they rank among the respecters—in a certain sense the admirers—of Jesus; whose disciples still, THEY ARE NOT. Favourable opinions may be entertained of this greatest of all teachers; benefits may be enjoyed that could flow only from his gospel; a man may be separated widely from the openly opposing foes of Jesus; and yet he approves not those who rank him as *a* prophet, and not THE prophet; and the reply of a true disciple differs far from any which these would render.

But the remaining view is that of Christ's true disciples. Our Lord then asked his followers, "But whom say ye that I am?" Peter promptly answered for them all, "Thou art the Christ, the Son of the living God." This is his personal confession: but they all shared it. For three things especially is it remarkable.

First, For the excellence of this great truth itself. It is the full acknowledgement, at once of the peculiar personal dignity, and of the peculiar official character and work of the Lord Jesus Christ. It is not needful for us to say that Peter fully understood at this time all he afterwards knew of the force of his confession; we must acknowledge that his own conduct was not always in full harmony with what he here declares. But if the grand belief of the gospel truly possesses the heart, it will show and cast out in due time the errors and inconsistencies which linger still in the regenerate mind. But the language of Peter implies his cheerful recognition of the claims of his Lord. He was the Son of the living God: here is the divine dignity. He was the Son of man: here is his mediatorial office. He was the Christ: this is to attribute to him and to find fulfilled in him all those remarkable types and prophecies by which God had foretold the Redeemer's coming, by the mouths of all the holy prophets since the world began; and we need not wonder that our Lord should follow such a confession by teaching his disciples more than they then understood—more, manifestly, than Peter now intended to imply—concerning his redeeming work upon the cross; which was the great work of his redemption; and which had been so abundantly attributed to the coming Messiah, both by the voices of the prophets and by the bleeding sacrifices of the old economy from the days of Abel onwards. These things—all the things of Christ—are better understood now, than when he was on the earth; indeed the imperfect knowledge of his disciples was more than was given to the people while his atoning work was still unfulfilled; and in our making reply to the same inquiry, "Whom say ye that I am?" "What think ye of Christ?" there ought to be that full recognition of his divine dignity and mediatorial work, which implies a confession of our guilty and lost estate as sinners: and our cheerful and happy dependence upon him for our salvation. True thoughts of Christ may mingle with various imperfections, but they imply that sense of our sin and of his grace; of our weakness and his dignity which leads us to recognize his divine mission, to own him as our Master, and to receive him, as he is offered in the gospel, as our mighty Redeemer.

It was a *second* excellency of Peter's faith that he made this confession at a time when the rulers of the Jews were already manifesting that hostility to the Redeemer's claims, which not long afterwards brought him to Pilate's hall and Calvary. He had indeed proofs enough of the authority of his Lord, in his workings and in his words. But this is a noble confession, while many stand in doubt or indifference; and many of the influential men of the nation stood opposed. Thus is it in every age. Reasons enough exist to lead any man in our day to see and acknowledge the claims of Christ and the excellence of his service. Yet it requires more than mere reflection and decision to come forth, not only apart from the opposers of religion, but from the mass of those who pay it some measure of respectful deference; and with a holy boldness make such a confession, as will call forth the benediction of the Lord. Happy indeed are they, and they only, who range themselves decidedly upon the side of Messiah—our Redeemer and King—and hear from his lips the commendation, "Blessed art thou!"

But thus are we reminded of the *third* and greatest excellency of this notable confession. Peter says this great thing, not through the force of superior discernment on his part; nor by reason of his natural boldness of character: but under the influence of divine teachings. "Flesh and blood hath not revealed this unto thee; but my Father which is in heaven." True piety in the heart of every disciple of Christ is due to the grace and power of God's Holy Spirit, who works to regenerate the soul. Without this working of the Spirit, this revelation of Jesus Christ by the Spirit of God, there is no true faith, there is no true blessedness. We do not mean that this internal spiritual experience is without any external teachings of the grace of the Redeemer. It was not in the case of Peter; it will not be in any of ours. Peter was under the teachings of Christ, as in no inferior sense we all are. And attentive and serious hearing of the word of truth has its proper place in the economy of salvation. But we need something more than can be secured by any resolutions we can form, any decision we can exhibit, any attainments we can reach by our unaided powers. We may be conscious of our sinfulness; we may fear the wrath of an offended God; we may recognize that in the atoning work of Calvary alone is God reconciled to the guilty sons of men. But we need something more than all this. All our views of sin, all our indefinite thoughts of the divine mercy are vain for our salvation, if we stop short of the revelation of God reconciled in Christ, brought home to our hearts by the Holy

Spirit. "Sense can never find him; only faith." If we are perplexed to know how we may secure this greatest of all blessings—the revelation of Christ to the soul and in the soul—let us learn that only the Spirit can reveal him. Nothing is more important than to know that the piety which springs not from the Spirit's workings, is insufficient and vain; that our dependence is upon the Spirit; that our prayers should be for his gracious power. The most eloquent teachings of men; the most impressive teachings even of the Bible; the greatest thoughts man can have of Christ, how powerless they fall, unless the Spirit breathes upon the truth. *How* the Spirit works we may not decide. But that only is true piety in us, which leads us to long for and cherish the Spirit's workings; that brings forth the Spirit's fruits in penitence and faith and meekness and holiness; and that recognizes our dependence, not only upon the truths taught by the Spirit, but upon the workings of his grace.

Blessed are they in whose hearts this revelation of the Son of God has been made. And if we were standing by him to-day—as his little band were with him by the towns of Cesarea Philippi—and not through curiosity or for information, but with infinite concern, for our sakes, and to call forth our faith towards himself—he should ask us individually, "Whom say ye that I am?" Happy indeed if we could reply,

"Dear name! the rock on which I build,
My shield and hiding-place;
My never-failing treasury, filled
With boundless stores of grace."

The world is as full as ever of various opinions concerning Christ. To some he is a root out of a dry ground; he has no form or comeliness; he is a rock of offence and a stone of stumbling. But to them that believe he is precious; the chief among ten thousand and altogether lovely. Blessed art thou, O believer in Jesus; renewed by his Spirit, led by his Spirit. If any man have not the Spirit of Christ, he is none of his.

CHAPTER XVIII.

THE CHURCH FOUNDED ON THE ROCK.

"Upon this rock I will build my church."

DOUBTLESS no passage, of all those recorded from the lips of our Lord, has been the ground of more vehement and abundant dispute, than this one, in which he speaks of the rock upon which he will build his church. An old writer in expounding the place gives it a fourfold meaning.* It is *first* instructive, *i. e.* it teaches us true doctrines; it is, *secondly*, vindicatory or controversial, *i. e.* it refutes the errors of false teachers; it is, *thirdly*, consolatory, *i. e.* it sustains and comforts those who receive it; and it is, *fourthly*, persuasive, *i. e.* it exhorts us to maintain and exemplify the teachings here given. Of course, the foundation of all is the true understanding of his word. What did the Saviour mean, when he said, "Thou art Peter, and upon this rock I will build my church?" It seems impossible for us in these later days to examine the matter without putting its controversial aspects first. For the church of Rome claims that by these words of Christ,

* Chemnitz Harmon., 1603, 4.

Peter is recognized as primate among the apostles; that Peter is the rock upon which the church shall for ever rest; and that the church of Rome, as founded by Peter, and possessing a succession of bishops in an unbroken line from him, is therefore the only and the truly apostolic church. This is indeed a stupendous claim to found upon these words. And the whole question may be narrowed down into these two inquiries. 1st. Does our Lord mean at all to say that Peter is the rock upon which his church should be built? And, 2d, Does he so mean Peter as to sustain any of the pretensions of the Romish church?

Now, while both these questions are well worthy of our thoughts, we cannot here pretend their full discussion. Yet neither can we allow them to remain undiscussed. Some brief suggestions therefore may be made upon them both.

We should consider *first* whether our Lord meant Peter by the rock.

The earliest question naturally pertains to the meaning and connection of his language. In the original the language is, "Thou art πετρος and upon this πετρᾳ." "Thou art a stone and upon this rock will I build." It is affirmed by Romish writers that in the language, in which it is likely our Lord spoke, no such variation of the words,* through their grammatical terminations, could be made. But it is impossible for any modern critics

* Dens' Theology, ii. 148. So also, Rosenmüller and Bengel.

to prove that no such variations could exist in the old Syriac; in fact, a high authority declares that these two forms, cephas and cepha, do really exist; and indeed so long as the inspired evangelist wrote in Greek, the singularity of his language is none the less remarkable.* The very thought that the words of Christ contain a kind of enigma, not to be obviously understood, but whose meaning must be gathered from other teachings, would but make them more characteristic of himself. Upon one occasion he was in the temple and the Jews asked a token of his authority, and he said, "Destroy this temple and I will raise it up in three days." They thought he meant the temple in which they stood: how could they then think otherwise? Yet the evangelist tells us, "He spake of the temple of his body." Jno. ii. 18–22. The change of words is significant here. Indeed a stone is not a rock. It is but a fragment of a rock. The rock is the Son of God himself, whom Peter had just recognized, not of himself; but as it was revealed to him by the Father. The Master was the rock; of this rock the disciple was a fragment. We may prefer this interpretation for these reasons:

1st. Thus we account for the change of the words: if there was no change of meaning from *πετρος* to *πετρᾳ*, why change the word at all?

2d. This is quite in keeping with our Lord's manner of speaking.

*Lightfoot. See J. A. Alexander and Pool's Synopsis.

3d. Thus we more fully maintain the propriety of the figure here used. We build upon a rock; we build with stones. Christ as the foundation is truly a rock; Peter as a part of the building is a stone. Christ is indeed called the Foundation-Stone; yet, as we shall see, no other is called a rock.

4th. To maintain that by the rock, Christ himself is meant, is agreeably to a most wonderful unanimity in the Scriptural writers. The divine nature is in the Scriptures called a rock, times almost numberless; and no instance can be pointed out where any human being is called so. According to Scriptural teachings, we cannot trust in man; we may ever trust in God. And there is no one figure applied to our Lord Jesus Christ himself more abundantly than that he is the foundation which God has laid in Zion. In Ps. cxviii. a head or chief corner-stone is spoken of, which has indeed found rejection by Jewish and papal builders, but which Christ himself interprets of himself. So, not to multiply passages, in Isaiah xxviii. 16, God promises to lay in Zion a foundation, evidently thereby meaning Christ. So it is interpreted by Peter himself, not only when he declares that Christ is the stone, the chief of the corner in whom alone is salvation, Acts iv. 12, but also when he quotes the very words of Isaiah, explains them to signify Christ, and speaks of believers as living stones built into the spiritual temple. And so Paul expressly affirms that the only foundation of the church is Jesus Christ.

This he repeats in different passages of his writings. 1 Cor. iii. 11: Eph. ii. 20: Rom. ix. 33: 1 Cor. x. 4. And it seems strange indeed, if this verse was meant to teach any superiority of Peter, that the other evangelists who mention this conversation, should yet omit so important a clause as this. Rather, we judge that it may be said here, as of the rock in the desert, "That rock was Christ." 1 Cor. x. 4.

5. The opinions of many in the church from the earliest ages agree to this understanding of the passage. The church of Rome lays great stress upon the opinions of the ancient fathers; but they do not support her interpretation of this important word. Some have understood that by the rock is meant neither Peter nor Christ, but the confession which had just been made. Upon the settled truth of the Sonship—upon the divine dignity of Christ, the church should be founded. And truly there is no doctrine of all the Scriptures that may more properly be regarded as lying at the foundation of all—none that has been more truly a criterion of the church. So the passage was understood by Hilary, Cyril, Chrysostom, Theophylact, Ambrose and Gregory of Nyssa,* and the authority of these men is not despicable in the Romish church. But others suppose directly that Christ is the rock. Among these Augustine must be reckoned. He reasons, in

* Pool's Synopsis, Chemnitz, 1606, Dens' Theology, ii. 149, Turrettine, iv. 103.

two* different passages that Peter is derived from the rock, and not the rock from Peter—as Christ is not derived from Christian, but Christian is derived from Christ. Augustine had in earlier days applied the word to Peter; but in his Retractations, a work expressly written to correct his early errors, he distinctly recalls this, and says, "*Petra autem erat Christus*,"—the rock was Christ.†

But we have asked the second question. Supposing that the rock does refer to Peter, does this sustain any of the pretensions of the Romish church? Surely it does not. It goes not the slightest step towards proving assumptions which are necessary to the support of the apostate church, which can never be vindicated by evidence or argument. They claim that Peter was the first bishop at Rome, and yet cannot prove that he ever was at Rome. They regard the popes as the successors of Peter, while it is false that the apostles can have any successors, or that the marks or duties of apostles belong to them. They pay no attention to the difference of the words here used; and destroy the consistency

*See one quoted by Dr. J. A. Alexander. The other may be found in Oper. Aug. 7, 1194. "Tu enim Petrus. A petra, petrus, non a petro petra. Sic a petro Petrus, quomodo a Christo, Christianus. Vis nôsse de qua petra, petros? Paulum audi. 1 Cor. x. 4. Ecce, unde Petras." Dr. Alexander shows that even Pope Hildebrand recognizes *Christ* as the Petra.—Commentary on Matthew. See notes in Lange on Matthew.

†Aug. Opera, i. 36. Yet Dens notes that he allows his readers to choose which sentiment they prefer.

of the figure, as if the foundation of the building was constantly changing. They assume that Peter is addressed here as an individual, and that to him is granted a primacy among the apostles, of which important teaching not a word is said in other passages, not even when the other evangelists speak of this very same transaction; and which indeed is contrary to the representations of the New Testament elsewhere. The most that can be meant of such a designation applied to Peter is that to him was granted the privilege of doubly laying the foundation of the Christian church, *first*, by preaching the first discourse after the resurrection of Christ, and with such signal success upon the day of Pentecost; and, *secondly*, by preaching the first discourse in the house of Cornelius, for the introduction of the Gentiles into the Christian church. These two things in Peter would be in an important sense a fulfilment of all that can be meant in the Saviour's words to make them at all consistent with what he adds to them, with the teachings of the Scriptures elsewhere, and with the restrictions which must be put upon the evident meaning. For the Romish theologians are themselves obliged to admit that "Christ alone is the essential and primary foundation, because he stands by himself, and can be based upon no other, but sustains all things which pertain to the church, and so also Peter himself."* And what is subsequently said of the keys of the kingdom of

* Dens, ii. 149.

heaven, manifestly refers to authority in the church, not to him personally, but to the others as well; for there was no power exercised by Peter that did not belong to the other apostles, as the council held at Jerusalem, Acts xv., evidently shows. So Augustine does not say only once, but repeatedly, that these words were spoken not to Peter alone, but to the whole church in him.* What is thus said to Peter, is said of him not as an individual, but with him are associated all his fellow-apostles and the church of Christ. And thus the true test of the church is an abiding in the teachings of Christ.

It should serve as additional proof that no especial primacy was given to Peter that the keys of the kingdom of heaven are no more given to him than to any other of the ministers of Christ. Two things only need be said in regard to these declarations. First, The power of the keys—or the thing signified by giving the keys of the kingdom of heaven—seems

* Petrus enim in multis locis Scripturarum apparet quòd personam gestet Ecclesiæ: maxime illo in loco ubi dictum est. Tibi trado claves regni, &c. Numquid istas claves Petrus accepit et Paulus non accepit? Petrus accepit et Johannes et Jacobus non accepit et ceteri apostoli? Aut non sunt istæ in Ecclesiâ claves, ubi peccata quotidie dimittuntur? Sed quoniam in significatione personam Petrus gestabat Ecclesiæ quod illi uni datum est, Ecclesiæ datum est. Ergo Petrus figuram gestabat Ecclesiæ, Ecclesia corpus Christi est."—Opera x. 438. De diversis Sermon. xxvi.

"Si hoc Petro tantum dictum est, non facit hoc ecclesia . . . . . si hoc ergo in ecclesia sit, Petrus quando claves accepit, Ecclesiam sanctam significavit . . . . . si bonus es, si ad corpus pertines, quod significat Petrus; habes Christum in præsenti, et in futuro."—Opera ix. 370.—Sermon l. in Johannem.

simply to be the grant of authority to exercise government and discipline in the church. The church of God is a kingdom. In a kingdom authority is to be exercised, not by those who have merely the capacity, but by those to whom power is entrusted in an orderly manner. The nature and limits of authority must be determined by the laws of the kingdom. The question whether any minister of Christ's church has power to forgive sins must always find its answer in full harmony with the principles of Christ's gospel. So long as men have no power to search the heart, they can never do more than declare that the truly penitent are forgiven. It is undesirable, inconsistent with the honour of Christ, destructive of every important influence, that to any man should be entrusted the power of granting or withholding the blessings of the Most High, so that impenitent sinners should be forgiven, or so that penitent and humbled souls should find it impossible to find pardon. Christ can have no such meaning as this. So the Romish church is obliged to acknowledge that her sacraments are often void of power, and of no avail to the rebellious. Every grant under the gospel is entirely according to the gospel. The power given to Christ's ministers in these words, can be none other than the power elsewhere spoken of in the Scriptures. To Peter was granted the power to administer all the ordinances of the house of God; but these of course in their own proper meaning and force. The laws of

Christ govern his kingdom; and Peter as a faithful servant must use the authority here granted accordingly. And so Peter understood it. For indeed no portion of the New Testament more directly refutes the preposterous claims of the popes, as the alleged successors of Peter, than the two epistles written by Peter. Had they followed *him*, they would never have claimed a primacy; nor lorded it over God's heritage; nor assumed power over kings; nor have been so notoriously greedy of filthy lucre. See 1 Peter v. 1–3: ii. 13–17. The meaning of our Lord in these words cannot be more or less than the power of executing the laws of the kingdom of heaven in the church, according to the nature, spirit, and design of the church.

But, *secondly*, this power of the keys was given to the other apostles and rulers in the church as truly and fully as to Peter. There is no trace of prerogatives belonging to him alone among the servants of the same Lord. Christ expressly told his disciples that though there was lordship in earthly kingdoms, "it shall not be so among you." Matt. xx. 26. And though here he says to Peter, "Whatsoever *thou* shalt bind," yet in a subsequent passage of this same gospel, Matt. xviii. 18, he extends this to the church, "Whatsoever *ye* shall bind on earth shall be bound in heaven." And so we actually find that Peter, save as the *first* preacher at Pentecost and to the Gentiles, did nothing that was not done also by others. He preached the gospel; so did they all; he baptized; so did Philip the evangelist; he rebuked with severe authority the sin of Ananias and Sapphira; so did Paul the wickedness of Elymas the sorcerer, and of the incestuous Corinthian; he administered the Lord's supper; but Paul has given us our plainest teachings respecting this. So in the ordination of deacons and presbyters, in the ordinances of the council at Jerusalem, and in the whole administration of the church no evidence appears that Peter was vested with powers that differ in nature or in degree from the powers given to other rulers in the kingdom of heaven.*

In all then, Peter *personal* is not the rock. Peter *representative* of the church is Peter as standing himself upon the great foundation. We are thus forced to this substantial interpretation that Christ is the rock; Peter himself was, to use his own words, a living stone, 1 Peter ii. 5, built upon the true foundation: and only they are the followers of Peter

Chemnitz Harm., 1620. Many Protestant writers on this matter appropriately notice that Peter, in a remarkable degree, refutes the claims made in his name by the Romish church. In addition to the citation already made from Chemnitz, we may notice this from Stier's Words of Jesus. "Peter must needs testify in the Scripture against almost all the principal parts of the papacy. Against lordship over the church. 1 Peter v. 3, 4. Against a separate priesthood, ch. ii. 5–9. Against assumption over a civil magistrate, verses 13–17. Against silver and gold and shameful gain. Acts iii. 6: 1 Peter v. 2. Against unbecoming marks of honour and slipper-kissing. Acts x. 25, 26. Against infallibility, verse 34. Against celibacy. 1 Cor. ix. 5. Against all righteousness by works, in harmony with Paul. Acts xv. 10, 11: 1 Peter i. 13, &c."

*Stier, (Clarke's Foreign Library,) ii. 342.

who follow his teachings. In how many points the church of Rome differs from the simple teachings of Peter, it would not be difficult to show.* Whether we interpret the rock to be Christ or Peter, the claims of Romanism are equally unfounded. No superiority over his brethren is given to Peter. The apostles and prophets are the foundation of the church in no such sense as to make any one of them the corner-stone; and though the stability of the church is here declared against all the raging of secret and open foes, there is no such infallibility promised, as would preclude many a fall to error, on the part of either individuals or judicatories; or make unnecessary many signal deliverances by the power and grace of God. And so it occurs, that the claims of the church of Rome are ever shaken, when men have free access to the Scriptures, and can compare her assumptions with the spirit of the gospel of Christ.

Let these thoughts suffice upon the controversial aspects of our Lord's words, which naturally need our consideration. The *instructive* teachings they present should possess more interest. Here we are called upon to consider the noblest institution on our fallen earth, THE CHURCH OF CHRIST. No more important inquiry can occupy our thoughts than when we ask, "What constitutes a church?" The entire tenor of the Scriptures teach us that the church exists in no line of persons as such. Where

* See on this Chemnitz Harm. 1609.

the principles of the church are held, there the church is to be found. Men tend to change. Again and again has the church been rescued from destruction by the revival of her principles. Men have ever been prone to boast of ecclesiastical descent, as did the Jews in the days of Christ; but John the Baptist declared that God could raise up children to Abraham from the very stones; and our Lord declared that the true followers of Abraham and Moses were they who held their faith and did their works. The calling of the Jews was to preserve the faith of God's people; for their departing from the faith, they were cut off; and the express threatening was made that any of later times departing from the faith should also be cut off. Rom. xi. 21, 22. And Paul explicitly declared that an apostacy upon a grand scale should really occur. 2 Thess. ii. 3 seq. So the succession of the church is to be tested by her conformity to truth, not the truth by a succession of men. The church of Christ is made up of Christ's humble, believing followers.

> "For where but two or three,
> Whatever place, in faith's communion meet,
> There, with Christ's presence, is a church complete."

The church of Christ is of all ages, times, people. It admits of diversity of forms and views; so long as the Head, even Christ is firmly held, and the common bond of faith unites all in one glorious body.

But how delightful is the assurance that this

church is the church of Christ. So he says, "*My* church!" In every respect the church belongs to Christ. As we have seen already he is the foundation upon which it rests. Not upon any created being can so noble a structure stand; but only upon the Rock of Ages. And Christ is the proprietor of the church in every respect. He planned the church. He chose the place where it should be established, on this earth where we now are; he chose the materials of which it should be built, not the angels that sinned, but sinners of Adam's lowly race; he chose the workmen that should be employed upon it. The ministers of the gospel are the servants of Christ, and according to our Lord's own rule they are to be known by the conformity of their teachings and success to the precepts he has given. "By their fruits ye shall know them;" and they who have the true teachings of Christ, they who have Christ's approval in souls converted and sanctified under their ministry, have a legitimate seal. But we are further directly taught that Christ builds the church. Whatever instrumentality man has, Christ has the efficiency. "Paul plants, Apollos waters, God gives the increase." The wisest servants indeed understand but a small part of the immense plan of this church of Christ. What a figure is this for the church; a grand temple that occupies all the ages of the world for its erection. In this new world upon the western continent, we have no old buildings, and we scarcely know what a splendid and costly temple is. We have no wealth to spend in such ways; we do not comprehend what sums, what thought, what time may be laid out in the stable magnificence of a grand architectural pile. St. Peter's church at Rome cost immense sums for its completion. Nearly two hundred years passed after it was begun before it was ready to be dedicated; and it was finished more than a century and a half later. Notre Dame in Paris took four hundred years to find completion; and the cathedral at Cologne, one of the most imposing Gothic structures in Europe, begun over six hundred years ago, remains yet unfinished. Generations of workmen labour on such buildings; the architects change the plans; no one man can superintend the whole. But the church of Christ is one, as to the great Master Workman. He indeed bought all the materials at a costly price, 1 Peter i. 18, 19; he employs all the labourers and gives them their reward. 1 Peter v. 4. Mortal men no more can foresee the changes and duties of the church in advance, than they can anticipate and control the workings of Divine Providence; and so Christ keeps the whole in his own hands. "*I* will build."

But the instruction assures us further that Christ is the preserver of his church. He declares that the gates of hell shall not prevail against it. By the "gates of hell" he means the power and malice of Satan, however these may attempt to destroy or injure the church. He does not say that Satanic power should not rage against the church. Rather he intimates that it will. The history of his church is a history of conflicts and deliverances. There is no pledge here of infallibility in the opinions and decisions of the church. God has never so dealt with his people as to preserve his wisest and holiest servants from error. This would be to change entirely the great principles upon which his church has ever been governed. How lamentably did the people of God err in the desert, where even with their high priest at their head, they made and worshipped the golden calf at the very foot of Sinai! How sadly did they wander when the greatest living prophet thought himself alone in all Israel! 1 Kings xix. 10. How humbly does Daniel lament, "We have not obeyed thy servants, the prophets who spoke to us in thy name." How plainly are we warned against false prophets and apostacies in far later days. Christ promises not infallibility in his church; he promises stability. And the very pledge implies dangers of every kind; errors, assaults, temptations, but deliverance; not exemption, but final safety. And so has it come to pass. "Many a time have they afflicted me from my youth up, ... yet have they not prevailed against me," is the song of God's Israel in all generations. "The time would fail," as the apostle says, not only to enumerate the troubles of Zion, but also the means by which her troubles have been brought upon her. Superstition, infidelity, heresy; curses, crosses, inquisitions; flatteries, falsehoods, hypocrisies; every force and every fraud have assailed the church. Sometimes the enemies of the church have seemed to prevail; and her people have been almost disheartened and ready to give up hope; as men's hearts often fail for fear, when the earth shakes beneath their unsteady feet. In Satan's rage against the church, not long after this promise of her stability was made, he so far prevailed as to lay her Head in the sepulchre of Joseph. But that hour of his triumph was the hour of his most complete discomfiture! A type, this, of every succeeding time; when most perplexed, Christ's people may take the very darkness as a sign that their deliverance will not long delay. And indeed the promise belongs not only to the church, but to every individual believer, toward whom the pledge of Christ is, "None shall pluck them out of my hand." John x. 28.

And now, to follow the thoughts before indicated, what consolation there is for the humble believer in Jesus in the assurances thus given! Could we stand by the blessed Redeemer as he uttered these words; could we know more than did the listening disciples of his infinite power and wisdom and grace; could we anticipate all they experienced of grief and perplexity and darkness, and indeed all that has been known by his people in all the intervening centuries, we might rejoice in his assurance that no power of earth or hell could prevail against his kingdom.

Blessed are our eyes, for they see far greater things. All the varied experience of eighteen hundred years may help us to interpret the promise, and give us confidence that it shall be fulfilled. How many empires have risen and fallen while the church of Christ is more widely known on the earth now than ever; possesses more vitality than ever; has sent forth the sacred Scriptures in more languages, in wider dispersion, in more abundant copies, and to more numerous and intelligent hearers than ever before; and has had larger experience of the grace of the Divine Spirit to accompany the footsteps of his servants as they fulfil their Lord's command and preach the gospel in all the world. It is a wonderful support to our faith in these words of that incomparable Teacher, that no human wisdom could have anticipated their fulfilment either upon a scale so grand, or with mercies so truly beneficent. It is exceeding consolation to judge that every past deliverance is a pledge of future blessings. The time has long since past for any thought of failure to the church of Christ. If he could ever think of abandoning his cherished plan of salvation, it must have been before he suffered so much for his church. Before his sufferings he promised that the gates of hell should not prevail. Now that the worst is all over; now that his feebleness on earth has given place to power in heaven; now that his humiliation is past and his exaltation begun, there is no reason for the doubt of his power and willingness to save.

Every past interference for the deliverance of his people is a pledge that he will still deliver. So that this is the believer's constant encouragement, "Now is our salvation nearer than when we believed." Rom. xiii. 11. This indeed may be our song in the house of our pilgrimage, that our Lord's leadings are pledges for the future. He who begins the work in us will perform it. Phil. i. 6.

> "Can he have taught me to trust in his name,
> And thus far have brought me to put me to shame?"

Nay, rather:

> "His love in times past forbids me to think
> He'll leave me at last in trouble to sink;
> Each sweet Ebenezer I have in review,
> Confirms his good pleasure to help me quite through."
>
> NEWTON.

And not less have we in these teachings of Christ the voice of mingled warning and exhortation calling the sons of men to put their trust in One who can fulfil a promise so grand as this. The disciples who stood beside him had but feeble thoughts of that grand pledge that his church should rest upon an immovable foundation, against which all raging of earth and hell would be in vain. But we may understand how dignified are his claims as the proprietor and builder and preserver of the church. Truly we need the confession of Peter as the interpreter of his character, who makes claims like these. The Son of the Living God is here indeed. And quite as blessed now as then, are those to whom this great truth is made known, not by flesh and blood, but by the Father. Our opportunities for knowing the superiority and the truth of his great claims are greater far than the apostles had. Nothing can be more important than for us to know Christ. How happy are the hours we may spend in following his footsteps; in dwelling upon his gracious words; in pondering his wonderful works; in spelling out the precious meaning of each significant thing; and in tracing in pious experience the rich fulfilment of his great promises. How miserable and unhappy are they who have no care to linger on the sacred places where Jesus loved to abide; who find no interest in thoughts that make him known; who have felt no need of him as their Teacher, King, Redeemer; and who have neither eyes to see nor ears to hear those great things which prophets and righteous men longed in vain to know. We may not forget that alike to those who saw Christ, and to us who live in far later ages, no knowledge is saving that flows not from the illumination of the darkened understanding by God's Holy Spirit! Not only Peter and Paul, that they may be apostles, but every man that he may be a believer, needs that which flesh and blood cannot impart. We must be born of God, or we cannot see the kingdom of heaven. We may have some knowledge of our sin and of the gospel as its proposed remedy; we may have concern for our interest in this great salvation; but to see the truth and excellency of Christ, to realize our need and his power to save, to be drawn to him that we may truly repose upon him, with a cheerful, loving faith, we need the light of the Divine Spirit. God alone, who commanded the light to shine out of darkness, can shine thus in our minds. We need eyes as well as light. We need to come, like the blind beggar of Jericho, forgetful of everything but our blindness; undeterred though the multitude bid us hold our peace; and earnest only with this great request, "Lord, that I may receive my sight!" Luke xviii. 41. But now, as when Christ was upon the earth, many say, "We see," therefore their sin remains. John ix. 41.

CHAPTER XIX.

THE SCRIPTURES FULFILLED IN CHRIST'S DEATH.

"He must go unto Jerusalem and suffer."

COMMENTATORS generally agree that this period in our Lord's life marks a striking and important change in his ministry. Some judge that from this time forward, he speaks less to the multitude, and more directly to his band of disciples. More agree that henceforward he speaks more plainly respecting his death and resurrection, now near at hand. On those topics he had not, before this, been wholly silent. At an early period of his ministry he had spoken of the great object of his mission to earth. John iii. 17. But here is a special record. "From that time Jesus began to show unto his disciples how he must go unto Jerusalem, and suffer many things of the elders and chief priests and scribes; and be killed, and be raised again the third day." We can easily understand why he should say less about his death before its actual occurrence; yet we would be greatly surprised if he had been entirely silent upon this topic; and we would rather hear him speak upon this greatest of all themes, than upon any other. He came into the world thus to lay down his life; he knew well the goal towards which he now pressed; and he would give his disciples teachings to be recalled with the deepest interest when time had unfolded their entire meaning.

We may plainly see here, on the one hand, that his disciples do not comprehend his words; and on the other, that he himself attaches especial value to this particular teaching. Between the reception and the rejection of the great necessity he here affirms, runs the dividing line that separates divine thoughts and inferior thoughts—separates the kingdom of God and the kingdom of Satan. Even an apostle—even one upon whose head so lately descended a precious benediction, as upon one divinely taught, must not question the necessity of his sufferings at Jerusalem, upon pain of being repulsed as a very Satan whose evil suggestings the Messiah could not endure. These are teachings essential to the gospel. That he gave them with some degree of publicity before his death, his enemies have proved. For the Jewish rulers set a guard at his sepulchre; and thus witnesses chosen by themselves attested first to them the resurrection of Jesus. His disciples had forgotten the words so carefully treasured by his foes. But the faith of the apostles was greatly confirmed afterwards in the remembrance of the words which now foretold these events.

Some commentators suppose that the reproof here given to Peter was chiefly for his presumptuous manner of addressing his Lord. We cannot so think.

There was doubtless an error here. This ardent disciple is often upon extremes. He had just been commended, and now he is unduly elated. He now presumes upon a familiarity that can have no place in any supreme respect for Christ. "Peter took him and began to rebuke him:" perhaps in the sense of our common phrases, *took him up*, or, *took him in hand.* Yet his words express a deference, though he speaks forwardly. They may be rendered, "Pity thyself, Lord," or rather, "May God be gracious to thee, this shall not be unto thee."* But he was stopped short by a pointed and severe rebuke; was even addressed as a very Satan for words like these. We cannot believe that it was either the manner, or the spirit of the disciple which our Lord here chiefly reproves. Peter needed a lesson in humility; but our Lord corrects more than mere forwardness. The false thought of Peter is far worse than his temper or manner; he has no adequate conception of the MUST which his Lord had just declared: and the promptness and emphasis of the reproof forbid us to confine its meaning to the narrow occasion on which it was uttered.

Meekness so blends with the Redeemer's dignity that he would hardly utter so severe a reproof to a warm-hearted disciple for a breach of decorum. And so far as Peter's error was one of fact, it would soon be sufficiently corrected. In a little time the events here foretold would be past; the brief triumph

*Bengel, Alford, &c.

of Jewish and Satanic malice would be over; and the cross would stand, the great historic scene of the world's annals. There was little danger that succeeding ages would copy the form of Peter's error. But against the principle which Peter's words imply, we must guard as carefully as our Lord's zealous warning would here admonish us. To the apostles, the thought of Christ's death was new and strange and startling; to us it is familiar. The fact announced troubled Peter; he could not anticipate it, much less discern the necessity for it. To us the fact is sufficiently obvious; but neither he nor we must deny, through human reasonings, or Satanic suggestions, the *must* which our Lord here asserts. Peter's confession of the Redeemer's dignity must not be annulled by his denial of the Redeemer's work. The *must be* of the death accomplished at Jerusalem is a truth inferior to none of all that pertain to human salvation. Human folly or Satanic malice can suggest none more false, or more dishonouring to the plans of infinite wisdom than to declare that Christ need not die, and died therefore in vain. "The things that be of God" include a just understanding of the death of the Mediator as the needful means, divinely chosen for man's redemption.

Few single words ever uttered by those incomparable lips, possess the emphasis which the word and the providence of God have thrown around the important MUST with which our Redeemer here inaugurates this new era of his life and ministry. Could we indeed stand by and hear this word, how should it fill our minds with busy thought! Even if we stood as did Peter, and appreciated the prejudices of his age and people, such a word as this should strike a key-note in full harmony with many a song that had been long familiar to believing ears. And if now we should attempt to array before our minds the evidences which tell us that Christ must needs die that man might know salvation, we would turn our thoughts to those things that were already before the eyes of our Lord's disciples, and consider,

I. The Prophetic Proof that Christ must die.

There is immense force in the great truth, undeniable to all who possess the Old Testament Scriptures, that long before the ministry of Jesus of Nazareth, the Jewish people looked for the coming of a great Messiah; and were held together as a most peculiar people by a religious system, whose types and prophecies were scattered all along a venerated history from the earliest knowledge of man. No principle seems more prominently set forth or more closely interwoven with this whole system, than that an apostle so plainly enunciates, "Without the shedding of blood there is no remission" of sins. The worship, the types, the teachings, the expectations of the Jewish church from the beginning onward, seem to say the same things. Not only do we find the bleeding victim at the altar of God from the first trace of sin in Eden; but after the establishment of the Levitical economy, "almost all things under the law were purged with blood." We should not wonder if, at our Lord's words, his disciples had consented that the Messiah's death did agree to the voices of their prophets. When we think of Israel's bleeding victims; when we recall their significant types; when we read their pages where Moses and David and Isaiah speak so plainly, we wonder that the ancient church could read these same truths, and still not understand that the Messiah must suffer and die.

In that beautiful philosophical instrument of modern days, we have sometimes been unable to see more than an ordinary picture. The peculiar *relief* which the stereoscope was designed to give, we could not perceive. Yet perhaps after gazing a while upon it, the eyes adjust themselves to the instrument, the difficulty disappears, and the very same figures which, a moment before, seemed so dull and lifeless, not only stand out full and fresh, but appear so vivid and life-like, that now we cannot but see them in these better forms. And now since our Lord, after his resurrection, took especial care to open the understanding of his disciples to see his necessary sorrows foretold in the Scriptures, how can we doubt that the scattered but numerous hints which "all the prophets" give us since the world began—of suffering and sorrow in HIM that was to come—are so many rays of light that were divinely designed to converge upon Calvary. Like the undesigned coincidences of many independent witnesses to the same events, the seeming insignificance of various words, and their wide dispersion through so many books and over so many ages, gives additional force to their bearing upon that distant and august event. The woman's seed in conflict with the adversary, must be bruised; the promised son of the believing father must be devoted to the altar and significantly restored on the third day, as if from the dead; the blood of deliverance must put its redeeming token upon every door-post in the night of Egypt's terror; the healing serpent must be lifted up in the wilderness, though the nation was not as yet born whose cruel mode of capital punishment was to raise the Messiah to the cross! And that the true method of redemption might be studied in its mysterious significancy; should be recognized as inadequate and typical by its very repetition, Heb. x. 1, 2; and yet should never pass out of sight with God's worshipping people, twice every day must costly victims bleed at his altars. What less, or what else, could all these things mean, in an expecting church, than that the coming Deliverer should himself be a sufferer? And if these hints, taken alone, could scarcely be understood; if these typical and significant services seemed but dark enigmas, too deep for man's solution, yet their very existence and continued observance by a believing people cannot be accounted for, on any less supposition than intelligent and authoritative, and, because so anticipatory, therefore divine enactment. Nor can we believe that an array of sacrifices and services and priests and symbols, so magnificent, so costly and so singular, would be adopted by that ancient people, or commended by their God, yet involving no permanent principles, teaching no abiding doctrines, confirming no stable covenant, proposing no valuable example for our imitation,* but vanishing away from the church, like the shadow of a passing cloud, whose influence is lost the moment the sun shines out. Rather, these forms of the old economy—like the chaff which covers and nurtures the growing grain, and yet falls from it dry and useless at the maturity of the harvest—drop off from the unchanging principles of the church when they are better known than ever. Death and the sprinkled blood are the unchanging lessons of the church of God.

But all these things are clearer when we add to them the more explicit teachings by which the prophets sometimes declared the Messiah's sufferings. How can we read the complaints which fell from David's lips, but which express sorrows that David never knew; or the description given by Isaiah in that remarkable passage, ch. liii., which stands by itself in all the records of the past; or the statement of Daniel that Messiah should be "cut off;" or Zechariah's later words, which tell of his piercing; and not agree that to fulfil the

* Turrettine, iv. 402–3.

voices of the prophets Christ *must* suffer? We indeed cannot now look on these teachings, and shut out the later light which gives them such illustrious clearness. Some of these old teachings have a later and most wonderful counterpart, like a new view of the same scene; and we may place two passages side by side and look upon both together until they blend into one. For in the stereoscope of this two-volumed book, the Old and New Testament prophets prove their common inspiration by the same Spirit, by presenting us with harmonious views of the same subject. Place side by side the twenty-second Psalm and the twenty-seventh chapter of Matthew. Look at them both at once; for, though they are not alike, their subject and their teachings are evidently the same. Behold in both an illustrious Sufferer. Hear the same language of complaint from his lips, as of one forsaken of his God. Witness the gathering multitudes with reviling tongues, and shaking heads, and taunting gibes that this man trusted in his God. See the bitter rage of angry men, the barking of Gentile dogs, the tumultuous swelling of wicked assemblies. Testify that his garments are parted and by lot; that his hands and feet are pierced; that in his racked and distorted frame upon that cross of agony you may count the staring bones; there is no mistaking the identity of the pictures; they are, they are the same! No two such scenes, in so many points alike, can all the world produce here is indeed the double glass of prophecy; prophet and evangelist speak of Christ and Calvary. And we who look upon both, should not fail to see that the cross is the central figure in all the Scriptures; should expect the living Jesus to anticipate and foretell his death by cruel hands at Jerusalem; should recognize that for the fulfilment of the Scriptures Christ *must* suffer; and should agree to call that a Satanic sentiment, even from apostolic lips, that gainsays the necessity for such a death.

Now while it is both impossible and undesirable—as we have frequently said—for us to take our stand by the disciples who heard the Lord, to see with their eyes, to hear with their ears, and to understand no more than they; while we find it difficult to make due allowance for their ignorance and prejudice; there is an important sense in which the very inability of the apostles and of the ancient prophets themselves to interpret these great oracles, enhances the value of the testimony which they bear to Christ. When we can see the evident meaning of the types and prophecies, and then know that those who wrote them aforetime did not comprehend them, we are certain that they were, in no proper sense, the authors of them. If a messenger brings me a letter written in plain English, of which language he understands not one word, need I any better proof that he is not its author? The prophets, moved by the Holy Ghost, wrote words they did not understand. And after his resurrection from the dead our Lord opened the understandings of his disciples to see in all the prophets that the Messiah ought to suffer these things before he entered into his glory. And nothing is more characteristic of the ministry of the apostles than their alleging out of the Scriptures that Christ must suffer. So did Peter at Pentecost and in the epistles that bear his name. Acts ii. 23: 1 Peter i. 10, 11. So did they in every synagogue, arguing with the Jews. So Philip preached Christ from Isaiah's great prophecy. Acts viii. 35. So Paul in his life-long ministry said, "None other things than those which the prophets and Moses did say should come, that Christ should suffer." Acts xxvi. 22, 23. As a matter of certainty, according to the teachings of all God's previous prophets, these new teachings of Jesus to his disciples are true. "He *must* go to Jerusalem and suffer many things . . . . . and be killed."

CHAPTER XX.

THE "MUST BE" OF THE DEATH OF CHRIST.

"The things that be of God."

It may justly be said that the more closely this prophetical proof of the necessity of Messiah's sufferings is studied and understood, the more complete will be the strength of our convictions, and the more wonderful the establishment of the authority of the Scriptures. This however is but one branch of the proof of this important teaching, which Peter cannot be permitted to gainsay. It would be easy to set forth,

II. The Didactic Proof that Christ must die.

For not only do our Lord's words here assert that he must; but he repeats afterwards, thus it *must* be, Matt. xxvi. 54; Christ *ought* to suffer these things, Luke xxiv. 26; and thus it *behooved* Christ to suffer, v. 46. So the apostles teach in later days, "It *became* . . the Father . . . to make the Captain of our salvation perfect through sufferings." It was necessary to purify by better sacrifices than those of the old economy, Heb. ii.

10: ix. 23, those who should enter the heavenly sanctuary.

But we may read, as these disciples could not,

III. The Historic Proof that Christ must die.

He *did* die we know; and in the knowledge of this is the clear proof that he must needs suffer. Before us we set illuminated prophecies, plain declarations, and indisputable providences. Predictions that thus it *should* be, declarations that thus it *must* be, have been succeeded by historic records that thus it *has* occurred. Here again our deepest study brings most profound conviction. Every just thought of that great event, when Christ did die upon the cross, under the government of a holy God, and directly according to the divine will, demands that a righteous necessity, for some adequate end, should exist for a scene like this. The dignity of the sufferer, who was the Son of God, and but voluntarily subject to the law for redemption's sake, Gal. iv. 4, 5; the excellence of his personal character, well pleasing in the Father's sight, and found without fault before the earthly judge who condemned him; the representations of the Scriptures so abundantly made that his death was public and official, and not private and personal, for others and not for himself; their constant teaching that love prompted himself to offer and the Father to give him, though there can be neither wisdom nor love in sufferings that may be easily and righteously avoided; the terms applied to that death, that he was a surety, a curse for us, a ransom and a propitiation; that he bore our sins, takes away sin by the sacrifice of himself, brings redemption to us, and reconciles us to God by his cross; all these things bid us recognize these sufferings as ordered by Providence, and as the needful means by which the Divine ruler would secure the Messiah's glory in man's salvation.

Now in speaking of the providential aspects of this great matter,—in justifying the Saviour's words that he *must* suffer—one sorrowful record in his life brings this necessity directly before us. In the great enterprise upon which the Mediator had now entered, he delights to do God's holy will, Ps. xl. 8: Heb. x. 7, and is actuated by a holy and steadfast purpose that is straitened till his fearful baptism is accomplished. Luke xii. 50. Yet he did not undervalue the heavy griefs through which his soul must pass. If the infinite wisdom of this suffering Mediator could have found any cheaper method of securing the same great end, that method he would have chosen. He chose the cross for its end, not for itself; as a *needs be*, not as an expedient: to save men who otherwise could not be saved. Could he have gained the same end in the avoiding of the cross, he would have done it. He passed on a willing victim to the cross; yet its gathering terrors filled his soul with anguish; he poured out his soul in strong crying and tears unto him who was able to save; and asked the Father to remove the bitter cup, with an earnestness that three times repeated the wonderful request. Yet he just so asked as to prove that its removal was not possible, consistently with those great designs which no sorrows could make him surrender. The Father heard, Heb. v. 7, but he did not save his beloved Son from death. Can we imagine a better proof in fact that the sorrows of his incarnate Son were necessary to the salvation of man than is furnished by the refusal of this submissive prayer? The Father would have removed it, if it had been possible. It was not. Christ must die. The pleading Redeemer DID suffer; the strongest possible proof that he MUST.

But besides this wonderful pleading in Gethsemane, these gospel narratives set before us two grand mysteries, springing out of two great facts, that seem capable of but a single sufficient explanation. Taken by themselves, we can explain neither. They seem altogether inconsistent with proper ideas of divine justice. One mystery is that Christ Jesus—whose innocence is acknowledged, and rendered indeed preëminent, by virtues the most extraordinary—suffers at the hands of man, is deserted by his God, and seems peculiarly to bear the curse of a law which truly he never broke. He restored that he took not away. The other mystery is, that many sinners—known as flagrant violators of the law, and themselves candidly confessing their guilt—are set free from the law's condemning sentence, are reconciled to God, and are rewarded with his favour.

Separated, neither of these things can be comprehended. Taken together they may be solved; for the innocent takes the responsibilities of the guilty, and the guilty are set free from the sentence which he endures for them. These two things equally demand our faith in the necessity of the sufferings of Christ.

We have spoken of Divine justice. This we should more carefully consider. It leads us to notice,

IV. The Ethical Argument for the Necessity of Messiah's Death.

How can we understand a great moral question, without going beyond facts and statements to inquire into the moral principles it involves? All the various points may be in harmony. Let us strive to see this. Prophecy foretold; wisdom taught; providence accomplished; thus events answer to God's intelligent designs. The prophets, looking forward, declared that Messiah's death *should* certainly occur; the Redeemer says it *must* be; and the evangelists, looking backward, narrate that it *did* take place. Can we pass deeper down than prophet, and teacher, and historian, and ask of Him from whom time and the things of time proceed—from the common Controller of prediction and event—what righteous principles underlie the whole? In the Saviour's reproof to Peter, he declares that the "must be" of his death is one of the "things of God." Is there that, in God and his government, which declares that Christ to save man ought to suffer? We have the *shall* of the prophets; we have the *must* of Christ's irrefragable word; we have the *did* in the evangelistic narratives; can we find the *ought* in the decisions of infinite righteousness; and find these all harmonious elements in the loving cross? Yes, we can. So we understand the Scriptures; so we interpret the scenes of Calvary; so we comprehend our Lord's reproof to Peter, far above the offence of forward zeal or rash presumption; so we draw the line between the decisions of divine wisdom and righteousness, and those offending suggestions, from whatever quarter, to which our Lord would say, "Get thee behind me, Satan!" The necessity for the death of Christ is not one of mere expediency, even to fill up the harmony of God's prophetic and providential plans: it was itself according to the preceding plan from which prophecy and providence themselves have sprung; and infinite grace and wisdom and righteousness meet in the cross of Calvary.

We can address ourselves to no higher thoughts than those which consider God himself. Let us study his works and his word; but through creation and through providence, through revelation and through grace, and, as superior to them all, let us study HIMSELF. And in all that we can know of God, no truth is of value or interest at all to be compared with the sure conviction of his unchanging righteousness. "Shall not the Judge of all the earth do right?" Everything he is and does, must be capable of vindication upon righteous principles. By declaring that God is just, we mean that he will deal with moral beings as they deserve—either directly punishing sin, or so dealing with it as to call forth confessions of his righteousness from the intelligent universe. It is unspeakably more important that God should be infinitely perfect in righteousness, than even in his natural attributes of wisdom and power. We could not respect even an angel upon whose robes was found one spot of falsehood or injustice. Wo to the universe, if the Most High is of infinite exaltation and of unchanging excellence, except in the most important of all things—his own moral principles. And here, above all, the character of God is incapable of the least deflection. Even in judging of men, "He who keeps the whole law and yet offends in one point, is guilty of all." He is no longer sinless who has spoken one untruth, or done one wrong. It arises from the infinite perfection of Jehovah, that he is incapable of the slightest decline from entire righteousness. "He cannot deny himself." 2 Tim. ii. 13. He is "God that cannot lie." Titus i. 2. Falsehood or injustice would be weakness, in One who has no weakness; he has no capacity for evil, but every excellence dwells in him; and all his attributes are in a harmony as excellent and glorious as themselves.

Of every man and of every thing must this holy

God form a just judgment. He cannot but know the sins of men; he cannot but approve or disapprove. But disapproval is condemnation; in a just judge the difference between right and wrong can never be trivial; and a righteous condemnation must go the full length of the ill desert it condemns. When we say that God is just, we can mean nothing less than that he will deal with sinners as they deserve. This his nature requires; this his law demands; this his word declares; and every just argument drawn from either, confirms this most, in its fullest strength. But sinners do not deserve approval, pardon, reward; and the judge who deals thus with acknowledged offenders must vindicate his decision for good reasons assigned, or lose his reputation for justice. God himself—indeed we should say, God *preëminently*—cannot arbitrarily forgive sinners.

This is the true reason for the necessity of Christ's death. Caprice cannot be introduced into God's government, or the foundations are destroyed. If he may smile upon any sinner, why not frown upon any holy being? If right no longer governs, anarchy sends dismay through the universe. This cannot be. Righteousness must reign—unswerving righteousness. Nowhere less can we tolerate the slightest defect—the least change from perfection—than in the truth and righteousness and purity of the divine character. In the sufferings and death of God's incarnate Son Jehovah "declares his righteousness in the forgiveness of sins." Rom. iii. 25. Proper ideas of this scheme, devised by love, wisdom and righteousness, divine and infinite, alone can explain why the holy should suffer, or the sinful be set free from suffering. *Personally* considered, neither was Christ, nor are Christ's people treated as they deserve. Christ, as innocent, deserved not to die; yet he did die. His people, as guilty, deserve condemnation; yet are they justified. So we are told that Christ took their place and suffered in their stead. Love and grace prompted his mediation. The claims of divine justice are made upon a sufficient and voluntary surety; these righteous claims are transferred from his people; this transfer presupposes the movements of infinite grace. The MUST BE of Christ's death was not absolute, but relative to man's salvation. Man must suffer for his own transgressions, in which sense no salvation was possible; or another must bear his guilt. So our great poet says,

> "Die he or justice must, unless for him
> Some other, able and as willing, pay
> The rigid satisfaction, death for death."

The apostle clearly argues that when God forgives sin, he vindicates the righteousness of so doing by setting forth the propitiation of Christ. Rom. iii. 25. If man is forgiven Christ must die. This is the counsel of God. This justifies even the death of the innocent, when he stands voluntarily in the stead of the guilty. This declares the divine rectitude when the believer on Jesus is justified. This explains how impossible it was to answer the prayer of Gethsemane; and to put away that bitter cup from a Saviour's lips.

There are not wanting other reasons to show the necessity of that death which our Lord now predicted to his astonished disciples. But we will not now present any others in the form of arguments. We may simply suggest that only by the death of a Redeemer is there any semblance of satisfaction made to the righteous demands of God's law, or to the expectations of man's enlightened conscience; while in the atonement of Jesus a complete answer is made to every inquiry which justice and intelligence can ask. Penitence, of itself, cannot answer the law, remove guilt, satisfy the conscience, or repair consequences; if indeed penitence could be exercised apart from the atonement. Perhaps especially we should say that,

V. The efficacy shown by experience to belong to the death of Christ is an important proof of its necessity.

This is a two-fold argument. On the one hand, it is notorious that lax views of morality, of sin, of divine righteousness, prevail among those who deny the doctrine of the atonement. On the other hand, those who recognize the necessity and efficacy of the death of God's own Son for human salvation, have the most profound views of man's sin, the highest views of God's justice, the most penitent thoughts of themselves, the most careful endeavours to keep holy the demands of God's law. The character and government of God are matters of the deepest concern to those who have learned their lessons at the cross of a redeeming Jesus. We put the Lord's own test to the Lord's own work. "By their fruits ye shall know them." The world over, no man ever becomes interested in the atonement of Calvary without higher views of the law of God, and more careful efforts to honour and keep it. This experimental test may be applied to this teaching, that it has every tendency to maintain the honour of God and of his law; that it makes men the cheerful and obedient subjects of his authority; that its fruits are holiness; and that those who decline from this doctrine of the atonement, decline to lax views of divine rectitude and of human duty.

The error of Peter was not one of mere form or temper. It was one of vital principle, when he did not recognize the *must be* which his Lord asserted. And no age, and no man can safely deny the necessity of his sufferings on the tree. Let us understand the position occupied by the great Mediator; let us rejoice in his willingness and his ability to do that most necessary work. The guilt of man is open, flagrant, manifold; the law of God is plain, and strict, and changeless; the divine justice demanded that the sinner should meet its claims. In the voluntary shedding of Christ's blood we recognize the plan of redeeming love and wisdom. Mercy and truth meet; righteousness and peace embrace. This satisfies our just reasonings respecting divine righteousness. This explains the scope of Scriptural teachings from Genesis to Revelation. Death and the sprinkled blood—without this, no remission—is God's wise method for man's forgiveness. To any that "for any reason" would deny this great teaching—the Son of man *must* suffer—should our reply be, "Get thee behind me, Satan! thou savourest not the things that be of God!"

Now all these thoughts are corroborated by the evident prominence and importance of the death of Christ in the gospel narratives, and in the teachings of the apostles. In no sense can his be thought an ordinary death. For the innocent to die at all is extraordinary; for such an one as he to fear death for any personal considerations is nearly as extraordinary;* for so much stress to be laid upon his death in the New Testament church, except as it was needful, vicarious and efficacious, is inexplicable. For the church to celebrate his death in a solemn sacrament that excludes all former sacrifices, and is itself to last till he shall come; to repeat this so often, with impressive words and actions; to make it the most affecting solemnity of her latest and most glorious dispensation, may sufficiently prove that we are in no danger of overestimating the cross of Christ. Let us beware of any leanings towards

* See the striking remarks of Saurin. Sermon on the Crucifixion, vi. 84.

the error of Peter. We cannot indeed even wish to stay the Redeemer's footsteps as he presses towards Jerusalem. The work of Calvary is "finished." It is too late to stop it, as Peter would have done. But it is not too late to misunderstand it; and against this we must guard.

If any sinful man needs an interest in the atoning work of Christ, every man does. If that death was at all needful, it was needful both for you and for me. Any failure to appreciate this; any neglect to seek the "blood of sprinkling" for our own souls; any confidence in other means of safety is to repeat the error of Peter. Let us rather believe that Christ has not died in vain. Neither was his death uncalled for by our necessities; neither is it inefficacious for the largest guilt; neither is it withheld from our humble and penitent application; neither can we slight it, but to our eternal undoing. Oh, foolish hearers of the gospel of his grace! who hath bewitched you that ye should not obey the truth, before whom, so frequently, Jesus Christ has been set forth evidently crucified!*

* On the necessity for the atonement see Turrettine, vol. iv. pp. 385–435; Witsius, Econ. Cov., book i. ch. v. § 23, seq., book ii. ch. viii.; Buddeus Inst. Theol., 870.

CHAPTER XXI.

TAKING UP THE CROSS.

The wisest teachers often perplex their disciples; and the most thoughtful scholars are the most likely to be perplexed. Careless hearers of the truth dismiss at once the instructions they do not readily understand: as if the thoughts that cannot be immediately comprehended, were thus proved wanting in intelligence or value. But thoughtful minds, really desirous of instruction, are awakened to more careful attention when the meaning of the lesson is not obvious. Of all teachers none give lessons more worthy of our earnest study than our Lord Jesus Christ: yet many of his words must have been obscure and enigmatical to the most intelligent of his apostles. We know no better illustration to explain the crude views and wild anticipations of that band of twelve, who gathered around him for three years, than to compare him to a father, and these to the children, whom he instructs by precepts, direct and indirect; by examples, copied more through an imitative instinct than by intelligence; by teachings, some of which are now understood, some half understood, and some not understood at all. How little does a child enter into sympathy with the parent. A thousand reflections, plans, fears, hopes, pass every day through a father's mind, of which the child can have no knowledge. Yet no one can doubt that the child learns in this parental school: indeed, reason as we may, of the strangeness of a scholar's learning where so many things are so long above his capacity and outside of his sympathy, experience tells us that there is no better method of training minds than in the family—a providential seminary of the wisest adaptation. Our Lord's disciples were his family; and if we wonder at their early misconceptions of his words and character and plans, we may acknowledge that in due time they knew his doctrines and sympathized with his designs.

As little as the children of our families know of the world before them and of their life in it, knew the disciples of Jesus of the spiritual kingdom that was to be established through their means. We talk to our children of life and its duties; and they learn to use language similar to our own; while yet only a practical experience of life's own changes can teach them the full meaning of the words we thus use. They often get false ideas from our teachings: not because we have taught falsehood, but because they have been incapable of appreciating the true meaning of our words. They are often at a loss to understand things, which may be recalled and understood better at a later time. True teaching is worth far more than its present apparent value.

When our Lord said to his disciples that they must deny themselves and take up the cross and follow him, he used in their ears the language of enigma. They had but a low conception of the meaning of the cross upon his lips. If he refers to his own sufferings upon the cross, they were not so familiar with that Roman mode of capital punishment; and they had not yet arrived at the conception that their Lord should indeed die a violent death. Yet doubtless they had seen or heard of the cross; they knew that the unhappy victims must carry the means of their own torture to the place of death; and must linger in cruel agony until they found a slow relief from every pang. And thus his words, dark though their meaning was, were a faithful forewarning that his service was not one of pleasure simply. He gives fair notice of suffering rather than of joy; of reproach rather than of honour.

Now if we may hear our Lord's words more intelligently than they, we should desire to know their true meaning in this especial case. He is willing—indeed desirous—that men should take distinct forewarning of the certain and unavoidable difficulties that attend their discipleship to him. He would not win a single follower by any bright representation of the joys or advantages attending his service; especially by any holding back of sacrifices to be made, or sufferings to be endured. He makes the cross an early, a prominent, a continual lesson of the Christian life. So no man can have it to say that the Scriptures beguiled him to embrace a service that turned out harder than had been represented. Those who would follow Christ are expressly directed to sit down and count the cost, that they may decide for, or against him, in view of intelligent considerations. So men who have once taken up the Saviour's service should be expected to press steadily forward, even through difficulties and self-denials; since they are not only supported under them, but have been forewarned of them. When we meet self-denials, difficulties and the cross, let us not judge that we have mistaken the path. For it could not be THE PATH, if it led us where we had nothing like trials or self-denials to encounter. And let it be known, the world over, that Christ Jesus has no other terms to offer that he may win the most illustrious disciple. No mortal man confers an honour on Jesus, when he is numbered among his followers; for no mortal man will any decline be made in the duties of his service; he that shrinks back from the cross is not worthy of this Lord; and while he speaks graciously, he ever speaks as a Sovereign to all the sons of earth.

Since we have good reason to believe that the Master expresses no special rule for his apostles when he speaks of the cross; but rather that his language can mean nothing less than a permanent rule of Christ's kingdom, we may the more thoughtfully listen while he speaks to us. Time has not faded a single letter; distance does not dim our reading of a single word; changing circumstances cannot transpose a single expression; nor can the pervading principle of this great sentence ever be wisely lost sight of by any of Christ's disciples. In view of the profession his followers must make of his name, of the sacrifices they must make, of the griefs they must endure, and of the services they must render, he had once before said, "He that taketh not his cross and followeth after me, is not worthy of me." Matt. x. 38. And now having spoken of his own needful sufferings for our salvation, he resumes the same topic, and asserts its universal necessity for all his people. "If any man will come after me, let him deny himself and take up his cross and follow me."

But this teaching of Christ, though a just forewarning of trials, is not, merely in this aspect, a strange thing for a religious teacher. For it would be difficult to point out any system of religion on earth, that does not enjoin its self-denials. Far more importance is to be attached to the true nature of Christian self-denial, than to the mere fact that self-denials are enjoined in the teachings of Jesus. If we look over the earth at this very hour; if we make ourselves acquainted with the gross impostures of paganism and of the corrupted forms of Christianity, we may well be surprised, not only at the sacrifices, personal and pecuniary, which they everywhere demand; but at the willingness with which their votaries pay the exactions that seem to us the extreme of absurdity and even wickedness. The Hindu will undertake protracted and dangerous journeys; will endure frightful and long-continued tortures; will pay liberally—from his poverty or from his abundance—if thus his gods command. Pilgrimages and penances, fastings and mortifications, alms-giving and self-denials form a prominent part of every kind of religion on the earth. Perhaps it is so, that man's sense of his fallen, degraded, sinful estate is so thoroughly felt by the conscience, that no man can consent to take the natural actings of his mind for religion. Religion, by the unanimous verdict of mankind, is self-denial, not self-gratification: it runs counter to man's natural impulses, not in the same channels with them; it testifies that man has departed from his God, and needs a painful restoration: and thus the world bears witness—in its very falsehoods against Christ—to the propriety of the claims which he here makes. This great fact, indeed, so universally recognized, is not properly interpreted anywhere else than in the gospel of Christ. False religions take this great truth as the basis,—that man needs self-denials,—and upon this they invariably build for man a superstructure of self-gratification. This wide and essential difference exists between the sacrifices and self-denials required by the gospel, and those demanded by every form of false religion; that false systems regard these as sufferings, sacrifices, efforts, COMPENSATORY; they are matters of *penance*, into which the idea of making amends for sins essentially enters; rather than matters of *penitence*, which indeed includes efforts for the amendment of the life, but which possesses no value as making amends to the law. The self-denials of the gospel are self-denials of another order, and hold quite a different place. So an apostle assures us that a man may give away all his goods to the poor, and give his body to the fiery stake: and yet in all this, offer a profitless sacrifice to that God, who asks a nobler offering still.

The self-denial required in the gospel may extend to personal suffering and include pecuniary sacrifice: but it is something very different from the senseless mortification of our persons, or the useless or reckless sacrifice of our property. It is easier to understand the object we should keep constantly in view, than to enumerate the details of a duty that influences all possible characters, situations, engagements and times of our earthly life. Interpret the words of Christ plainly, and you have the whole of it. Deny self, take up the cross, and follow me. Even the fearful requirements of false teachings; the evasions, which our depraved natures, instinctively keen to avoid every cross, would prompt us to make of true teachings; and the penances of a spurious devotion, yet allow men to gratify self.

They enjoin self-denials in voluntary and useless mortifications, that have no tendency to do good to ourselves or to others, or to glorify God; and especially they build up the pride of man's heart, and beget an esteem of his own righteousness, in which thing they are the furthest removed from the spirit of the gospel.

At the foundation of the self-denial enjoined in the gospel lies an utter renunciation of our dependence upon our characters or doings, as the ground of our acceptance before God. This is the denial of self. Nor is it easy. Self-righteousness is a root of bitterness not easily extirpated from the soil of the human heart. In the spirit of dependence upon Christ, we are to take up the cross he lays upon us, and to follow him in all his teachings and in all his leadings. Christian self-denial is to follow the Lord's leadings, to submit to the Lord's will, to do the Lord's bidding, and to promote the Lord's glory, out of love to the Lord, undeterred by painful, costly, difficult or unpleasant sacrifices, or engagements. It is nothing more nor less than giving ourselves to Christ—to have our souls imbued with the holy principles of his gospel; to have every rebellious passion brought into subjection to his holy will; to have every step of our earthly path taken cheerfully by the direction of his providence; and to have our souls upon the constant watch, not to seek our own honour, but to seek his glory, for whom we live, and for whom we are ready to suffer the loss of all things. It is to live in the world in constant contact with things that are unfriendly, yet also to live above the world. It is to find that the changes of life, as we grow older, as we grow wiser, as we grow richer, or as we grow poorer, even indeed as we grow holier, still bring us no relief from the law that yet rests upon us to take up our daily cross and bear it after Jesus. We may learn to glory in the cross we bear for him, we may count it all joy that we are esteemed worthy to suffer or endure for his sake; we may lighten the burden by holding it closely to our hearts; but still will we find it THE CROSS: like our afflictions, not in themselves joyous, but grievous: rejoiced in not as pleasant, but as working afterwards the peaceable fruits of righteousness. As our sorrows often wither our brightest hopes, sever our tenderest ties, and grieve our dearest affections; and submission under them is most the fruit of grace when we feel the most keenly: so the cross borne in our following after Jesus may be the heaviest, the hardest to bear just when our patient endurance may enable us most fully to glorify the name and the principles of Christ. And it should be no mean support under the heavy burden of some special cross, to remember that the infinite wisdom of our King has appointed our place in his kingdom; and has laid upon us the very duties wherein we may get the most good to our own souls, do good to those that are around us, and glorify the great name of our Redeemer.

Notice, in our Lord's phraseology, it is the *believer's* cross, as well as *Christ's* cross. It is Christ's cross because borne at his bidding and to glorify him; it is the believer's cross because he must bear it; yes, indeed, suffer upon it! And because the cross you bear is divinely designed to mortify your members that are upon the earth, and to enable you to adorn the gospel, the especial weight of this cross as borne by you, is divinely adapted to form your character and to mould your life in Christ's service. We often feel like complaining that we have special griefs to bear, special hardships to encounter, special losses to endure! And so we all have! Not in the sense that our crosses are heavier than any ever before borne; but in the better sense that divine wisdom has made no mistake in the burden specially allotted to him, let every man take up HIS cross.

CHAPTER XXII.

BEARING THE CROSS.

"Must Jesus bear the cross alone,
And all the world go free?
No, there's a cross for every one,
And there's a cross for me."

PERHAPS it may be well for us to specify some of the forms which the cross assumes, as the disciples of Jesus must bear it after him.

First, then, it is an important part of Christian duty that we must not be ashamed of the teachings of Christ before men. He himself expressly forbids his disciples to be ashamed of him or of his words. The teachings of Christ are so excellent that men are everywhere willing to applaud; and that many even wear the name of Christian who still are far from following where Jesus leads. It is not enough that we should honour some of the teachings of Christ. He claims to be the greatest of all teachers, infallible in the correctness of his doctrines, consistent in their entire harmony, and legitimate and supreme in the authority with which he calls his disciples to embrace them. Yet there are many of Christ's teachings not readily received among men:

and the man who dares to hold consistently all the teachings of such a Lord must expect to be reproached as bigoted and illiberal by that wisdom of the world, which refuses to be instructed even when the Son of God is the teacher. The followers of Christ must belong to a sect that is "everywhere spoken against;" they need not wonder if many slanders are heaped upon the truth; they may expect that their Lord's own words will be perverted to uses far different from his designs. Among the variety of opinions among men touching religious doctrines, every disciple of Christ should learn and should firmly maintain the teachings of Jesus; he should be undismayed, if indeed special denial is made of important doctrines, and special reproach is cast upon them; he should even anticipate this, as the offence inseparable from the cross.

If the authority of the sacred Scriptures is called in question; if men deny the divinity of Christ, the necessity and efficacy of his atonement, the power or freeness of his grace, or the worthlessness of human merits; if the doctrines of the resurrection, the final judgment, and the future perdition of ungodly men are called in question, we are not at liberty even to seem indifferent or neutral in matters so important as these. To argument we can often reply; by sneers we must be unmoved; it is foolish and perilous to avoid the cross. We must not be ashamed of the words of Christ. We are often tempted to compromise the truth that we may not vex opposers. But it is our duty to be both wise and bold; and the prudence that allows error to triumph and truth to fall in the streets is more timid than faithful. Nothing is more noble than for a disciple of Christ to be ready anywhere and at any time to speak firmly in vindication of every doctrine that has been delivered to us in the teachings of our Lord.

Secondly, the service of Christ often lays a cross upon us in reference to our ordinary duties of life and to our tenderest relationships.

Our Lord Jesus Christ does not intend that his people should separate themselves from other people; but that they should live in a mixed state of society, and show their discipleship by their principles rather than by their abodes, their professions or their apparel. And men can be known by their principles as certainly as by anything else. If Christians tried to live in separate towns or streets by themselves, many people would crowd in there who were not true Christians. If they wore any special dress, other people could put on similar clothes. Christ enjoins no such separations. His people are thoroughly mingled with the world; and all their attempts to stay too much together he thwarts; as when the apostles tarried too long at Jerusalem against his bidding, he scattered them by persecution. So you can hardly find a family that has not its ungodly members; and sometimes a single person in a family has alone tasted of the grace of Christ, and is called to bear the cross for Jesus in the very circumstances thus surrounding him. For though persecutions are not known among us, in the same gross sense that pertained to the earlier ages; though the trials of many converts from heathenism, who must surrender their earthly goods and part from their earthly friends, are not the trials endured in a Christian community; it is as true now as ever, that the spirit of Christ is not the spirit of the world; that every Christian will be closely watched by those who are about him; that he will find a cross in the differences which true piety puts between himself and others. Christ's words are still true that he has come to set at variance the most intimate relationships of life. If a wife is a Christian and the husband is not; the parent is and the child is not; the sister is and the brother is not, here is room for cross-bearing.

The engagements of the family may not be changed; the affections of the family may be as warm as ever; they live still beneath the same roof, and are upon the best of terms with each other. But the member of the household that loves Jesus has new views in which the others do not sympathize; new affections and tastes that agree not with theirs; and it is worse, that conscience often takes the differences as a protest against a worldliness that would otherwise remain unreproved. It is very hard always to maintain a truly Christian temper; especially when the mildness that yields is reproached as inconsistent and unfaithful; the firmness that refuses to yield is branded as stubborn and unfeeling; the zealous care to keep a good conscience is thought overscrupulous; and watching against sin is esteemed the bigotry of a sect. Many a time are the warm affections our tempters to do what we hope may be for good; and it is a cross to be misinterpreted by dearly loved friends in our best intended services. This cross is infinitely various, as it rests here or there; it must be borne faithfully wherever it rests; and every wise disciple will judge *that* the most dangerous of all mistakes, which lays off the cross itself to avoid the reproach of the cross. Faithfulness to Christ is the very first requisite in all true affection and faithfulness to the souls of others. Compliances with their wishes against the duty we owe to the Saviour will both entangle our souls and lay stumbling-blocks for theirs. Many of our most delicate duties—especially for younger Christians—arise in these social relationships. The firm, kindly, consistent exhibition of Christian principles; the denial of self in a thousand ways, which every intimate friend must see; the constant humble care to honour the Saviour and to let nothing stand before him, is the best proof of piety in the eyes of unconverted friends. We all have our opportunities for such service in the cause of Jesus; and just the cross we each arc called to bear has been fitted to our shoulders by One who will bless us and glorify himself as we faithfully bear it.

Thirdly, the service of Christ lays a cross upon his disciples in respect to their conformity to the world.

Christians are still in the world; they mingle with its business; they partake of its prosperity; they share its pleasures. It is impossible, it is undesirable; we may go still further, it would be wicked for Christians to stand wholly aside from that world which they should do so much to save, and which they cannot save if they withdraw from the sympathies of men. As before remarked, Christ designs a separation in principles rather than in place. There are many self-denials in worldly business. The Christian desires success as truly as another man; he may be tempted to use means for this end which others use; and in the exciting whirl of life, he is often on the point of saying and doing things that are forbidden by the holy teachings of his Master. To curb the temper that is naturally so quick; to repress the passions that are naturally so strong; to keep in check our interest in worldly things, that it gets not too powerful, at the same time that we must give our careful attention to business in order to secure its success; to be actuated by principle, and not by impulse and feeling; these things are the daily duty of Christ's followers in the business of this life; and these things are the denial of self and the bearing of the cross. Many a gain could the Christian make, many a thing could he do, many a word could he say, many a feeling could he cherish, did not Christian principles forbid; and he who ever acts thus denies self and bears a daily cross.

So are Christians, for the Master's sake, called to bear the cross with reference to the pleasures of this world. Men love pleasure. Christians love pleasure. And many of the world's pleasures they can innocently enjoy. And many that are ensnaring have their strong attractions. We may have a natural taste for them; this may be stronger because we have formerly indulged it; and it would be very easy to acquire so strong a passion for earthly and sensual pleasures that reason and conscience would try in vain to hold us back from their indulgence. But Christ's disciples are not to be governed by their tastes. Deny thyself, is a fundamental rule in his service. All our engagements, pleasures, pursuits, must be subservient to an all-possessing desire to glorify Christ. If the world claims any pleasure for its own and triumphs over my religion to see me indulge in it; if Christian people withdraw from vain scenes and are grieved to see me there; I would rather give up all the border pleasures that lie between the church and the world, than inflict one pang upon the friends of my Master, or allow one feeling of exultation in his foes. No doubt it is often a difficult thing for young Christians to bear the cross meekly in reference to the world's pleasures; yet just in proportion to the difficulty of maintaining a firm and holy standing as a youthful disciple, is the honour put upon Christ and the good accomplished for others, when such a position is held. Let every Christian in regard to the pleasures around him, notice what those are that belong to the world, are claimed by the world, and ever promote only a worldly spirit; and let him refuse entirely and always to indulge in these. Let him notice those that are innocent in themselves, and that may be safely indulged in their proper time and measure; and let him form such rules in regard to these as becomes his Christian character.

For example, he cannot be a Christian at all if he finds his highest happiness in any earthly thing. He should let the world know that he has sources of enjoyment better and purer than any it can give. So then with him religious engagements should take precedence of the calls of earthly pleasure; and nothing of an earthly nature should be allowed to create a disrelish for pious enjoyments. In this unfriendly world it is unwise for a disciple of Christ to allow anything to weaken or to clash with his religious principles; and it is safer to err on the side of self-denial, than to run the risk of bringing reproach upon his consistency, or of ensnaring the conscience by doubtful compliances.

Fourthly, Christ's disciples must bear his cross by their efforts to advance his cause among men.

The church is a vineyard into which Christ's servants come to labour. It is a home for weary souls; but it is not a lounging-place for the indolent.

Here as elsewhere the divine rule is, "If any man will not work neither should he eat;" the divine economy gives the sweetest rest to those who most faithfully toil; and many lose the rest and peace of Zion, because they do not Zion's work. The happiest Christians are those that are cheerful in labouring for Christ. The work he gives us to do is very different; but he is well served when we have a mind to seek his glory, no matter that it costs us some inconvenience. Every Christian has an example to set which proves his attachment to his Lord. Some indeed excuse themselves upon frivolous pleas. Their influence is small. They are too shrinking and timid to let their voices be heard in social or even in family prayer. They have no time or talents to teach in the Sabbath-school. If all the servants of Christ did as some do, we would have no prayer-meetings, no Sabbath-schools, no cross-bearing among us. What if it is hard? Who ever told you that the cross was easy? Is it a cross for you to do this thing for Jesus? You feel that it is. Does that prove that therefore you may shrink? Are you justified in the life-long neglect of a serious work which your Lord lays before you, because you fear that your discharge of it may be difficult or imperfect?

We must deny ourselves that we may aid in the spread of the gospel. Our Lord designs to send these great teachings to the whole earth; and to do this by the instrumentality of his people. So he calls upon us to do this work with our might. The work has a thousand various forms, and should tax our energies and resources in every way. In one sense it is a most exalted privilege that we are permitted to carry forward the work for which Christ died; in another sense it is like Christ's own work, a matter of great self-denial. As it cost our Lord himself so much to win salvation, so it costs his people labour to spread the tidings. There are two departments of service, giving from our substance as the Lord has prospered us, and labouring ourselves directly in the same service. We have no right to neglect either of these as our opportunities offer; nor should we allow one to serve as compensation for the neglect of the other. Every disciple should be glad to do either; though indeed many give much who can work little, and many work much who have nothing to give. But he is unworthy the name of a disciple who stands back from this cross, not through inability but through indisposition. Every disciple of Christ should from principle support the ministry of the church to which he belongs; sustain all the institutions of religion about him; and labour and pray and give for the conversion of souls elsewhere. We speak not now of amounts. If there be first a willing mind it is accepted according to that a man hath, and not according to that he hath not. But the more there is of the true mind that was in Christ, the more liberal things will we devise for the promoting of his cause.

But we may attempt to specify no more particulars touching this great duty. It is the life-work of the Christian to bear his cross after Christ; and he can spend no hour upon earth that will not afford him an opportunity for cross-bearing. Nothing is of greater or more pressing or continual importance than an entire self-renunciation, so that the soul's full dependence for acceptance before God is upon the finished righteousness of this glorious Redeemer; and in full consistency with this, we should press on in his steps who for us "endured the cross, despising the shame." We have indeed self-denials which he could not have. We have passions to subdue, affections to mortify, tendencies to correct, even follies of our very worship to watch, that could not belong to him; and the argument for our watchfulness and prayer is stronger than for his.

Nothing is to be gained by efforts to avoid the cross. Self-imposed penances are indeed of no account in the service we should render to him; but, truly, joys sought in the shunning of duty are of as little worth. Christians would undoubtedly be happier, if they endured self-denials more abundantly and more cheerfully for the dear sake of Christ. The joy of being like Jesus, the privilege of doing like him, the happiness of suffering as he did and for his sake, these things his loving disciples should highly prize. Little wonder is it that so many complain of the absence of pious joys, when they so much neglect pious duties; little wonder that they taste not the Redeemer's gladness, who avoid his bitter cup of sorrow. As our Lord passed to his crown by his cross, his people must expect to follow him. This, indeed, is an old watch-word of Christianity,—"No cross, no crown."

If any man will come after Christ let him deny himself, take up his cross, and follow him. Men like not the path of self-denial; but Christ calls us to it. And unhappily too many persons fail to look far enough, when they ponder the question of taking up the cross. It lays burdens on us. Does it relieve us of none? Is Christ Jesus exacting only? Does he not promise really also? Let us take both worlds into the account, when we hear his calls who has the keys of hell and of death. And his very language holds forth our unspeakable privilege. He addresses not simply those who stood by him on that eventful day; but his terms are extended also to us. If any man will come, let him! He holds forth a cross in one hand; he points to a crown with the other. The two are one. The cross is a seed to fall in our hearts and die; the crown is the fruit to satisfy us in glory for ever.

"The consecrated cross I'll bear
Till death shall set me free;
And then go home my crown to wear,
For there's a crown for me."

CHAPTER XXIII.

THE SAVIOUR'S GREAT QUESTION.

"What shall a man give in exchange for his soul?"

WE cannot accompany the footsteps of Jesus, and carry with us our present knowledge of his character and mission to the earth, without desiring to hear something from his lips, not only of sympathy and encouragement, but also of awakening. Any just understanding of his errand to earth will assure us that if love prompted, justice demanded his condescension and sacrifice; and that therefore the voice of warning to sinful souls sounds as clearly in his gospel as the voice of invitation and mercy. We listen to the words of this Teacher as the Saviour of sinners; yet we need not a Saviour except as we are lost; and to need such a Saviour and such a method of redemption implies that man's lost estate is one of the deepest wretchedness, and that only he could save. And upon the subject of the soul's worth, who can know more than Jesus? Surely we should listen reverently when this is the theme of his remark. If now we were walking with him and his disciples, when he declared the necessity of self-denial to follow him; if we heard him ask the momentous question, "What is a man profited if he shall gain the whole world and lose his own soul? Or what shall a man give in exchange for his soul?"—could we help but esteem this as a most solemn inquiry to reach our ears from his lips? Recognize his character, and then ask, "Who could better know the soul's excellence and the value of its salvation than he?" Himself the Son of God and possessed of every attribute of divinity, yet also the Son of man, possessed of a human soul, and knowing its joys and sorrows and longings and attachments; himself the Maker of the soul, and well knowing its capacities and its immortality; and beyond this, himself the soul's Redeemer, exposed to scorn and suffering and the death of the cross, that he might ransom it; surely he has a right to make this inquiry; and it has an emphasis upon his lips that it cannot have from any other prophet. And if now we stood among the people around that great Teacher; if now he should fix his eye upon you and inquire of you personally in these solemn terms; if with his emphasis it should fall upon your ear, could you fail to ponder it? Indeed he does speak to you! His words have addressed myriads, but they always mean to reach the individual; and if you have a soul to save, the inquiry is as pertinent and as important to you as ever it was to any man. These are living words of Jesus, though thousands that have heard them are numbered with the dead; these are words in which indeed Jesus does address us, as truly as if we stood beside him; the tones are not here, but the principles are. This is certainly the most momentous question of life; and practically it must be answered by every man. Men may put religion away from them; they may dislike to listen to thoughts which bring it home to personal reflection; they may hate the message and refuse to ponder what even Jesus speaks. But they cannot evade the responsibility laid upon them by divine authority. The anxious and the careless, the humble and the scoffing, the penitent and the unbelieving do all decide, in their different ways, the same unavoidable question. The soul must be gained through Christ, or lost in neglecting or rejecting him.

We may well ponder the great question proposed by our Lord for human solution, as a remarkable example of the power of the great Teacher to compress the most mighty and suggestive thoughts into the compass of a brief and simple sentence. Few words and many thoughts may better describe what he here says, than almost any other passage of even his teachings. And this inquiry should follow us and be often repeated by us, in the house and upon our beds, till it has profited us in the soul's eternal gain.

His language implies, we can easily see, that the soul of man is of infinite value. He does not argue this question, nor suggest reasons why it is of more value than the whole world; he assumes the fact, as one that needs but be stated, to secure the assent of every thoughtful mind. It is not wrong for us to argue upon this, or upon other subjects. Yet indeed we would never need to argue upon this or any other matter but for the weakness of the human intellect and the ignorance of the understanding. All truth is intuitive before the infinite mind of God; and the larger man's knowledge and intellect, the more fully he perceives truth without needing the processes of argumentation. The weaker the mind is, the more must we descend to minute details to convince it by an argument. So then the power to argue denotes vigour of intellect, and his is a master-mind who can set truth before men in the clearest and most convincing forms. But if the necessity for argument denotes weakness of intellect, he has the feeblest mind who needs the most numerous stepping-stones to cross over from a statement to its conclusion. Some great things every man should see at a glance. Argument is possible, but not needful. We might speak of the soul's origin and nature and capacities and immortality; we might elaborately show that the man who loses his soul loses himself, and can hold nothing else he gains; yet the question is itself sufficiently suggestive; it carries its own argument to the humblest mind; we may leave the statement where the Master does, to make its own way; the incomparable value of the soul we all may grant.

But the suggestive language of the great teacher

further implies that men ought to ponder the loss or the salvation of the soul; that we are placed in circumstances where either of these is possible; and that the very pondering of this inquiry has its bearing upon the momentous issue. We may justly say indeed that in the nature of the case and in all the teachings of the Scriptures, the loss of the soul is not its destruction, in the sense of annihilation; its loss is all the more dreadful, because this cannot occur; it is not the loss of being, for the soul is immortal; but it is the loss of WELL-BEING, for the soul is sensitive and rational. In one important sense, every sinful soul is already lost, because already condemned by God's righteous law; and so Christ says he came to save the lost. But the lost condition of sinful men is not as yet beyond a remedy. Condemnation is pronounced, but the sentence is not yet executed. The mission of Christ is to save; and the preaching of Christ promises salvation to every believing disciple. Every man then who hears Christ's gospel is called to consider the soul's perdition or salvation; and the question would not be asked at all, but for the responsibility that rests upon every man for his own soul's gain or loss.

We could not listen to this great question from the lips of Jesus, without understanding him to admit that the loss of the soul is quite consistent with the enjoyment of the present life; that men may lose the soul and be insensible to any deprivation, so far as their present consciousness goes; because, in the supposition, the gain of the world is expressly set over against the loss of the soul. He does not mean that every man who loses the next world gains this; but simply that a man may gain this and lose that. We may turn our thoughts to any desirable form of worldly prosperity, and reflect that the possessor of this may be one who after all may lose his soul. See the honoured of the earth, holding their eminent dignities; see the rich, amassing their treasures; see the voluptuous, enjoying their pleasures; see the learned, studying lessons of various wisdom; but these things may all belong to men who are righteously condemned by God's holy law; and in their best estate, these earthly things are not evidence of the soul's acceptance before God. A man may gain as much of this world in any of its forms as ever a man gained, and yet lose his soul.

But the Saviour's words imply that any man is guilty of inexpressible folly who chooses this world to the loss of the soul. He recognizes the danger that men will do this; that they will prefer a flattering and seductive world to a strict and self-denying religion; that neglecting him they will lose the soul. And the interrogative method of instruction implies that even the great Teacher could not express in direct words the folly of the choice. The burden of such a thought, human language is too weak to bear. On both sides of the subject—looking on what men gain, and on what they lose—this folly is palpable.

For the gain of the world is but a partial, short-lived, and unsatisfactory acquirement, when men make the most of it; and nothing can be more complete and irrevocable and miserable than the loss of the soul. Consider both, if you can; and let the sum of your thoughts lead you humbly to that Redeemer, by whom alone the salvation of the soul can be secured.

No man has ever gained the whole world, or enjoyed to the full even one single kind of earthly good. Earth's sons of unbounded ambition have run for a few years a career of splendid glory; but a drunken revel cuts an Alexander off in the flower of his youth, or a foreign island holds the imprisoned Napoleon. How few of the world's honours or pleasures or riches can any one man enjoy? And those that have the most that earth can yield may repeat the experience of Solomon. They may build houses; they may gather delights about them; they may seek all their hearts can wish; and confess after a fair trial as the final result, "All is vanity!" "All is vanity and vexation of spirit!"

The result of all earthly experience, expressed by a modern poet in a single line,—

> "Vexation, disappointment, and remorse,"

is necessarily reached by all those who seek their happiness in this world. For many reasons it is impossible that this experience should be different to any one who chooses earth as his portion. For whatever of earth any man has, he is liable to lose at any time; and this mars his enjoyment. The highest honours often suddenly change to shame and contempt; wealth deserts a man, and he sinks to poverty; health leaves him, and he declines to feebleness and pain; friends forsake him, and he is miserable. Even social joys, the holiest and purest on earth, cannot be retained. Our best beloved distress us, pine away before our eyes, are suddenly removed. Every man is liable to lose every earthly thing at any hour; or he may at any time pass away from them. Even while he holds them, his enjoyment is far from perfect. Honours are harassing.

"Uneasy lies the head that wears a crown."

Wealth fills a man with cares, draws the envy of others upon him, and even exposes his life to violence. How easily may he lose his relish for any earthly good. The aching of a single nerve gives torture which honour, wealth, and respect cannot remove; the king cannot sleep when the labourer finds repose; and but little is required to unbalance reason from her seat, and to make a man, though surrounded with every earthly good, that most pitiable object among the objects of human pity, a lunatic. At the very best and when most firmly held, the world cannot satisfy the mind of man. God never intended that a rational, immortal soul should be satisfied with earthly good. And the very sinfulness of man, which gives him a morbid and unnatural thirsting for these earthly joys, tends also to make him more and more dissatisfied; the more exclusively and sinfully he seeks pleasure in the world, the more constantly will it elude his grasp; and he who makes the world his portion may well expect to be dissatisfied with his choice.

But their folly who prefer the world to the soul's salvation is more manifest, as we look upon the other side of the subject. The loss of the soul we may contemplate, but we cannot fully comprehend. The loss of the soul is the loss of God's offered and eternal favour; it is the incoming of God's threatened and everlasting wrath. This is the constant contrast set before us in the teachings of Jesus; no prophet ever invited more kindly or warned more fearfully than he; his lips declare that the lost shall go away into everlasting punishment, and the saved into life eternal; and his own mission to die upon the cross can be justified only by the fearful destiny of the lost whom he came to save. Let us not close our eyes to the solemn truth, so clearly revealed in the entire word of God, that the difference between the salvation and the loss of the soul can be measured only by the contrast between the favour and the wrath of God for ever. "Eye hath not seen, ear hath not heard," imagination has not conceived the eternal weight of glory; and no conception can make too fearful the wrath of God abiding upon the sinner. The man who loses his soul loses himself, in the worst form of loss, and beyond remedy for ever!

All we know upon this subject we know from the teachings of the Scriptures. Men may argue profoundly; they may bring their selfishness to aid them; they may refuse to believe the teachings of truth. But this is a topic upon which we want INFORMATION, not argument; though correct arguing may teach us the same things, and forewarn us of God's righteous judgments. Information man cannot give. Passing constantly into eternity, no traveller comes back to tell its wonders; and it remains to us an undiscovered country. What we know, we know only because God has revealed it to us; and if conscience and reason ratify these Scriptural teachings, still it is chiefly from what HE says that we can know the great truths of eternity.

Among the things we learn from the sacred Scriptures respecting this fearful thing, the loss of the soul, are such as these.

I. The loss of the Soul is not the loss of its Existence.

The soul is immortal. The last enemy which Christ shall destroy is death; and there shall be no more dying. In the sense of terminated existence or even changing existence, there shall be no death in the world to come. Satan can never die; his angels will live and suffer for ever; and though the spirits of lost men may wish, they will ever vainly wish for death.

And if the soul of man lives for ever, it must still live *as a soul.* All the faculties which make it a soul will still belong to it. No essential change can affect its nature. It may think more truly, but it will still think; it may feel more keenly, but it will still feel; and whatever changes take place, understanding, and conscience, and will, and memory, and imagination, and the affections, must still belong to a living soul.

II. The loss of the Soul is not the loss of the Understanding.

The soul will be intelligent still; and its capacities and its actual knowledge will doubtless be greatly enlarged. The man will there understand his own capabilities, and the holy and just character of God better than ever before. No ignorant man will there charge God with too great severity. Every mouth will be stopped; and the justice of the sentence of wrath will be in every case undeniable. And as our Lord in one parable speaks as if the inhabitants of hell are able to look across the impassable gulf, directly into heaven, we may learn that the lost will see the glories they can never reach, as well as feel the sorrows they can never escape.

III. The Soul in Eternity will not lose its Conscience and its sense of Accountability.

The conscience of man is an essential and distinguishing characteristic. Brutes have limited powers of reasoning and affection; but they have no moral sense. Man is an accountable being. Here indeed his conscience is often stupid; yet even here no sufferings are so severe, so incapable of alleviation, as those which the guilty sometimes endure from an awakened conscience. If men may argue what the conscience *can* do, from what it *has* sometimes done, they may well fear the day when it shall lash them with remorse. Here there are many ways in which men are able to silence the voice of conscience. They can consciously do wrong, and yet be little troubled by it; they can forget, in the busy cares of life, the wrongs they have already done; they can neglect many duties, and feel no regret. But the veil of delusion will drop as the soul passes to the eternal world. A just sense of accountability will no longer be lost in pressing cares; and the dull conscience will arouse from its apathy, never more to slumber.

And we may well think what a different judgment from that of earth will be passed by an enlightened understanding and an awakened conscience, between the worth of the world and the worth of the soul. If the question were now proposed to a soul in perdition, "What is a man profited, if he should gain the whole world and lose himself?" what would be the answer? Aside from the question of the malignant affections, the lost soul would not answer as sinful men now act. Would he reply, "Place me back in the world again, and again I would choose it as my portion? I would neglect religion; I would close my Bible; I would refuse to pray; I would reject the offer of heaven; I would hear the preacher speak of the loss of the soul; I would follow the footsteps of the Son of God, and hear his startling and momentous question; and yet I would be just as indifferent, and as prayerless, and as idle as ever?" Is it possible that the lost soul, with its new views of heaven and hell, could use such language? Is it not more likely that eternity will change these earthly delusions? Would you not expect to hear from that abode of despair, according to Christ's own teachings, a voice like that of the rich man? "I have five brethren; oh, I have five brethren; let me go and tell them, lest they also come to this place of torment." Ah, if the truth could resound from the depths of the abyss, it would come in a voice louder than seven thunders; and the united confession of innumerable lost souls would declare, "We would not purchase the world's highest honours, and riches, and pleasures for the longest life, if at the end of all, we were doomed for them to experience only one hour of hell!" There will be an amazing difference in the judgment which the sinner forms in time, and that which he will form in eternity of the worth of the soul. The loss of the soul is not the loss of understanding or conscience.

IV. The loss of the Soul will not be the loss of its Affections.

There may be no objects upon which love, and joy, and hope can rest, but fear, and hatred, and malice will dwell there. The malignant affections will darken the lost world with infinite gloom and misery. Who could live in a village on earth, where every man hated God and hated his neighbour? How wretched will hell be from passions unrestrained, desires ungratified, the reign of despair, and the tormented, tormenting each other.

V. The lost Soul will not lose its Memory.

If the past was blotted out, the soul might be comparatively easy. But the mind will constantly revert to the scenes of earth, its various engagements, its lost opportunities. Memory will recall years of false peace, promises never fulfilled, and hopes that proved vain; and these will awaken many feelings of bitter remorse. Hours of giddy mirth, moments of sensual guilt, aspirations for honour, strivings for wealth, words of boasting, thoughts of vanity, will each be remembered; and the memory of each will add its sting. The desire for vain display, the fear of ungodly associates, the pressure of worldly business, the determination to seek one more pleasure, the oft-urged plea, "a more convenient season," those trifling hindrances, which turned the soul away from piety, memory will bring up, and will contrast them with the solemn calls, and warnings, and seasons of peculiar solemnity, that urged the man to forsake the world and secure salvation. Many a son of believing parents has sold his precious birthright cheaper far than Esau, and shall find no place of repentance, though he seeks it carefully with tears.

Let the sinner now reflect that through a never-ending eternity, the memory will have time enough to think again and again over the whole life. The attention will be fixed, the faculties exercised, and nothing will be forgotten. There are instances of astonishing vigour and accuracy of human recollection. Drowning people have said that, at the moment of sinking, the whole past life came up before the mind with wonderful vividness, as the eye sees a landscape at a glance. What a power will memory be in eternity. There will be no Bibles in hell; but on the pages of many a memory, too faithful at the last, will be deeply engraved those solemn warnings and those precious invitations, whose truth is seen too late. It is hard to treasure up these teachings now; but chapters even rarely read, will be well remembered there. Memory will bring up many sermons now not easily recollected. Memory will recall the form of every pastor that has ever preached to you the blessed gospel, the tones of every voice, and the solemn pleadings and tender entreaties that are now unheeded. The appearance of the sanctuary, the solemnity of the people, the songs of praise, the voice of prayer, the sacramental table, the baptismal water, will be well remembered. You have been asked to go into your closet; the call of the Spirit has touched your heart; you have quenched his strivings and refused to pray. His serious seasons; the times when he was almost persuaded to be a Christian; the deep conflict, known only to himself and his God; the uprisings of pride; the victory of unbelief, the man who loses his soul will never forget. The lost soul will not lose its memory.

VI. The loss of the Soul is not the loss of its Sensibilities.

These will indeed be keener than ever. Desires for sympathy, relief, and happiness will still exist. These are inseparable from the soul's existence. But they must for ever remain ungratified. Our sorrows on earth are lightened by human sympathy; but the relief of sympathy will be unknown there. The soul is ruined, and its every power will fill it with misery; it is a world of wailing; and the torment is unceasing, unmitigated, and for ever. The soul's own endowments will increase the blessings of heaven, and the curses of hell. Immortality, conscience, intelligence; the affections and sensibilities of the soul; the memory; how precious will these be in heaven; how awful in the abode of despair!

We cannot decide that the great question which the lips of Jesus asked of the multitude around him would fall on our ears with any saving power, if now we stood beside him, and heard its solemn emphasis from his living voice. But this we can easily know, that the words mean no less for us than they did for those to whom they were first directed. This is a question for the world and for every heart of man; and whether pondered in the sanctuary or in the place of secret solitary meditation, let us reflect that it embodies the truth, and the wisdom, and the grace of Christ. Christ teaches us here that the soul may be lost, that its loss is possible when the world is gained, yet that its loss is dreadful beyond all comparison or conception. Yet would his lips have been silent, indeed his mission to earth would not have taken place at all, and a less charge of folly would be made against man for the soul's loss, but for this other truth, that the soul's salvation may be secured. There is an aspect of Christ's question which makes it fearful; so that indeed men like not to hear the perdition of the soul discussed as even possible; but there is another aspect of the question that is exceedingly precious; and the Saviour speaks and his ministers may repeat his words in tones of richest mercy. If his question implies clearly that the soul of man may be lost, that this loss is unspeakably great, and that through man's folly and sin it may occur; it just as clearly implies that the soul may be saved, that its salvation is precious beyond all price, and that man's wise efforts should be directed to secure it. Let us fix our minds chiefly on this thought, for it filled the Saviour's heart when he made this great inquiry, man may secure the soul's salvation. We do not lose sight of that atoning blood by which he bought our souls upon the accursed tree; but we make this the basis of our hope, as we draw near a sin-forgiving God. We do not forget that these our sinful souls need the renewing power of the Holy Spirit as an essential part of their salvation: but we desire to plead for the Spirit's grace, to receive his teachings, and to obey his promptings. But with these truths fully in view, and the rather because we are made so fully acquainted with them, we dare not forget the very object which alone could prompt this question from the lips of the great Teacher. If there is any meaning in these words at all, they impress the folly and the guilt of any man who hears the gospel and neglects to secure according to it the salvation of his soul. The words are spoken in infinite mercy. If they teach solemnly that man may be lost, they assure us, just as plainly, that he may be saved. And surely it is only for the greater encouragement of our humble prayers for divine deliverance that assurances are given us of the grace of God in the salvation of the soul.

If we could bring up before our minds at this hour the deep importance of this question in the eyes of him who asked it, with what different interest would we ponder it! The soul's Redeemer talks with man about his soul's worth. He, who made our souls, who saw their ruin by sin, a ruin hopeless and irrecoverable, so far as created wisdom and power could go; who came himself from the joys and glories of heaven to the griefs of earth and the shame of the cross, was able surely to estimate the worth of the soul; and he knew what his words meant when he called our thoughts to its salvation. If we could see these great truths as Christ saw them, could we be indifferent? Yet we ought to know that his judgment is just, and his words should awaken our concern for salvation. And there is one thought, infinitely serious for our reflection, in any comparison we may make between the estimate he put upon the soul, and that which we may put upon it; that the soul of each individual is more valuable to himself than it can be even to the soul's Creator and Redeemer. The soul of man to man is his all. It robs not the Redeemer of his glory, if even the foolish and guilty sinner departs with those that shall perish for ever. This great question of the soul's salvation is of infinite importance to every man who hears it; a value as great to every one, as if the voice of Jesus spoke it in his ear alone. Concerned we may be for other men's lives; but death comes to each man for himself as no other man's death can affect him. Concerned we may be for the salvation of other souls; but God has laid upon each individual a responsibility for his own soul, and for securing its salvation, unspeakably more pressing than any care or obligation he may have for others. This responsibility in its just bearings does not interfere with any other duty upon us. The man who cares most for this great first duty, will be least prone to neglect any other. But he, who fails to ponder the Saviour's great question, loses all else to which he has ever given his thoughts.

Many persons who acknowledge the infinite value of the soul, will yet fail to secure its salvation. Multitudes lose their souls through neglect. Possibly they make many fine promises, indulge many serious thoughts, and flatter themselves with hopes that they may yet inherit everlasting life. And alas for what a miserable price do men barter heaven and eternal glory. Let us ponder the Saviour's words as we never have before. He warns us, but he warns in mercy; he speaks of the soul's loss, he calls to its gain; he tells us of perdition, he offers us salvation. Do you think you would listen eagerly, you would take home the lesson seriously, you would seek the soul's salvation, if you could sit down with the multitudes around the living Jesus, and hear from his lips this impressive inquiry? You will lose your soul, if you never repent till then. And you will perish in your own guilt, for you reject the same truth which the men around him heard; you despise Christ's own chosen method of bringing his truth to your thoughts; and you lose your soul under more favourable circumstances for securing its salvation than belonged to those who lived while Jesus was here upon the earth.

CHAPTER XXIV.

SCENES OF TRANSFIGURATION.

We have already said that the wonderful scene which is now to pass before our thoughts, did not perhaps occur within a week of our first interview with the Son of man. But it will be none the less instructive though we are unable to decide its exact chronological place. If we were accompanying the footsteps of Jesus during that eventful year, we would not wish to lose sight of him upon that wonderful night; we would desire to be eye-witnesses of his majesty on the holy mount; we would prize the privilege of beholding the glimpses of his glory through the veil of his flesh, and of seeing his companions from the celestial world; and we would listen reverently to hear their conversation and the approving voice of the Father concerning his beloved Son. And we may see here, as truly as anywhere else in all these meditations, how important it is for us not to see as the apostles then saw, but to see with our better knowledge of the character and mission of our Lord. For the truth will bear repetition that we know Jesus better than they then did, and that we stand in more favourable circumstances for a just comprehension of the words and scenes of his earthly life.

We may not be able to decide fully what was the design of the transfiguration scene. It may have had its important teachings and supports even for the Mediator himself; and it seems to mark the beginning of a new era of his life. It is deeply interesting to notice that the nearer the Redeemer came to the death of the cross, the more was his soul occupied with the grand theme of his sufferings. Before the transfiguration he had spoken of his coming death; but it was his more abundant teaching from this time until it occurred. The transfiguration marks the beginning of the second grand period of our Lord's public ministry. The first period began at his baptism, and was specially the period of active labours and diligent obedience to the law; the second began on the holy mount, and was specially the time of sufferings unto death, anxiously and yet cheerfully anticipated, spoken of, and endured. These two periods are both marked by the same approving voice from heaven: "This is my beloved Son;" and if we regard the baptism of Jesus as foreshadowing the sufferings he must endure, and which he himself expressly calls a baptism, Luke xii. 50, we may take the transfiguration as anticipating the glory which was to follow his death accomplished at Jerusalem. And several things seem to teach us that upon that holy mount our Lord stands to look both backward and forward, to the past designs of God touching his church, and to their coming fulfilment. Especially the presence of Moses and Elijah, the great representatives of the old economy, and at the same time the representatives of the church of the first-born above, reminds us that God's people belong to one church, no matter if they are widely separated on earth by changing times and dispensations; no matter even if they are separated by the dividing line that runs between earthly darkness and celestial glory.

The sacred writers do not tell us where the transfiguration occurred. Tradition, since the fourth century, has declared that it was upon Mount Tabor, an affirmation which it is impossible for us either to sustain or disprove, and which may therefore be received or classed among the legends which superstition has so largely prepared for almost every spot in Palestine. Mount Tabor may have been the place. "No more noble or appropriate theatre for such a glorious manifestation could be found or desired."* Perhaps one of the strongest reasons against judging that it is the proper spot, is found in the silence of the evangelists respecting the name of the mountain; for Tabor was so famous in the Hebrew annals, that the mention of its name seems almost certain, if there these things occurred. It was upon a high mountain, with perhaps more than

* The Land and the Book, ii. 139.

ordinary care to secure a retired spot, that this extraordinary scene took place.*

If we accompany the footsteps of the three favoured disciples, let us do it with deeper than usual reverence. Few spots on earth are holier ground than this meeting-place of celestial visitors and their Lord; few sights are greater than the Redeemer lighting up his transfigured person; no theme is nobler than that which formed the topic of this remarkable conversation. Let us not forget that our Lord went apart to pray. His life was so eminently devotional that prayer marks every movement; and we should learn to abound in prayer from the example of Jesus. We are not told the object of his prayer, and we cannot listen to his words. Perhaps, if we could listen to one prayer from his lips, we would learn ourselves to pray as we have never yet prayed. And yet it is easy for us to decide that in one especial and most essential element of our prayers, we have reasons to pray almost infinitely beyond the necessities which his petitions could express as he bowed before his Father. That sinfulness, which forms the chief burden of our prayers, formed no part of his confession; and our true reasoning from the devotion of Christ is simply this, if he prayed constantly, *much more may we!* If our Lord seems like ourselves, when he felt the necessities to which prayer gives expression; if we have no greater example of

* Lange judges it was Hermon.

the propriety and value of prayer; surely it is also true that prayer to us is a privilege the more indispensable for the very weakness and wants which bid us pray.

We learn from him that prayer is not necessarily the language of guilt, seeking forgiveness; but it is the language of dependence, of weakness, of inferiority, looking upward to God for blessings he alone can grant. *We* are never able to separate from our prayers the tones of penitence, the confessions of unworthiness, the pleadings for mercy; and in this particular our supplications are widely separated from the devotions of our spotless Lord. *He* prayed not as we do. But while it is of great importance for us to understand the words of Jesus when he declares, "My Father is greater than I," and of as great importance to comprehend his teachings when he says, "I and my Father are one," it is of no less interest to be able to reconcile these in the teachings of this scene on Tabor. When we see this wonderful person spending so many hours in humble prayer, we cannot but recognize that strength is not here, but weakness; sovereignty is not here, but subjection; riches are not here, but poverty. And our souls are drawn out towards that brother, who so evidently feels our necessities, endures our temptations, and shares our sympathies. Well may we study the prayerfulness of Jesus; but we need some deliverer stronger than he seems to be in these hours of weakness. And so, if we look on while he bows before God, we may see the proof we need. While he was praying the fashion of his countenance was altered. He rises above weakness. He appears as the Son of God. Yet it is the same person. This is the excellency of the transfiguration. This is the proof of the great mystery of godliness. God is manifest in the flesh. The humility of one moment, succeeded by the dignity of the next, gives us the needed evidence of the two distinct natures in one mediatorial person; and we may bow before him, who is at once the Son of man, the Son of God.

We need not attempt to explain the appearances upon the mountain. While he prayed, he changed. His face, his whole appearance, his clothes shone with a glorious brightness. Of something like this we have two other records in the Scriptures; for the face of Moses, after his communing with God on Sinai, was so radiant that the people dare not behold it; and those who stood about the dying martyr, Stephen, saw his countenance as the face of an angel. But these were reflections from the glory of Jehovah upon the faces of mortal men; while the glory of Christ upon that mountain, as the sun gleams brightly through a floating cloud, was the forth-shining, through the veil of his human nature, of that personal dignity which essentially belonged to the Son of God, and which the Father proclaimed in a voice from heaven. How could we look upon the bright form of Jesus, or hear that voice from heaven, without reverencing his majesty, without believing in his divine commission, without longing to share that glory which is to be revealed when all his people shall be like their glorified Lord!

But what lessons may we learn as we look upon the celestial visitors, who now stand beside him upon the holy mount. We are told that Moses and Elijah appeared by him, and that they appeared in glory. How they appeared we cannot declare. We think we can better conceive of the appearance of Elijah, for he never tasted death; and we do not wonder that his appearance should be in the body. But it seems more strange that Moses should be there in a bodily form, especially when we read of his burial where no man knew, and of a mysterious contest respecting his body. Jude 9. Yet let us acknowledge that we know too little concerning the departed to reason upon the matter; and let it suffice us to be taught that both Moses and Elijah appeared in glory. Doubtless they came as representing the Old Testament church; perhaps particularly the Jewish dispensation, soon to pass away. Thus they give their homage to the great Messiah, in the presence of the three greatest of the college of apostles. Some suppose that Moses appears as the lawgiver, and Elijah to represent the prophets; or it may be that Moses was the great giver of the law, and Elijah the great reformer of Israel's degeneracy.

How gladly would we listen if we could draw

near and hear the conversation of these glorified prophets and their shining Lord. If one of the heavenly inhabitants should appear upon the earth, how would we desire to learn the glories of the place. And indeed heaven itself, we learn from many teachings, has no greater theme for the thoughts of happy saints than that very thing about which Moses and Elijah speak on this holy mount. If we cannot hear their words, we know the subject of them; and perhaps Peter, and James, and John were astonished to find these two speaking of that very thing which had excited the surprise of the impetuous disciple but a little while before. When Christ had told them that he must suffer at Jerusalem, Peter could not bear the thought, and even ventured to rebuke his Lord concerning it. Yet here the topic is renewed; and Moses and Elijah spoke "of his death, which he should accomplish at Jerusalem."

If we accompany the footsteps of the Son of God as he treads the earth, we may both desire and expect to hear something from him respecting the chief object of his errand from the skies. Christ came to bleed and die. Yet we hear less from his lips respecting his expiatory death, because it was not yet accomplished; after the scenes of Calvary this great thing was better understood by his disciples; and it is our privilege to know more than they then comprehended. The teachings of Christ during his life-time were entirely consistent with the later teachings of his apostles; but the instructions which succeed his death are plainer, fuller, and more easily understood. The death of Christ "to be accomplished at Jerusalem" is the great theme, alike of the Bible and of the church of God; our teachings respecting it begin before the birth of the eldest prophet; before a word was penned of the sacred writings; and as we stand before the first smoking altar. From the days of Abel's sacrifice onward, how many bleeding victims spoke typically of his availing blood; how many prophets, taught by the Holy Ghost, spoke of his sufferings unto death; how many righteous men longed to bathe in the fountain of his atonement. And the interest belonged not only to earth. The very angels stooped to look into these things, 1 Peter i. 12; and when Moses and Elijah come down to earth for a brief season, it is to speak of this absorbing topic. No wonder for this. The redeemed from among men owed their seats in glory to that glorious covenant which demanded the death upon the cross, and which was not fulfilled until his death was accomplished. Though there was no possibility that he could fail in the great work he had undertaken; though thus their crowns were secure before the price was paid, yet could they not be uninterested in the accomplishment of that great event.

It is not for us to know what communications are made to saints and angels respecting the future events of our earthly history. We may understand that in our life of faith there are reasons for concealment which do not pertain to them; thus they may be able to see things in our future of which we are ignorant; and yet, doubtless, to all finite beings, there is a gradual unfolding of the divine plans. They eagerly inquire into the things of earth, and learn progressively, as we do, the great things which lie in the pathway of Providence. Providence itself is above all creatures. God alone directs its march; God alone foreknows its revealings. Yet it may be that in the clearer light of heaven and in the purity of heavenly minds, there is a far further discernment in advance—especially a clearer understanding of those prophetic revelations which God has been pleased to make for human teaching. One of the favoured three, who was an eye-witness of this glory on the holy mount, tells us that the angels of heaven, with anxious searchings, were wont to study those great words which, of old time, were spoken by inspiration of the Holy Ghost respecting the sufferings and glory of the Messiah. 1 Peter i. 10–12. These things were not understood when they were first spoken. The time was not yet. First, he declares that the prophets who foretold these sufferings could not themselves understand the words which the Spirit spake by them, but searched diligently, and, as to some points at least, in vain. Then he declares that the angels found in them matter of profound inquiry. Repeatedly in the Scriptures we are told that angels wonder at and adore God's great scheme of mercy for man's salvation, as it is accomplished by the death of his Son. What profound amazement must have filled the mind of Gabriel, when he first heard the grand revelation that the Son of God had laid hold on sinning man, and purposed by his own sufferings to secure his salvation. Perhaps no thought of grace divine to sinning rebels ever entered the minds of angels, when they saw Satan and his hosts cast down from their seats of shining bliss to the abode of darkness and despair; and even holy angels may have trembled when they saw God's fearful wrath. It may be they looked for new thunderbolts of vengeance, to lay waste Eden and to smite men down, when Adam fell. But now they heard, with wonder and with joy, Jehovah's words of mercy. Here was heaven's new, everlasting theme, thenceforth to be the greatest for heaven's study. How can we conceive the thoughts which would fill the minds of angels, when they first learned that the glorious Son of God was himself to be man's Redeemer; how can we trace the growing interest of angelic minds, as they studied the increasing evidences of God's grace for man's salvation; now reading the prophecies which the Holy Ghost spake by man; now ministering about the heirs of glory upon the earth; now welcoming the souls of the redeemed to their abodes of bliss. But how wonderful, in the gradual unfolding of the scheme of salvation, was that period when angels saw their

Lord empty himself of his glory and descend from the throne to the manger. If they wondered, they also rejoiced, and filled the air with their songs of congratulation to man. And even angelic recollection can recall no period of more eventful scenes, of more wonderful instructions, or calling for deeper adoration before the God of grace, than the three years spent by the Son of God upon earth; and specially the three days which witnessed his death and resurrection accomplished at Jerusalem. Surely there can be no question in angelic minds, on the one hand touching the necessity of the death of Christ; and on the other touching its efficacy. Knowing God as they do, they are well assured that if justice had not demanded and wisdom approved, love and grace would never have provided such a sacrifice. And their greatest wonder, perhaps, as they know the history of redemption, is at man's indifference to a gospel of grace so unspeakable.

But, whatever may be in full the relationship sustained to the angels by the redeemed now in glory, we know they serve the same God, and share the same joys; we may believe that they study the same profound subjects; we must also think that their interest is far deeper in these thoughts of human redemption. It was no new theme of which the glorified Moses and Elijah spoke, when they came from heaven to earth to talk with Jesus on that shining mount. Surely, if the inhabitants of heaven study the death of Christ, the sons of earth, who owe their crowns to him, must be deeply interested. And when we consider how dimly these things were understood in the ancient days of the church; when we recall the perplexed faith of the ancient believers, as they gazed upon their dim types and through the smoke of their altars; when we are assured that the prophets did not understand their own predictions; we judge that with wonderful interest they would renew these studies in the light of eternity. Here Moses talks of the death of Christ. He had known him, he had talked of this long before. His mother's lips, by the reedy Nile, had first taught him of the faith of God's earthly people; and he esteemed the reproach of Christ greater riches than all the treasures of Egypt. He himself had ranked among the greatest of earthly teachers; and yet he knew but little of the meaning of those dim ceremonies and significant types by which the church in the wilderness were taught of the sufferings of the Messiah. Many prophets and righteous men longed to see things they never saw. How were these Old Testament prophecies studied to know their meaning; how would the spirits of the just renew their studies when they reached heaven. When Moses entered heaven, he began anew to study the great subject of salvation. What a sight that would be to look in upon the heavenly hosts and see Moses studying his own teachings! That eye, which six-score years of earth did not dim, is bright with unfading lustre; that face, which Israel could not behold, is far more radiant now; and he sees a glory, which he could not bear when he was hidden in the clefts of Sinai. But all the new light of heaven only imparts a deeper interest to that most sacred of all themes; and glorified spirits speak of the death of Christ, to be accomplished at Jerusalem.

But how strange it seems to speak of Christ's death at such a moment as that. The mountain around was lighted up with celestial splendour, which shone forth from his transfigured form; never before, since he came to earth, did he so seem the Son of God, and incapable of death; and who could judge that this glorious One could ever die? To speak of his glory, when he was so glorious, would seem a natural topic for their thoughts; but how is his death an appropriate theme for that time? What reflections would fill our minds if we could see that wonderful person, and hear these conversings respecting his death? Gaze, listen, reflect, as you would if you were among that favoured three upon the holy mount.

Surely, if this Jesus is to die, his death must be entirely voluntary. Not only may he avoid it, advertised of his danger, but such an one as this has power over every foe. No man can take his life from him: if he lays it down, he must lay it down of himself! And, in a higher sense than ever was true of any martyr upon earth, the death of Jesus WAS voluntarily met. Not even duty, but grace and love, bade him tread that painful path. The glory which he had with the Father before the world was, and which now shone in him upon the mount of transfiguration, may give sufficient proof that he at once knew the bitterness of that cup of sorrows, and voluntarily and cheerfully drank it to the dregs.

Moreover, we could not gaze upon that shining form and know that it must meet the stroke of death, without judging that extraordinary things belong to such an event as happening to him. If death comes to the feeble, how can this mighty One feel his power? If death is the wages of sin, this holy One is not a sinner. Yet no death in all the world was so anticipated and prepared for as his. It was not merely because he was a man that he must die. Elijah, though a man of like passions with other mortals, escaped death; and yet the Messiah, who plead three times for release, if it were possible, must bow his head in death. Nothing less than the representative, expiatory nature of the death of the Messiah can explain why he must die at all, or vindicate the propriety of his unparalleled sufferings.

But the chief thought that may attract our attention in the death of Christ, springs from the very glory that essentially belonged to him, that shone so brightly on the mount, that seemed to render it impossible that he should die, and that yet was his very qualification for that dying upon the cross. Instead of saying that one so glorious as he cannot die for man, it is far nearer the truth to say that only such a glorious One can suffer such a death. The wide extremes, of weakness that is capable of death, and of power that can again rise from the dead, must meet in OUR REDEEMER. These glorified prophets speak not simply of A DEATH to be accomplished at Jerusalem, but of HIS DEATH! It is Christ that died for us. This eminence belongs only to him, for he only is worthy. Only the transfigured Jesus can so pass through the realms of death as to come forth on the third day from humiliation to glory. And if our eyes could see his glory as it shone on that holy mount; if we could realize that he is to meet death for us, could we have any doubts that such a Redeemer was able to save to the uttermost?

Great as would be the privilege of seeing the transfiguration, and of hearing the voices of Moses and Elijah upon this greatest of all topics for human thought, we may be assured that we can now secure a better acquaintance with the death of Christ, than was gained by the three favoured apostles upon that eventful night. Alas for the infirmities of our poor human nature, which often prevents our appreciating the most delightful opportunities! Peter and his brethren were overcome by sleep, even in this august presence. Perhaps they did not hear what Moses and Elijah could tell. Perhaps their darkened minds could not understand what they did hear. This much we know, that after this, and even when their Lord was in his sepulchre, they did not comprehend the teachings of the Scriptures concerning the death of their Master; and he must, after he had arisen from the dead, explain the teachings of Moses, and the prophets, and the psalms, respecting himself.

Let us understand our opportunities. We do not see that transfigured form: but we know who he was; and we do not wonder that the Son of God could look so glorious. We do not hear Moses and Elijah talk of that death to be accomplished: but we look back upon the finished work of redemption, and are permitted to know more than his most favoured disciples then knew of the nature, and aim, and efficacy of his cross. Peter might say, "It is good for us to be here;" yet Peter himself says that our word of prophecy is more sure than that transient vision. It is good for us to be here. We may learn of Jesus and of his death; we may secure an interest in it; we may see in him a glory above all that could merely meet the eye; indeed, we may be prepared to share that glory through the death accomplished at Jerusalem.

CHAPTER XXV.

IT IS GOOD FOR US TO BE HERE!

We may sympathize with Peter when, beholding the glory of his Lord, he said, "Master, it is good for us to be here!" And yet we wonder that these disciples learned less from these scenes, and knew less their true power and glory, than we may learn and know from our opportunities. That it was a great privilege to see Jesus in the flesh, to witness his wonderful deeds, to hear his gracious words, to accompany his footsteps, especially to behold his honour and majesty in this transfiguration scene, we readily grant. But that we should long for such opportunities, in comparison with those we now enjoy; that we should think they could learn more than we, or draw near to God in closer communion than we, or rise more above their own infirmities than we, or have more convincing proofs of the divine origin of our holy religion, are all matters, respecting which many are tempted to judge unwisely. In a fair comparison we live in times more favourable than theirs for an acquaintance with Christ and his gospel, and for a cordial embrace of its claims. They were eye-witnesses of his majesty, as we cannot be; and this had its advantages; but the prejudices of their early education, the darkness usually gathering about the unfinished plans of Providence, and the unrevealed things of the gospel, put them under other serious disadvantages, which more than compensate to us; and with the full records of all they saw in our hands, with the opportunity of repeatedly pondering upon the sights and words that were transient to them, with the clearer knowledge of things they so imperfectly understood, and with the accumulated evidences which support the authority of the sacred writers, we have no reason to envy even the favoured disciples who saw our Lord in the flesh. Our walks with Jesus may give us, by the blessing of his Spirit, as large an acquaintance with the grace of the gospel; we may know him as truly, and secure as precious and true communion with God; indeed we have a "more sure word of prophecy."

Our profit depends not only upon our opportunities. Some of our best advantages secure us small return, through the weakness of our poor human nature! How do we think we would enjoy the sight and the conversation on the holy mount! Jesus is transfigured; Moses and Elijah talk with him; redemption is the theme! Yet, behold, Peter and James and the beloved disciple were heavy with sleep. Even such a sight fades from their eyes; even such a conversation cannot fix their attention. The topic is noble; the speakers are glorious; the occasion is once in the world's history; the audience is select; but the hearers are asleep.

That the chosen three were overcome with sleep may suggest to us one of the advantages which we now possess for learning the great teachings of the gospel, over those who were eye-witnesses of the Saviour's earthly majesty. We may suppose that this drowsiness on the part of the disciples was merely natural; the demands of the physical system claiming ordinary repose in its appropriate and customary time. Our Lord, we know, sometimes spent the entire night in prayer; he had gone up upon this high mountain to pray; it is likely that these scenes occupied the whole night. For we are expressly told that they came down from the mountain upon the next day, Luke ix. 37; and perhaps not at a very early hour of it. Night is the time to sleep; and though there are occasions when our untiring attention may be fixed for successive hours, even through the night watches, it is not surprising to see men sleep in the night. The opportunities enjoyed by those who saw Christ in the flesh in themselves were transient; they must be embraced as they passed, or be lost; and yet nature's feebleness might mar the improvement of their best seasons. To some extent this is still so with us; yet the written and inspired record of these scenes in the life of Christ, is far better for our profit than the sight first and the memory afterwards, to those who saw these things. Our opportunities are not transient, but are repeatedly offered. We may take our freshest hours to the study of these sacred scenes; we may keep them before us when the attention is most fixed; we may refresh our memories by hearing of them again; we may weigh every important truth; we may lie down to night's slumbers in night's season, not fearing that the vision will be for ever gone before we wake again. What if we had been with Peter, and, like Peter, upon the holy mount? Peter knew more of these scenes when the Spirit of inspiration brought them to remembrance, than he did in that hour of infirmity.

But perhaps the disciples slept, because the glorious scene before them was more than our mortal frame can bear; the sleep was supernatural, and necessary for them in such a scene as that; and thus we know not what we ask, when we would share the privileges they enjoyed. We are abundantly assured in the sacred word that communications of the glory of God are more than man can bear. Jehovah assured Moses that no man could see his face and live. Paul heard in paradise words unspeakable and unlawful to be uttered. The beloved Daniel twice expressly tells us that when divine communications were made to him, he fell on his face in a deep sleep; and Zechariah declares that the angel awakened him "as a man is awakened out of his sleep." The disciples may have been unable to bear the flood of glory that shined forth from their transfigured Lord; they were unable to hear the language of heaven respecting the death to be accomplished at Jerusalem; they were not as yet prepared to be the companions of Moses and Elijah; and, in the divine mercy, they sank into the repose of deep slumbers. But the communications of divine truth to us are large enough for us, and they are every way suited to our present capacities. We read, but not with such overwhelming emotions as forbids us to understand; the words are more than celestial; they are the teachings of the Holy Ghost; yet the language is human language; and the thoughts are not all that God could teach, but all that infinite wisdom has chosen to express for our profit.

In reflecting upon our comparative advantages over those who witnessed these scenes in the life of our Lord, it is exceedingly difficult to realize how much better is our position than theirs, because of the clearer knowledge given us of the true nature of Christ's character and kingdom. There is an important sense in which it is impossible that the men of any age can understand the scenes going on around them, as they will be known to later times. No man knows his own times, as he may know the generation before him; in our personal experience we often see better what we should have done, when the opportunity is passed for ever, than when it is present with us; in the present we are like men who wander through the mists in the valley; in the future we ascend the mountain, the sun clears the air around us, we look forth over a larger view, and understand all these various objects better than when we were down among them. It is, perhaps, true that there are scholars now upon the earth whc understand the Greek language more critically than the men who spoke and wrote it two thousand years ago. Histories of ancient times have been written in the present age, far superior to any that could have been written by the nations of whom they speak, and far in advance of any that have been written, by even profound scholars, for twenty centuries back. No candid and intelligent man can question that we are capable of knowing the principles of the gospel of Christ, and the historical and moral evidences of Christianity, and of arriving at as great and as intelligent certainty of all these things as they could who were the eye-witnesses of his majesty. The principle upon which we urge this is given by our Lord himself, when he says, in one of his parables, "If they hear not Moses and the prophets, neither would they be persuaded though one rose from the dead."

We do not call in question the evident truth that things which are seen to pass before our eyes may awaken our interest, may convince us of their reality, and may be adapted to make upon us a salutary impression. If the gospel of Christ was simply an array of FACTS, then the advantages of being an eye-witness would be greater than we now allow. But it is far more than a system founded upon historical verities. It is a great system of holy PRINCIPLES; and these may be far better understood by those who never saw Jesus than by those who saw him. Whether we look at the evidences of Christianity, or its spiritual teachings, or its influences upon the minds of men, or at the responsibilities which rest upon those who now read the sacred writings, the times in which we live enable us to know Jesus, to walk with Jesus, and to find our salvation in him, quite as easily as if we were among those who knew him in the flesh.

If we speak of this in reference to the evidence that Christianity is from God, we find no serious objection in the fact that infidel men now live upon the earth, and even take rank among the learned of a polished age. For unbelievers looked upon the miracles of Jesus, heard him who spake as never man spake, and knew that he had arisen from the grave. We never expect to array such proofs of the divine commission of Christianity, as will force conviction upon every unwilling mind; especially we do not expect that men who study only the false side of a question shall reach the knowledge of the truth. Indeed, in the orderings of God's inscrutable providence the infidels of every age are among the witnesses to testify that our religion is true. Unquestionably no book but the Bible can claim to be a divine revelation, and stand the test of any examination; but this system has stood the severest tests during every age. These teachings, openly and publicly proclaimed, amidst the most violent opposition, eighteen centuries ago, have never since wanted either friends to uphold, or foes to resist; and it is not in a trifling sense that the foes of religion are witnesses as truly as its friends. If it is true that there are now infidels among men, it is also true that infidelity has given occasion to some of the most important teachings which support the authority of the Scriptures. Infidelity has never arrayed intellect and learning against the Scriptures, that have not been met by learning as profound, and by as vigorous thoughts; every changing and reviving age of skepticism has been of brief duration, and has been succeeded by the more rapid spread of the truth; and Christianity is purer and better understood to-day, because opposition so fierce has so often assailed her.

It is no small task to bring into view, at a glance, the various evidences which support our faith; yet there is no presumption in saying that to spend a year in the personal society of Jesus upon earth, would give no more intelligent reason for believing his gospel, than a man may now possess who studies the evidences of Christianity. Reasons for doubting might arise anywhere: these may spring from our depravity, and may be made confirmatory of a more settled faith. But the evidences of Christianity are stronger now, to any man who will candidly examine them, than ever they were.

Look at them *historically*. Consider this church of Christ, with all the influence she has exerted upon the earth, for eighteen centuries back; see how the changes among the nations, the rise and downfall of empires, the wars and revolutions, the discoveries, the arts, the commerce, the civilization of men, have been originated, or modified, or controlled by the influence of this religion; see how human laws, benevolent institutions, language, and the social manners of the nations, bear testimony to its power; see how the Sabbath and the sacraments of the church have been adopted and variously corrupted among men; and an array of historical evidence gathers here which makes it madness to question the reality of those events in the life of Jesus and his apostles which attended the setting up of the Christian church. These things we may reasonably believe, as truly as if we saw them before our eyes. There is an array of testimony, gathered from so many quarters, embracing so many independent witnesses, corroborating each other in so many unlooked for ways, that the proof is as strong as any evidence of the senses. Consider also this Bible. Half the literature of the Christian world, far more than half that is worth anything, is written about it. Every thing has been attacked, sifted, defended. Many errors have been controverted, many given up among Christ's professed followers. But the sacred volume itself has passed unscathed and victorious through a thousand fierce attacks. It is the simple truth to say that more is known of the Bible in our age than in any preceding generation. Not only has every book in it been attacked and defended, but even every word has been critically scanned, every letter has been investigated The various manuscripts have been compared with profound and various learning, with laborious industry, with unwearied perseverance; yet, whatever conflicting views may prevail touching minor passages, we have no reason to believe that one single doctrine is different in the entire Bible from the original teachings of the inspired writers. All this is the more remarkable, because the foes of revelation are continually changing their ground; the infidels of each succeeding age are ashamed of the cavils and arguments of their predecessors; no careful, candid, systematic refutation of the best Christian writers has ever been attempted; and the infidelity of all the ages has no other bond of union than that it ever possesses a like bitter spirit, and is ever unscrupulous in using any means of hostility against the Scriptures.

But let us not forget to say that there is one part of the evidences of the Christian religion, that is of itself sufficient to vindicate any man's faith. This is open to every man who intelligently reads THE BOOK, and may be independent of every other evidence. The book commends itself. There is a purity and a power in these teachings which only truth can possess. There is an adaptation to the necessities of sinful men; there is a revelation of help for our distresses; there is a sympathy for the hidden griefs of a wounded heart, which divine teachings alone can afford. These words of Jesus cannot possibly come from an inferior teacher; and yet so connected are his words, his life, his mission, and his superior character, that we cannot consistently admit any of his claims, without admitting all. Take Christianity in its chief claim as a system of holy principles, and we are as capable of understanding and receiving them as the men of any age; we may know Jesus more fully, and be his disciples as truly as any who saw him on earth.

Indeed, we see upon this mount of transfiguration how Peter misconceived the kingdom of Christ. "It is good for us to be here; and let us build three tabernacles." Ah, short-sighted and erring Peter! Evidently the church of God and the triumphs of Christianity were never planned by him; evidently these apostles did not control the great revolution that established the Christian church, but were borne along with it, themselves ignorant of the results they did so much to bring about. Peter would have Jesus set up an earthly kingdom; he would even have Moses and Elijah come down from heaven to take part in the new commonwealth. He knew not what he said. Christ planned the church better than the apostles thought; and we know better the nature of Christ's spiritual kingdom, the excellency of his doctrines, and the precious blessings he secures to his people, than did that favoured three upon the holy mount. We know the Son of God, we know the death of Christ, we know all the truths of his salvation better to-day than if we were merely eye-witnesses of that glory. As they came down from that mount, Jesus charged his disciples not to make these things known, until the Son of man was risen from the dead; and they understood not his words, but inquired among themselves what the rising from the dead should mean. If the transfiguration foreshadowed the resurrection, it was not to their minds. After such a sight they knew more than others, which as yet they must not tell; but they knew less than they afterwards knew, and less than is known to us.

But we do not wisely institute any comparison between the advantages we possess, and those that belonged to them or to any previous time, if we do not use them to impress upon ourselves our own responsibilities, and to learn what further needs we have, beyond the teachings that address our eyes and ears. It would be a great thing to be allowed to walk with Jesus for a few brief days, to see that blessed form, to hear his gracious words, and to receive from his lips the delightful invitation to follow him as our Lord and Saviour. But there are two or three thoughts, with which now we may close these meditations, which it becomes every man seriously to ponder, touching the opportunities divinely afforded for our instruction in the things of "THIS LIFE." Acts v. 20.

1st. During our life-time must each one settle the great question that pertains to his immortality. Whether former times were better or worse than the present; whether others have had opportunities more or less favourable than our own, will make no difference as to this point. We cannot change places with others. God has chosen our lot; God has taught us the truths we know; God calls us to repentance and salvation by means of his own choosing for us. In some matters, all who hear the teachings of the gospel are much alike. All are sinners; all are in a sinful world; all are called to contend with difficulties. Temptations ever beset us, to delay the affairs of salvation, to think our circumstances peculiarly trying, and to wish we enjoyed the advantages of some of whom we have heard. Yet all have the important responsibility of securing or neglecting the soul's salvation, during that brief life which the casualty of any moment may so suddenly close.

2d. The privileges we enjoy are among the highest ever given to any land or race. They really leave us nothing to desire, so far as the full revelation of the duties or the privileges of piety are concerned. It might be a great privilege to spend a week in the society of Jesus; but, really, we may come into his society under more favourable circumstances than those who lived with him upon the earth. They saw him in his estate of humiliation, and it was by a slow process that they were brought to realize his true character and dignity; while we cannot remember the time when we first recognized his supreme claims, and regarded him as the Son of God. They were filled with many prejudices, could scarcely credit the fact or the need of his death, and had no just conceptions of a spiritual church; while the great principles of Christianity have been household words for us from the very lispings of our childhood. The miracles which they saw him perform were doubtless deeply impressive: but we may have a conviction, as thorough and as intelligent, that he did perform these wonders, as if we saw them done before our eyes; and the most important part—that is, not the mere wonder of the sight—but the moral impression, arising from the nature and design of Christ's miracles, we may possess as thoroughly as any of the original witnesses. The wondrous words of Jesus, what would we give to hear them? But here they are, better than any hearers ever had them from his lips. The same teachings, written down, put in print, put in our possession, so that no treacherous memory can deprive us of them, so that we may study every word, the very thoughts of Jesus, the words of everlasting life. We who think that if Jesus should warn, we would tremble; if Jesus should call, we would follow; if Jesus should assure, we would believe; if Jesus should promise, we would rejoice, may have all these things here; solemn warnings, earnest calls, firm assurances, precious promises, in his very words and addressed to our souls. Not a single lesson of the law of God is wanting for our teaching: every precious principle of the whole gospel of God's grace is given in his blessed instructions; and though there are temptations to turn our thoughts away from salvation, though this present world, with its pressing cares, withstands every movement towards piety, and every new year of life has its new dangers and excitements, yet, compared with other men and other times, "the times have fallen to us in pleasant places." God's full word is in our hands, and we are free to use it; God's holy Sabbath dawns upon us, and we may enjoy its richest privileges; and we need envy none the privileges they enjoy. Happy will it be for us if we are prepared to answer for the wise use of the opportunities God has given to us.

But, while it is true that our responsibilities are full, and we must surely answer if we neglect the privileges granted to us, it becomes us to remember,

3d. That the teachings of God's Holy Spirit are ever necessary to our spiritual profit, under any means of grace. He can make the very feeblest teachings and the very poorest opportunities effectual for the soul's salvation; and, without his blessing, Paul may plant and Apollos water in vain. The disciples of Christ often did not understand his words. Their minds were darkened, their eyes were holden, they saw and saw not. We need not only light, but open eyes to see. Men may have the gospel and love it not; the inhabitants of Christ's own city may perish in unbelief; while a poor woman from the coasts of heathenism may find the commendation of her unwonted faith. Unquestionably, the

Spirit of God, who opens blind eyes and awakens stupid hearts, is a sovereign, working when and as he pleases; but this in such a sense as to leave upon every man who hears this blessed gospel, the full responsibility that attends his rejection of it. It relieves us from no sense of obligation that we need the Spirit's regenerating power; it is our precious encouragement that he is a Spirit of infinite love, that we live in the age of his largest workings, and that his own word bids us seek his grace. Let our prayer ever be for the Spirit's teachings. To his more sure word of prophecy let us give heed "as to a light that shineth in a dark place." How long? As he bids. "Till the day dawn and the day-star arise in our hearts." Praying for the Spirit, let us follow his bidding, yield readily to his promptings, and beware of all resistance to his strivings. The Spirit speaks in his word; let us ponder it. The Spirit calls in the sanctuary; let us love the habitation of his house. The Spirit bids us pray; let us draw near the throne of grace.

Every soul truly led by the Spirit shall see Jesus, and be with him, and be like him, on a better mount than Tabor, to see and share more glory than at the transfiguration, to eat the living bread, and to enjoy, not a week, but an eternity with Jesus.

www.ingramcontent.com/pod-product-compliance
Lightning Source LLC
LaVergne TN
LVHW010145110826
845151LV00002B/431

* 9 7 8 1 4 2 5 5 3 8 4 1 5 *